Lecture Notes in Artificial Intelligence   11654

Subseries of Lecture Notes in Computer Science

Series Editors

Randy Goebel
University of Alberta, Edmonton, Canada

Yuzuru Tanaka
Hokkaido University, Sapporo, Japan

Wolfgang Wahlster
DFKI and Saarland University, Saarbrücken, Germany

Founding Editor

Jörg Siekmann
DFKI and Saarland University, Saarbrücken, Germany

More information about this series at http://www.springer.com/series/1244

Patrick Hammer · Pulin Agrawal ·
Ben Goertzel · Matthew Iklé (Eds.)

Artificial General Intelligence

12th International Conference, AGI 2019
Shenzhen, China, August 6–9, 2019
Proceedings

Springer

Editors
Patrick Hammer
Temple University
Philadelphia, PA, USA

Pulin Agrawal 🆔
University of Memphis
Memphis, TN, USA

Ben Goertzel
SingularityNET
Tai Po, Hong Kong, China

Matthew Iklé 🆔
SingularityNET
Alamosa, CO, USA

ISSN 0302-9743   ISSN 1611-3349   (electronic)
Lecture Notes in Artificial Intelligence
ISBN 978-3-030-27004-9   ISBN 978-3-030-27005-6   (eBook)
https://doi.org/10.1007/978-3-030-27005-6

LNCS Sublibrary: SL7 – Artificial Intelligence

This Springer imprint is published by the registered company Springer Nature Switzerland AG
The registered company address is: Gewerbestrasse 11, 6330 Cham, Switzerland

Preface

This volume contains the papers presented at the 12th Conference on Artificial Intelligence (AGI 2019), held during August 6–9, 2019, in Shenzhen, China. In addition to co-locating with the International Joint Conferences in Artificial General Intelligence (IJCAI 2019) held in nearby Macau, the Shenzhen location was designed to spur enhanced engagement and discussion between researchers from Europe and the Americas with the burgeoning Chinese research community. Building upon the palpable energy apparent during the 2018 joint Human Level Artificial Intelligence (HLAI 2018) conference, of which the Artificial General Intelligence (AGI 2018) conference was a part, AGI 2019 brought together researchers from at least 14 countries from around the globe, resulting in a robust set of stimulating, diverse, and extremely deep discussions.

Transfer learning, one-shot learning, meta-learning, causality, and unsupervised natural language processing are all becoming increasingly common topics in AGI research. Recent breakthroughs in hybrid neuro-symbolic systems are beginning to produce better results than more specialized sub-symbolic deep neural networks or reinforcement learning alone. In addition, new AI platforms are being developed to take advantage of blockchain technologies.

This volume contains the contributed talks presented at AGI 2019. There were 30 submissions. Each submission was reviewed by at least three (on average 3.0) Program Committee members. The committee decided to accept 16 long papers (53% acceptance) for oral presentation, and 5 papers for poster presentation. Once again the topics covered proved to be very diverse.

There are papers covering AGI architectures, papers discussing mathematical and philosophical foundations and details, papers developing ideas from neuro-science and cognitive science, papers on emotional modeling, papers discussing safety and ethics, and a host of other papers covering a wide-ranging array of additional relevant topics.

Keynote speeches were shared by the participating organizations, and were presented by researchers from both academia and industry including such experts as Hugo Latapie (Cisco), Zhongzhi Shi (Institute of Computing Technology, Chinese Academy of Sciences), Harri Valpola, (Curious AI), Wei Xu, (Horizon Robotics), and Yi Zeng (Research Center for Brain-inspired Intelligence, Institute of Automation, Chinese Academy of Sciences).

In addition, the AGI 2019 conference featured tutorials and workshops on the Non-Axiomatic Reasoning System (NARS) and on the OpenCog system.

We thank all the Program Committee members for their dedicated service to the review process. We thank all of our contributors, participants, and tutorial, workshop and panel session organizers, without whom the conference would not exist.

Finally, we thank our sponsors: the Artificial General Intelligence Society, Springer Nature Publishing, SingularityNET, Hanson Robotics, and OpenCog Foundation.

June 2019   Patrick Hammer
                                                                                          Pulin Agrawal
                                                                                          Ben Goertzel
                                                                                          Matthew Iklé

Organization

Program Committee

Pulin Agrawal	The University of Memphis, USA
Joscha Bach	AI Foundation, USA
Tarek Richard Besold	Alpha Health AI Lab, Telefonica Innovation Alpha, USA
Jordi Bieger	Reykjavik University, Delft University of Technology, The Netherlands
Cristiano Castelfranchi	Institute of Cognitive Sciences and Technologies, Italy
Antonio Chella	Universià di Palermo, Italy
Arthur Franz	Odessa Competence Center for Artificial Intelligence and Machine Learning (OCCAM), Ukraine
Nil Geisweiller	OpenCog Foundation, SingularityNet Foundation, Novamente LLC, France
Benjamin Goertzel	OpenCog Foundation, SingularityNET Foundation, Hanson Robotics, China
Patrick Hammer	Temple University, USA
Jose Hernandez-Orallo	Universitat Poliècnica de València, Spain
Matt Iklé	SingularityNET Foundation, USA
Peter Isaev	Temple University, USA
Garrett Katz	University of Maryland, USA
Anton Kolonin	SingularityNET Foundation
Francesco Lanza	Dipartimento di Ingegneria - Università degli Studi di Palermo, Italy
Xiang Li	Temple University, USA
Tony Lofthouse	Evolving Solutions, USA
Amedeo Napoli	LORIA Nancy (CNRS - Inria - Université de Lorraine), France
Eray Ozkural	Bilkent University, Turkey
Maxim Peterson	ITMO University, Russia
Alexey Potapov	SingularityNET Foundation, AIDEUS
Nico Potyka	Universitaet Osnabrück, IKW, Germany
Paul S. Rosenbloom	University of Southern California, USA
Rafal Rzepka	Hokkaido University, Japan
Oleg Scherbakov	ITMO University, Russia
Ute Schmid	Faculty Information Systems and Applied Computer Science, University of Bamberg, Germany
Javier Snaider	Google, USA
Bas Steunebrink	NNAISENSE, Switzerland
Kristinn R. Thorisson	CADIA, Reykjavik University, Iceland

Contents

AGI Brain: A Learning and Decision Making Framework for Artificial General Intelligence Systems Based on Modern Control Theory

Mohammadreza Alidoust[✉] (iD)

Mashhad, Iran

Abstract. In this paper a unified learning and decision making framework for artificial general intelligence (AGI) based on modern control theory is presented. The framework, called AGI Brain, considers intelligence as a form of optimality and tries to duplicate intelligence using a unified strategy. AGI Brain benefits from powerful modelling capability of state-space representation, as well as ultimate learning ability of the neural networks. The model emulates three learning stages of human being for learning its surrounding world. The model was tested on three different continuous and hybrid (continuous and discrete) Action/State/Output/Reward (ASOR) space scenarios in deterministic single-agent/multi-agent worlds. Successful simulation results demonstrate the multi-purpose applicability of AGI Brain in deterministic worlds.

Keywords: Artificial general intelligence · Modern control theory · Optimization · Implicit and explicit memory · Shared memory · Stages of learning · Planning · Policy · Multi-Agent · Emotions · Decision making · Continuous and hybrid ASOR space

1 Introduction

In this paper, AGI Brain, a learning and decision making framework for AGI is proposed which has a unified, simple structure and tries to emulate the stages of human learning. Based on Wang's classification [1], AGI Brain looks at intelligence as a form of optimality and tries to duplicate intelligence using a unified approach by applying state-space representation (e.g. see [2]) and neural networks as its modelling technique. In AGI Brain, intelligence is defined as "optimizing the surrounding world towards common goals", counting the agent's body as a part of the surrounding world. AGI Brain is a model based algorithm and delays its decision making stage until it built a model upon collected data from interaction with the environment. It estimates the reward value using feedforward neural networks. Like reinforcement learning (RL) [3], AGI Brain works in both continuous and discrete Action/State/Output/Reward (ASOR) spaces. But, unlike RL, AGI Brain works only in deterministic worlds with immediate rewards as yet. AGI Brain benefits from multi-agent capability. In the multi-agent case, the agents can share their experiences easily, and they can also benefit from shared memories.

© Springer Nature Switzerland AG 2019
P. Hammer et al. (Eds.): AGI 2019, LNAI 11654, pp. 1–10, 2019.
https://doi.org/10.1007/978-3-030-27005-6_1

2   AGI Brain

2.1   The Agent and the World

Consider an intelligent agent ω living in the world γ which also contains the object ψ. The agent ω benefits from an artificial brain Γ which controls the behavior of ω for achieving its goals (Fig. 1).

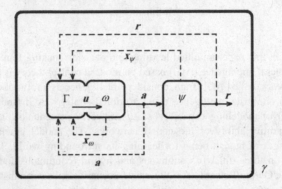

Fig. 1. The world γ consisting of the artificial agent ω and the object ψ.

At every time step n, the artificial brain Γ produces commands $\boldsymbol{u}$ (e.g. hormones or neural signals) which change the states of ω's body, i.e. $\boldsymbol{x}_\omega$, which then leads to performing action $\boldsymbol{a}$ on the object ψ. This action changes ψ's states $\boldsymbol{x}_\psi$, which consequently leads to ψ's response $\boldsymbol{r}$. Like a natural brain, the Γ can observe these values by its sensors.

We model the agent ω by its input $\boldsymbol{u}$, its states $\boldsymbol{x}_\omega$ and its output, i.e. action $\boldsymbol{a}$;

$$\omega : \begin{cases} \boldsymbol{x}_\omega(n+1) = \boldsymbol{f}_\omega(\boldsymbol{x}_\omega(n), \boldsymbol{u}(n)) \\ \boldsymbol{a}(n) = \boldsymbol{g}_\omega(\boldsymbol{x}_\omega(n), \boldsymbol{u}(n)) \end{cases} \tag{1}$$

And, the object ψ by its input $\boldsymbol{a}$, its states $\boldsymbol{x}_\psi$ and its output, i.e. response $\boldsymbol{r}$;

$$\psi : \begin{cases} \boldsymbol{x}_\psi(n+1) = \boldsymbol{f}_\psi(\boldsymbol{x}_\psi(n), \boldsymbol{a}(n)) \\ \boldsymbol{r}(n) = \boldsymbol{g}_\psi(\boldsymbol{x}_\psi(n), \boldsymbol{a}(n)) \end{cases} \tag{2}$$

The functions $\boldsymbol{f}$ and $\boldsymbol{g}$ are columns and they are, in general, complex nonlinear functions of the states and the inputs.

Please note that bold letters represent vectors or matrices. For simplicity, here we assume that both of ω and ψ change simultaneously.

From the Γ's viewpoint, the ω's body is an actuator for performing the Γ's commands, so, the world γ can be modeled by its input $\boldsymbol{u}$, its states $\boldsymbol{x} = \boldsymbol{x}_\gamma$ (vector of all states contained in the world γ, i.e. combination of $\boldsymbol{x}_\omega$ and $\boldsymbol{x}_\psi$), as well as its outputs $\boldsymbol{y} = \boldsymbol{y}_\gamma$ (vector of all outputs contained in the world γ, i.e. combination of $\boldsymbol{a}$ and $\boldsymbol{r}$).

$$x = x_\gamma = \begin{bmatrix} x_\omega \\ \cdots \\ x_\psi \end{bmatrix}, y = y_\gamma = \begin{bmatrix} a \\ \cdots \\ r \end{bmatrix} \tag{3}$$

Thus, the discrete time state-space representation of the world γ will be as follows;

$$\gamma : \begin{cases} x(n+1) = f(x(n), u(n)) \\ y(n) = g(x(n), u(n)) \end{cases} \tag{4}$$

And the continuous time state-space representation of the world γ will be as follows;

$$\gamma : \begin{cases} \dot{x}(t) = f(x(t), u(t)) \\ y(t) = g(x(t), u(t)) \end{cases} \tag{5}$$

2.2 Inside the Artificial Brain

As mentioned in the previous section, in AGI Brain we look at intelligence as a form of optimality. This optimality should be observable and also measurable during the artificial life of an intelligent agent (or a swarm of them). Therefore, an optimality criterion must be defined first. We define the artificial life of an artificial intelligent agent ω living in the world γ as completing a task Q (or a series of tasks) on the object(s) ψ (or on its own body). Completion of task Q requires maximization of reward function R as the task completion criterion, which is a linear combination of objectives J and their corresponding importance coefficients P called personality, as well as an artificial brain Γ which is responsible for this optimization procedure.

For the reward function R we have;

$$R = P^T J \tag{6}$$

Thus, completion of task Q will be as follows;

$$Q : Max \left[R = P^T J \right] \tag{7}$$

The aim of the artificial brain Γ is to complete Q by calculating and then producing the optimal control signal u^* such that the reward function R is maximized with respect to the state equations that govern the world γ, i.e. equation (4) (or (5)). So, in discrete time case, the brain Γ has to solve the following optimization problem at every time step n;

$$u^*(n) = \underset{u \in \aleph}{ArgMax} \left[R = P^T J \right]$$

$$s.t. \tag{8}$$

$$\begin{cases} x(n+1) = f(x(n), u(n)) \\ \quad y(n) = g(x(n), u(n)) \end{cases}$$

Where $\aleph$ is the set of all possible alternatives. The optimal command u^* is the decision made by the Γ and will be transmitted to the agent's body to produce a desired action. Please note that the same problem applies to the continuous time case.

Remark 1: Objectives. The vector of objectives J is a vector that contains the objectives of the agent ω on a benefit-cost basis and relates the components of the world γ to the agent's goals. In general, it is a function of time, input, states and outputs as well as the desired states x_d and desired outputs y_d of the world γ, i.e. $J = J(n, u, x, x_d, y, y_d)$.

Remark 2: Personality. Personality vector P is a dynamical vector which regulates the behavior of the agent and plays as the necessary condition for attaining an objective. Each element of the dynamical vector P, i.e. p_k, is the coefficient of a corresponding objective j_k at the current time. In general, P is a function of the current states and outputs of the world γ, i.e. $P = P(x_0, y_0)$, and based on the current situations alters the importance of each objective to be achieved, in order to regulate the behavior of the agent ω. For instance, P activates fight-or-flight behavior by deactivating other objectives when ω senses a predator approaching. Also it leads to more diversity in multi-agent environments.

2.3 Learning and Decision Making

Equation (8) has two parts; the reward function and the state equations that govern the world γ. For solving Eq. (8), the artificial brain Γ has to search its available alternative set $\aleph$. For each alternative $u^k \in \aleph$, the Γ must solve the state equations first and then evaluate the reward function. The reward function is pre-defined by the designer, but since most environments are unknown, the state equations of such environments are not available. Therefore, the agent does not know what the consequences of performing a command $u^k \in \aleph$ are, how it changes the world and how the world may seem after performing each command.

In this major case, the agent has to build a model of the world which enables the agent to estimate the consequences of performing each alternative $u^k \in \aleph$ on the world during the decision making stage. So, by using an estimator, the state equations of Eq. (8) turn into the following estimation problem:

$$\left\langle \begin{matrix} \hat{x}(n+1) \\ \hat{y}(n+1) \end{matrix} \right\rangle \overset{Estimator}{\longleftarrow} \left\langle \begin{matrix} x(n) \\ y(n) \\ u(n) \end{matrix} \right\rangle \tag{9}$$

Where $\hat{x}(n+1)$ and $\hat{y}(n+1)$ are the estimated states and outputs of the world γ after performing command $u(n)$ on the γ with initial conditions $x(n)$ and $y(n)$.

For building such an estimator the agent needs a set of collected data from the world, i.e. observations during its learning stages (which will be described in the following paragraph), as well as a memory to learn those collected data. In AGI Brain, due to the high power of function approximation of neural networks, the agent is equipped with two neural network memories: explicit memory (EM) and implicit memory (IM). The EM is used as the estimator model in Eq. (9) and the IM is used for direct production of the optimal command u^* without solving Eq. (8).

According to [4], there are three stages of human skill learning; (1) Cognitive: in which movements are slow, inconsistent, and inefficient, (2) Associative: in which movements are more fluid, reliable, and efficient, (3) Autonomous: in which movements are accurate, consistent, and efficient. Regarding the accuracy of the produced signals and with some connivance in the meanings, we implemented the above learning stages in our model as infancy, decision making and expert respectively. During these three learning stages, the artificial brain Γ produces three differently-produced control signals, and stores the consequences of them in its memories, EM and IM.

Infancy Stage. In the infancy stage, the agent tries to collect data from its surrounding world by interacting with it. During this stage, at every time step n, the artificial brain Γ exerts randomly-generated commands u to the world with initial conditions $x(n)$ and $y(n)$, and then observes the results $x(n+1)$ and $y(n+1)$.

Each observation vector o at time step n has the following form;

$$o^n = [x(n), y(n), u(n), x(n+1), y(n+1)]^T \tag{10}$$

The agent stores these data in its memories EM and IM. For the EM, each observation is split into vectors $I_{EM}^n = [x(n), y(n), u(n)]^T$ and $T_{EM}^n = [x(n+1), y(n+1)]^T$ which are trained to the EM as its inputs and targets respectively. And, for the IM, each observation is split into vectors $I_{IM}^n = [x(n), y(n), x(n+1), y(n+1)]^T$ and $T_{IM}^n = [u(n)]$ which are trained to the IM as its inputs and targets respectively. During this stage, these observations will not be used for producing the next commands.

Decision Making Stage. Using EM as the estimator in Eq. (9) and substituting Eq. (9) with state equations of Eq. (8), the decision making problem of Eq. (8) turns into the following equation;

$$u^*(n) = \underset{u \in \aleph}{ArgMax} \left[R = P^T J \right]$$

s.t.

$$\left\langle \begin{matrix} \hat{x}(n+1) \\ \hat{y}(n+1) \end{matrix} \right\rangle \xleftarrow{EM} \left\langle \begin{matrix} x(n) \\ y(n) \\ u(n) \end{matrix} \right\rangle \tag{11}$$

For solving Eq. (11), at every time step n, the artificial brain Γ searches $\aleph$ in three stages: (1) Estimation: using its EM, the Γ estimates how the world γ would seem after executing each alternative $u^k \in \aleph$, i.e. estimating the states $\hat{x}(n+1)$ and the output

$\hat{y}(n+1)$ of the world γ for each alternative $\boldsymbol{u}^k \in \aleph$, given the current states $\boldsymbol{x}(n)$ and outputs $\boldsymbol{y}(n)$, (2) Computation: computing the influence of the estimations on reward function $R = \boldsymbol{P}^T \boldsymbol{J}$ with respect to $\boldsymbol{J} = \boldsymbol{J}(n, \boldsymbol{u}, \hat{\boldsymbol{x}}, \boldsymbol{x}_d, \hat{\boldsymbol{y}}, \boldsymbol{y}_d)$ and $\boldsymbol{P} = \boldsymbol{P}(\boldsymbol{x}_0, \boldsymbol{y}_0)$, (3) Comparison: selecting the alternative which maximizes the reward function R the most as the optimal decision $\boldsymbol{u}^*$. The learning process of the agent is also continued in this stage by learning observations with its IM and EM at certain time steps.

Planning. Planning happens when the agent cannot solve a problem at once (because of its limitations) and has to solve it by making decisions in a series of consecutive steps. During this process, the agent estimates the total value of the reward function over different possible series of consecutive inputs, i.e. $U = \{\boldsymbol{u}(n_1), \boldsymbol{u}(n_2), \ldots, \boldsymbol{u}(n_f)\} \in \aleph$, that here we call them policies. Using its EM, the Γ estimates the consequences of the first member of each randomly-generated policy on current states and outputs of the γ, and then the consequence of the second input on the changed γ, and so on. By computing and then comparing the overall reward of all the policies, the Γ selects the optimal policy U^* which has the maximum reward value over the time horizon n_f. Thus, planning can be considered as an extension of decision making and we have;

$$U^* = \left\{ \boldsymbol{u}(n) \middle| \underset{\boldsymbol{u} \in \aleph}{ArgMax} \sum_{n=n_1}^{n_f} \left[R = \boldsymbol{P}^T \boldsymbol{J} \right] \right\}$$

$s.t.$

$$\left\langle \begin{matrix} \hat{\boldsymbol{x}}(n+1) \\ \hat{\boldsymbol{y}}(n+1) \end{matrix} \right\rangle \overset{EM}{\longleftarrow} \left\langle \begin{matrix} \boldsymbol{x}(n) \\ \boldsymbol{y}(n) \\ \boldsymbol{u}(n) \end{matrix} \right\rangle$$

(12)

Expert Stage. In the expert stage, the IM takes over the decision making unit. Given the initial conditions $\boldsymbol{x}_0$ and $\boldsymbol{y}_0$ as well as the desired states $\boldsymbol{x}_d$ and outputs $\boldsymbol{y}_d$, the IM produces the command $\boldsymbol{u}$ which transits the current states and outputs to the desired states and outputs. In this stage the commands are produced faster and they are more accurate and efficient. The learning process of the agent is also continued in this stage by learning observations with its IM and EM at certain time steps.

Role of Emotions (Stress). The role of stress as a key factor in decision making has been implemented in our model as the exploration/exploitation ratio regulator. It empowers the agent to a further exploration of the world during its second and third stage of learning. Here, we define stress as the distance between the agent's current state/output and its desired state/output, that produces stress signal s which changes the probability of selecting the optimal decision $\boldsymbol{u}^*$ (or optimal policy U^*) as follows;

$$p^{u=u^*} = \frac{1}{1+e^s}$$

(13)

Data Sharing and Shared Memories. In the multi-agent scenarios, the agents can share their experience in the form of observation vectors of Eq. (10). This helps the agents to benefit from the experiences of the other agents and make better decisions.

At a higher level, all of the agents can benefit from one shared explicit memory (SEM) and one shared implicit memory (SIM) which are trained with the observations of all of the agents. For training SEM and SIM, a matrix of observations O^n is formed from the observation vector o^n of each agent.

3 Simulation

3.1 Continuous ASOR Space

Function Optimization. Assume a world γ_1 which contains a function f as the object ψ_1 which is going to be optimized by a group of agents $\omega_1^1, \omega_1^2, \ldots, \omega_1^N$, who have these objectives: (1) j_1: finding the maxima of the function, (2) j_2: social behavior by moving close to the group, and (3) j_3: following the leader, i.e. the agent whose function value is more than the other agents. The agents have different personalities. Coefficient p_1 is positive but p_2 and p_3 are small normally distributed random numbers, so that some agents may try to get far from the group and/or the leader. Agents with negative value of p_3 get nervous when they are far from the leader and may not execute their optimal decision. They select their next moves during their three stages of learning using their SEM and SIM.

$$\gamma_1 : y = f(x_1, x_2)$$
$$= 20 \exp(-0.01 \sqrt{x_1^2 + x_2^2}) + \sum_{i=1}^{20} 10 \exp(-0.05 \sqrt{(x_1 - x_{1i})^2 + (x_2 - x_{2i})^2}) \quad (14)$$

Where x_{1i} and x_{2i} are random numbers that satisfy the equation: $x_{1i}^2 + x_{2i}^2 = 1000^2$. The simulation results are depicted in Fig. 2.

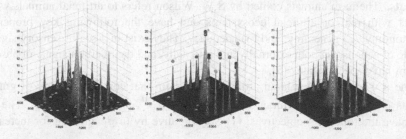

Fig. 2. Simulation results of AGI Brain on γ_1: small spheres represent agents' positions at: (Left) the infancy stage, (Center) At epoch 35 of the decision making stage some agents reached local and global maxima, (Right) Expert stage: Starting from any initial position, they all reached the global maxima using SIM.

Tracking Control of a MIMO Nonlinear System. Assume a world γ_2 which contains a continuous stirred tank reactor (CSTR) as the object ψ_2, which is a multi-input multi-output (MIMO) plant described by the following state-space equations[1]:

$$\gamma_2 : \begin{cases} \frac{dh(t)}{dt} = w_1(t) + w_2(t) - 0.2\sqrt{h(t)} \\ \frac{dC_b(t)}{dt} = (C_{b1} - C_b(t))\frac{w_1(t)}{h(t)} + (C_{b2} - C_b(t))\frac{w_2(t)}{h(t)} - \frac{k_1 C_b(t)}{(1 + k_2 C_b(t))^2} \end{cases} \quad (15)$$

Where $h(t)$ is the liquid level, $C_b(t)$ is concentration of the output product, $w_1(t)$ and $w_2(t)$ are input flow rates, $C_{b1} = 24.9$ and $C_{b2} = 0.1$ are input concentrations, and $k_1 = k_1 = 1$ are constants associated with the rate of consumption. The single agent ω_2 has to control the liquid level and product concentration on a predefined reference $y_d = [18, 20]^T$ by its available actions $u(n) = [w_1(n), w_2(n)]^T$. Figure 3 illustrates the results of simulation.

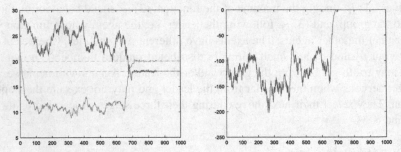

Fig. 3. Simulation results of AGI Brain on γ_2: (Left) Plant outputs during: Infancy stage ($0 \leq n \leq 650$), decision making stage ($651 \leq n \leq 850$), and expert stage ($851 \leq n \leq 1000$). Blue line: liquid level, red line: liquid concentration, dashed red line: level reference, and dashed magenta line: concentration reference, (Right) Total reward value.

3.2   Hybrid ASOR Space

Animats. The term animats coined by S.W. Wilson refers to artificial animals which interact with real or artificial ecosystems and have the following key properties: (1) autonomy, (2) generality, and (3) adequacy. They exist in a sea of sensory signals, capable of actions, act both externally and internally, and their certain signal or absence of them have special status [5].

Assume a world γ_3 which is an artificial ecosystem that contains a cattle of grazing animats $\omega_3^1, \omega_3^2, \ldots, \omega_3^N$, pasturages $\psi_3^{ps1}, \psi_3^{ps2}, \ldots, \psi_3^{psM}$, and a predator ψ_3^{Pr}. The animats have the following objectives: (1) Staying alive by (a) j_1: grazing for increasing

---

[1] Although the describing equations of the first and the second scenario are available, AGI Brain considers them as unknown environments, and from the observations that are gathered by interaction with these unknown environments, it builds their models in its memories and then completes its required tasks based on the models.

their energy, (b) not getting hunted by the predator by j_2: moving as far as possible from it, and j_3: by moving close to the cattle, (2) j_4: Reproduction by mating, and (3) j_5: Searching for new pasturages ψ_3^{psl}. The animats have the following discrete actions set: $\aleph = \{\text{up,down,right,left,eat,mate}\}$.

The rules of the world γ_3 are as follows: The animats can move by performing $u_1 = $ up,$u_2 = $ down,$u_3 = $ right and $u_4 = $ left. They can only increase their energy by performing action $u_5 = $ eat when they are near a pasturage, otherwise they lose one unit of energy. They can only reproduce by performing action $u_6 = $ mate when they are mature and they have enough energy. The animats get hunted and die by the predator ψ_3^{Pr} when they are very close to it. Also, they die whether their energy level is equal to zero, or they get old. Corresponding elements of the dynamic personality vector $P(x_0, y_0)$ will change when different situations occur, e.g. when the animat ω_3^k observes the predator near to it, $p_2(x_0, y_0)$ and $p_3(x_0, y_0)$ are increased while other elements are decreased to zero. They select their next actions during their three levels of learning using their SEM and SIM. Figure 4 illustrates snap shots of simulation.

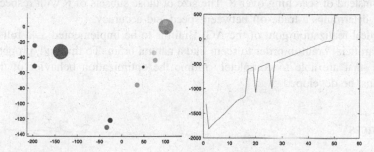

Fig. 4. Simulation snapshots of AGI Brain on γ_3: (Left) snapshot of the agents' positions during decision making stage. The big green circle represent a pasturage, small circles represent the agents moving towards the pasturage, big red circle represent the predator, and small circles with red star represent hunted agents, (Right) Reward value of agent ω_3^k during decision making stage (color figure online).

4   Discussion and Future Works

In this paper, the AGI Brain as a learning and decision making framework was introduced. The model utilizes optimization as its theory and state-space representation as its technique. It implements the three levels of human learning using its IM and EM. Also it incorporates planning as well as some mental factors of the human intelligence like emotions and different personalities. AGI Brain was tested on two category of problems with continuous and hybrid ASOR deterministic spaces.

As can be seen in the simulation section, the model returned successful results in the above-mentioned scenarios. Utilizing different personalities helped in different behavior as well as exploration/exploitation diversity. For instance, in the first scenario, agents with different personalities found other local maxima of the function. Also, implementation of the role of stress resulted in more exploration, e.g. in the second scenario. Additionally, the model benefits from ultimate learning power of neural networks. The learning problem of neural networks when dealing with discrete (categorical) ASORs was solved by incorporating pattern recognition neural networks, and high precision learning achieved, e.g. in the third scenario. In multi-agent scenarios, the agents utilize SEM and SIM where they can share their experiences with other agents.

Despite the successful results of AGI Brain on current scenarios, still more developments, implementations and tests on other scenarios must be performed, in order to guarantee the multi-purpose applicability of AGI Brain. Currently, the model is parameter-dependent, e.g. the time horizon of planning. In order to determining the *sufficient* amount of a parameter for successfully accomplishing a policy on a desired task, the model should also learn these parameters during its learning stages, preferably during its infancy stage. The model works only in deterministic environments as yet. For stochastic environments, the IM and EM must be empowered with memories which are able to correctly estimate, for example, the results of an action in a stochastic world. For large alternatives sets $\aleph$, the performance speed of the model can be improved by searching over smaller random subsets of $\aleph$ (whose elements are randomly selected from $\aleph$), instead of searching over $\aleph$. The size of those subsets of $\aleph$ with respect to the size of $\aleph$ determines a trade-off between speed and accuracy.

The ideal realization goal of the AGI Brain is to be implemented as a full-neural-network artificial brain in order to seem like a natural brain. To this end, proper neural networks -that are able to completely mimic the optimization behavior of the AGI Brain- must be developed.

References

1. Wang, P.: Artificial General Intelligence, A gentle introduction, [Online]. https://sites.google.com/site/narswang/home/agi-introduction. Accessed Jan 2019
2. Paraskevopoulos, P.: Modern Control Engineering. Taylor & Francis Group, Didcot (2002)
3. Sutton, R.S., Barto, A.G.: Reinforcement Learning: An Introduction, 2nd edn. MIT Press, Cambridge (2018)
4. Wulf, G.: Attention and Motor Skills Learning. Human Kinetics, Champaign (2007)
5. Strannegard, C., Svangard, N., Lindstrom, D., Bach, J., Steunebrick, B.: Learning and decision making in artificial animals. J. Artif. Gen. Intell. **9**(1), 55–82 (2018)

Augmented Utilitarianism for AGI Safety

Nadisha-Marie Aliman[1]([✉]) and Leon Kester[2]

[1] Utrecht University, Utrecht, The Netherlands
nadishamarie.aliman@gmail.com
[2] TNO Netherlands, The Hague, The Netherlands

Abstract. In the light of ongoing progresses of research on artificial
intelligent systems exhibiting a steadily increasing problem-solving ability, the identification of practicable solutions to the value alignment
problem in AGI Safety is becoming a matter of urgency. In this context, one preeminent challenge that has been addressed by multiple
researchers is the adequate formulation of utility functions or equivalents
reliably capturing human ethical conceptions. However, the specification
of suitable utility functions harbors the risk of "perverse instantiation"
for which no final consensus on responsible proactive countermeasures
has been achieved so far. Amidst this background, we propose a novel
non-normative socio-technological ethical framework denoted *Augmented
Utilitarianism* which directly alleviates the perverse instantiation problem. We elaborate on how augmented by AI and more generally science
and technology, it might allow a society to craft and update ethical utility functions while jointly undergoing a dynamical ethical enhancement.
Further, we elucidate the need to consider embodied simulations in the
design of utility functions for AGIs aligned with human values. Finally,
we discuss future prospects regarding the usage of the presented scientifically grounded ethical framework and mention possible challenges.

Keywords: AGI Safety · Utility function · Perverse instantiation ·
AI alignment · Augmented Utilitarianism

1 Motivation

The problem of unambiguously specifying human goals for advanced AI systems
such that these systems once deployed, do not violate the implicitly underlying
intended human conceptions by pursuing unforeseen solutions, has been referred
to as "literalness" [31,42] or also "perverse instantiation" [10,41] problem. A
higher problem solving ability does not necessarily entail the integration of the
contextual knowledge required from an advanced AI in order to accurately interpret human ethical conceptions. Therefore, it is of great importance from the
perspective of A(G)I Safety and A(G)I Ethics to a priori consider this crucial
issue when crafting quantitative utility functions for intelligent systems that
would operate based on the human goals these functions encode. Recently, a
novel type of such explicitly formulated utility functions denoted *ethical goal*

© Springer Nature Switzerland AG 2019
P. Hammer et al. (Eds.): AGI 2019, LNAI 11654, pp. 11–21, 2019.
https://doi.org/10.1007/978-3-030-27005-6_2

functions [2, 40] has been introduced as critical tool for a society to achieve a meaningful control of autonomous intelligent systems aligned with human ethical values. Departing from this, we show why in order to design ethical goal functions and avoid perverse instantiation scenarios, one needs a novel type of ethical framework for the utility elicitation on whose basis these functions are crafted. We introduce a new to be described socio-technological ethical framework denoted *Augmented Utilitarianism* (which we abbreviate with AU in the following).

While multiple methods have been suggested as moral theory approaches to achieve ethical objective functions for AGIs [16, 17] (including classical ethical frameworks like consequentialism or encompassing methods based on uncertain objectives and moral uncertainty [9, 15]), most approaches do not provide a fundamental solution to the underlying problem which wrongly appears to be solely of philosophical nature. According to Goertzel [20], *"pithy summaries of complex human values evoke their commonly accepted meanings only within the human cultural context"*. More generally, we argue that in order to craft utility functions that should not lead to a behavior of advanced AI systems violating human ethical intuitions, one has to scientifically consider relevant contextual and embodied information. Moreover, it could be highly valuable to take into account human biases and constraints that obstruct ethical decision-making and attempt to remediate resulting detrimental effects using science and technology. In contrast to the AU approach we will present, most currently known moral theories and classical ethical frameworks considered for advanced AI systems do not integrate these decisive elements and might therefore riskily not exhibit a sufficient safety level with regard to perverse instantiation.

2   Deconstructing Perverse Instantiation

In the following, we enumerate (using the generic notation < *FinalGoal* >: < *PerverseInstantiation* >) a few conceivable perverse instantion scenarios that have been formulated in the past:

1. "Make us smile": "Paralyze human facial musculatures into constant beaming smiles" (example by Bostrom [10])
2. "Make us happy": "Implant electrodes into the pleasure centers of our brains" (example by Bostrom [10])
3. "Making all people happy": "Killing all people [...] as with zero people around all of them are happy" (example by Yampolskiy [42])
4. "Making all people happy": "Forced lobotomies for every man, woman and child [...]" (example by Yampolskiy [42])

From our view, one could extract the following two types of failures out of the specified perverse instantiations: misspecification of final goal criteria and the so called *perspectival fallacy of utility assignment* [2] which will become apparant in our explanation. First, one could argue that already the proposed formulations regarding the criteria of the final goal do not optimally capture the nature of the intended sense from a scientific perspective which might have finally misguided the AI. While the concept of happiness certainly represents a highly ambiguous construct, modern research in the field of positive psychology [35, 39], hedonic psychology [23] and further research areas offers a scientific basis to assess what it means for human entities. For instance, one might come to the conclusion that a highly desirable final goal of humanity for a superintelligence rather represents a concept which is close to the notion of "well-being". In psychology, well-being has been among others described as a construct consisting of five measurable elements: positive emotions, engagement, relationships, meaning and achievement (PERMA) [38]. Another known psychological measure for well-being is subjective well-being [29] (SWB) which is composed of frequent positive affect, infrequent negative affect and life satisfaction [11, 13]. In both cases, happiness only represents a subelement of the respective well-being construct. Similarly, as stated by Diener and Bieswas-Diener [14], *"happiness alone is not enough; people need to be happy for the right reasons"*. Coming back to the provided examples for perverse instantiation, in the cases 1, 2 and 4, it is implausible that a pluralistic criteria of well-being like PERMA would have been met.

Second, it is however important to note that even if the final goal would have been specified in a way reflecting psychological insights, a perverse instantiation cannot necessarily be precluded without more ado. By way of illustration, we correspondingly reformulate the example 3 within a new type of perverse instantiation and provide an additional example. We thereby use the term "flourish" to allude to the achievement of a high level of well-being in line with a psychological understanding of the concept as exemplified in the last paragraph.

5. Make all people flourish: Killing all people
6. Make all people flourish: Initiate a secret genocide until the few uninformed people left in future generations all flourish

Despite a suitable final goal, value alignment is not succesful in 5 and 6 because the underlying assignment of utility seems to be based on a detached modus operandi in which the effects of scenarios on the *own* current mental states of the people generating this function are ignored. Thereby, it is assumed that during utility assignment, the involved people are considered as remote observers, while at the same time one inherently takes their perspective while referring to this mapping with the emotionally connoted description of a *perverse* instantiation. This type of detached design of utility functions ignoring i.a. affective and emotional parameters of the own mental state has been described as being subject to the perspectival fallacy of utility assignment [2]. Although most people would currently dislike all provided examples 1–6, the aggregated mental states of their current selves seem not to be reflected within the utility function of the AI which instead considered a synthetic detached measure only related to their future selves or/and future living people. In the next paragraph, we briefly introduce a known problem in population ethics that exhibits similar patterns and which might be of interest for the design of utility functions for advanced AI systems in certain safety-relevant application areas [15].

Population ethics [21] is an issue in philosophy concerning decision-making that potentially leads to populations with varying numbers or/and identities of their members. One interesting element of a population ethics theory is the derived population axiology which represents the total order of different population states according to their ethical desirability. As an example, consider the choice of either perform a policy measure that leads to a population A of ca. 10 billion members and a very high positive welfare or to rather prefer another policy measure leading to a population Z of ca. 10.000 billion members and a much lower only barely acceptable (but still positive) welfare. Intuitively, most people would rank the policy measure leading to population A as higher than the one leading to population Z. However, given the population axiology of total utilitarianism [21], Z might well be ranked higher than A if the number of people multiplied by their welfare is bigger for population Z in comparison to population A. This type of violation of human ethical intuitions when applying total utilitarianism to population ethics has been termed "Repugnant Conclusion" by Derik Parfit [34]. In this context, Arrhenius [3] proved in one of his impossibility theorems that no population axiology[1] can be formulated that concurrently satisfies a certain number of ethical desiderata.

However, as shown by Aliman and Kester [2], this type of impossibility theorem does not apply to population axiologies that take the mental states of those attempting to craft the total orders during utility elicitation into account. Similarly to the perverse instantiation examples 1–6, the application of e.g. total utilitarianism to the described scenario is subject to the perspectival fallacy of utility assignment. As in the case of these perverse instantiations, the fact that most people consider the scenario involving population Z as *repugnant* is not reflected in the utility function which only includes a detached measure of the well-being of future people. In practice, how humans rate the ethical desirability of for instance a policy measure leading to a certain population, is dependent on the effect the mental simulation of the associated scenario has on their corresponding mental states which inherently encode e.g. societal, cultural and temporal information. For instance, from the perspective of a current population Z_0 being similar to population Z both with regard to number of people and welfare level, it might instead be "repugnant" to prefer the policy measure leading to population A [2]. The reason being that the scenario leading from Z_0 to A might have included a dying out or even a genocide. The lack of the required contextual information in consequentialist frameworks (such as utilitarianism) has implications for AIs and AGIs that are implemented in the form of expected utility maximizers mostly operating in a consequentialist fashion.

3   Augmenting Utilitarianism

In the light of the above, it appears vital to refine classical utilitarianism (CU) if one intends to utilize it as basis for utility functions that do not lead to perverse

---

[1] Importantly, this also applies to non-consequentialist frameworks such as deontological ethics [21].

instantiation scenarios. However, as opposed to classical ethical frameworks, AU does not represent a normative theory aimed at specifying what humans *ought to do*. In fact, its necessity arises directly from a technical requirement for the meaningful control of artificial intelligent systems equipped with a utility function. Since the perverse instantiation problem represents a significant constraint to the design of ethical goal functions, a novel tailored ethical framework able to alleviate issues related to both misspecification of final goal criteria and perspectival fallacy of utility assignment emerges as exigency. With this in mind, AU is formulated as a non-normative ethical framework for AGI Safety which can be augmented by the use of science and technology in order to facilitate a dynamical societal process of crafting and updating ethical goal functions. Instead of specifying what an agent ought to do, AU helps to identify what the current society *should want* an (artificial or human) agent to do if this society wants to maximize expected utility. In this connection, utility could ideally represent a generic scientifically grounded (possibly aggregated) measure capturing one or more ethically desirable final goal(s) as defined by society itself. In the following, we describe by what type of components AU could augment CU:

– *Scientific grounding of utility:* According to Jeremy Bentham [7], the founder of CU *"by the principle of utility is meant that principle which approves or disapproves of every action whatsoever according to the tendency it appears to have to augment or diminish the happiness of the party whose interest is in question"*. For AU, one could for instance reformulate the principle of utility by substituting "happiness" with a generic scientific measure for one or more final goal(s). In the context of crafting ethical goal functions, the party whose interest is in question is society. Further, a crucial difference between CU and AU is that in order to assess the tendency an action has to augment or diminish the chosen ethical measure, AU considers more than just the outcome of that action as used in the classical sense, since AU presupposes the *mental-state-dependency* [2] of utility as will be expounded in the next subitem. With this application-oriented view, one could then argue that what society should ideally want an agent to do are actions that are conformable to this modified mental-state-dependent principle of utility. In this paper, we exemplarily consider well-being as reasonable high level final goal candidate which is e.g. already reflected in the UN Sustainable Developmental Goals (SDGs) [44] and is in the spirit of positive computing [12]. Besides SWB [29] and PERMA [38], multiple measures of well-being exist in psychology with focus on different well-being factors. For instance, the concept of objective happiness [23] has been proposed by Kahneman. Well-being has moreover been linked to the hierarchy of needs of Abraham Maslow which he extended to contain self-transcendence at the highest level on top of self-actualization in his later years [26,27,30]. (Recently, related AI research aiming at inducing self-transcendent states for users has been considered by among others Mossbridge and Goertzel [32].) For a review on relevant well-being factors that might be pivotal for a dedicated positive computing, see Calvo and Peters [11].

– *Mental-state-dependency:* As adumbrated in the last section, human ethical evaluation of an outcome of an action is related to their mental states which take into account the simulation that led to this outcome. The mental phenomenon of actively simulating different alternative scenarios (including anticipatory emotions [6]) has been termed conceptual consumption [19] and plays a role in decision-making. Similarly, according to Johnson [22] *"moral deliberation is a process of cognitive conative affective simulation"*. Moreover, it has been shown that for diverse economical and societal contexts, people do not only value the outcome of actions but also assign a well-being relevant *procedural utility* [18,25] to the policy that led to these outcomes. In light of this, AU assigns utility at a higher abstraction level by e.g. considering the underlying state transition (from starting state s over action a to outcome s') instead of the outcome alone as performed in classical consequential frameworks like CU. Furthermore, according to constructionist approaches in neuroscience [5], the brain constructs mental states based on *"sensations from the world, sensations from the body, and prior experience"* [33]. Hence, ethical judgements might vary with respect to multiple parameters encompassing e.g. psychological, biographical, cultural, temporal, social and physiological information. Likewise, the recent Moral Machine experiment studying human ethical conceptions on trolley case scenarios with i.a. autonomous vehicles showed *"substantial cultural variations"* in the exhibited moral preferences [4]. Ethical frameworks for AGI utility functions that disregard the mental-state-dependency may more likely lead to perverse instantiations, since they ignore what we call the *embodied nature of ethical total orders*. In the light of the aforesaid, AU considers perceiver-dependent and context-sensitive utility functions which could e.g. be formulated at the transition level leading to utility functions $U_x(s,a,s')$ for each perceiver x instead of the general $U(s')$ in CU.
– *Debiasing of utility assignment:* One might regard decision utility based on observed choices (as exhibited e.g. in big data [36]) as sufficient utility source for a possible instantiation of AU if one assumes that humans are rational agents that already act as to optimize what increases their well-being. However, utility as measured from this third-person perspective might not capture the actual experienced utility from a first-person perspective due to multiple human cognitive biases [8,24]. Since it is impossible to directly extract the instant utility (the basic building block of experienced utility [24]) of future outcomes to craft ethical goal functions, AU could – in its most basic implementation – rely on predicted utility which represents the belief on the future experienced utility people would assign to a given scenario from a first-person perspective. However, the mental simulations on whose basis predicted utility is extracted are still distorted among others due to the fact that humans fail to accurately predict their appreciation of future scenarios [24]. Therefore, it has been suggested by Aliman and Kester [2] to augment the utility elicitation process by the utilization of technologies like virtual reality and augmented reality within a simulation environment in order to be able to get access to a less biased *artificially simulated future instant utility*. (Thereby, simpler

techniques such as movies or diverse types of immersive storytelling are as well conceivable.) Analogous to the AI-aided policy-by-simulation approach [40], this technique might offer a powerful preemptive tool for AGI Safety in an AU framework. Overall, the experience of possible future world scenarios might improve the quality of utility assignment while having the potential to yield an ethical enhancement for one thing due to the debiased view on the future and secondly, for instance due to beneficial effects that immersive technologies might have on prosocial behavior including certain forms of empathy [12,28]. Interestingly, the experience of individualized and tailored simulations itself might provide an alternative simulation-based solution to the value alignment problem [43].

– *Self-reflexivity:* As opposed to CU, AU is intended as a self-reflexive ethical framework which augments itself. Due to the mental-state-dependency it incorporates and the associated embodied nature of ethical total orders, it might even be necessary to craft new ethical goal functions within a so-called socio-technological feedback-loop [2]. In doing so, ongoing technological progresses might help to augment the debiasing of utility assignment while novel scientific insights might facilitate to filter out the most sophisticated measure for the ethically desired form of utility given the current state of society. Advances in A(G)I development itself leading to a higher problem solving ability might further boost AU with an improved predictability of future outcomes leading to more precise ethical goal functions. Given its generic nature, what humans should want an agent to do might thereby vary qualitatively in an AU framework, since quantitatively specifiable observations at specific time steps within a socio-technological feedback-loop might even lead society to modify the desired final goal candidate(s) making it possible to ameliorate the framework as time goes by.

Table 1. Decision-making focuses within different possible ethical frameworks for AGI Safety. "S&T" denotes a foreseen augmentation of the ethical decision making process by science and technology including A(G)I itself. By "experiencer", we refer to the entities in society performing the ethical evaluation via the experience of simulations (in a mental mode only or augmented).

Ethics framework/Focus	Agent	Action	Outcome	Experiencer	S&T
Virtue ethics	x				
Deontological ethics		x			
Consequentialist ethics (e.g. CU)			x		
AU	x	x	x	x	x

– *Amalgamation of diverse perspectives*: Finally, we postulate that AU^2, despite its intrinsically different motivation as a socio-technological ethical framework for AGI Safety and its non-normative nature, can be nevertheless understood as allowing a coalescence of diverse theoretical perspectives that have been historically assigned to normative ethical frameworks. To sum up and contextualize the experiencer-based AU, Table 1 provides an overview on the different decision-making focuses used in relevant known ethical frameworks that might be seen as candidates for AGI Safety.

4   Conclusion and Future Prospects

In a nutshell, we proposed AU as a novel non-normative socio-technological ethical framework grounded in science which is conceived for the purpose of crafting societal ethical goal functions for AGI Safety. While CU and other classical ethical frameworks if used for AGI utility functions might engender the perverse instantiation problem, AU directly tackles this issue. AU augments CU by the following main elements: scientific grounding of utility, mental-state-dependency, debiasing of utility assignment using technology, self-reflexivity and amalgamation of diverse perspectives. Thereby, AU facilitates the explicit formulation of perceiver-dependent and context-sensitive utility functions (e.g. of the form $U_x(s, a, s')$ instead of $U(s')$ as performed in CU) for an aggregation at the societal level. These *human-crafted* ethical goal functions should be made publicly available within a white-box setting e.g. for reasons of transparency, AI coordination, disentanglement of responsibilities for AI governance and law enforcement [2] (which differs from using utility functions implicitly learned by AI agents or AIs learning moral conceptions from data such as e.g. in [36]). Besides being able to contribute to the meaningful control of intelligent systems, AU could also be utilizable for human agents in the policy-making domain. Overall, we agree with Goertzel [20] that the perverse instantiation problem seems rather not to represent *"a general point about machine intelligence or superintelligence"*.

One of the main future challenges for the realization of AU could be the circumstance that one can only strive to approximate ethical goal functions, since a full utility elicitation on all possible future scenarios is obviously not feasible. However, already an approximation process within a socio-technological feedback-loop could lead to an ethical enhancement at a societal level. Besides that, in order to achieve safe run-time adaptive artificial intelligent systems reliably complying with ethical goal functions, a "self-awareness" functionality might be required [1,40]. Moreover, the security of the utility function itself is essential, due to the possibility of its modification by malevolent actors during the deployment phase. Finally, proactive AGI Safety research [1] on *ethical adversarial examples* – a conceivable type of integrity attacks on the AGI sensors having ethical consequences might be important to study in future work to complement the use of safe utility functions.

---

[2] AU is not be to confused with agent-relative consequentialism which is a normative agent-based framework, does not foresee a grounding in science and seems to assume a "pretheoretical grasp" [37] of its "better-than-relative-to" relation.

Acknowledgements. We would like to thank Peter Werkhoven for a helpful discussion of our approach.

References

1. Aliman, N.-M., Kester, L.: Hybrid strategies towards safe self-aware superintelligent systems. In: Iklé, M., Franz, A., Rzepka, R., Goertzel, B. (eds.) AGI 2018. LNCS (LNAI), vol. 10999, pp. 1–11. Springer, Cham (2018). https://doi.org/10.1007/978-3-319-97676-1_1
2. Aliman, N.M., Kester, L.: Transformative AI governance and AI-empowered ethical enhancement through preemptive simulations. Delphi Interdisc. Rev. Emerg. Technol. **2**(1), 23–29 (2019)
3. Arrhenius, G.: An impossibility theorem for welfarist axiologies. Econ. Philos. **16**(2), 247–266 (2000)
4. Awad, E., et al.: The moral machine experiment. Nature **563**(7729), 59 (2018)
5. Barrett, L.F.: The theory of constructed emotion: an active inference account of interoception and categorization. Soc. Cogn. Affect. Neurosci. **12**(1), 1–23 (2017)
6. Baucells, M., Bellezza, S.: Temporal profiles of instant utility during anticipation, event, and recall. Manag. Sci. **63**(3), 729–748 (2016)
7. Bentham, J.: An Introduction to the Principles of Morals and Legislation. Dover Publications, Mineola (1780)
8. Berridge, K.C., O'Doherty, J.P.: From experienced utility to decision utility. In: Neuroeconomics, pp. 335–351. Elsevier (2014)
9. Bogosian, K.: Implementation of moral uncertainty in intelligent machines. Mind. Mach. **27**(4), 591–608 (2017)
10. Bostrom, N.: Superintelligence: Paths, Dangers, Strategies, 1st edn. Oxford University Press Inc., New York (2014)
11. Busseri, M.A., Sadava, S.W.: A review of the tripartite structure of subjective well-being: implications for conceptualization, operationalization, analysis, and synthesis. Pers. Soc. Psychol. Rev. **15**(3), 290–314 (2011)
12. Calvo, R.A., Peters, D.: Positive Computing: Technology for Wellbeing and Human Potential. MIT Press, Cambridge (2014)
13. Diener, E.: Subjective well-being: the science of happiness and a proposal for a national index. Am. Psychol. **55**(1), 34 (2000)
14. Diener, E., Biswas-Diener, R.: Happiness: Unlocking the Mysteries of Psychological Wealth. Wiley, New York (2011)
15. Eckersley, P.: Impossibility and uncertainty theorems in AI value alignment (or why your AGI should not have a utility function). CoRR abs/1901.00064 (2018)
16. Everitt, T.: Towards safe artificial general intelligence. Ph.D. thesis, Australian National University (2018)
17. Everitt, T., Lea, G., Hutter, M.: AGI safety literature review. In: Proceedings of the Twenty-Seventh International Joint Conference on Artificial Intelligence, IJCAI 2018, pp. 5441–5449. International Joint Conferences on Artificial Intelligence Organization, July 2018. https://doi.org/10.24963/ijcai.2018/768
18. Frey, B.S., Stutzer, A.: Beyond Bentham-measuring procedural utility (2001)
19. Gilbert, D.T., Wilson, T.D.: Prospection: experiencing the future. Science **317**(5843), 1351–1354 (2007)
20. Goertzel, B.: Superintelligence: fears, promises and potentials. J. Evol. Technol. **24**(2), 55–87 (2015)

21. Greaves, H.: Population axiology. Philos. Compass **12**(11), e12442 (2017)
22. Johnson, M.: Moral Imagination: Implications of Cognitive Science for Ethics. University of Chicago Press, Chicago (1994)
23. Kahneman, D., Diener, E., Schwarz, N.: Well-Being: Foundations of Hedonic Psychology. Russell Sage Foundation, New York (1999)
24. Kahneman, D., Wakker, P.P., Sarin, R.: Back to Bentham? explorations of experienced utility. Q. J. Econ. **112**(2), 375–406 (1997)
25. Kaminitz, S.C.: Contemporary procedural utility and Hume's early idea of utility. J. Happiness Stud. **20**, 1–14 (2019)
26. Kaufman, S.B.: Self-actualizing people in the 21st century: integration with contemporary theory and research on personality and well-being. J. Humanist. Psychol. 0022167818809187 (2018). https://doi.org/10.1177/0022167818809187
27. Koltko-Rivera, M.E.: Rediscovering the later version of Maslow's hierarchy of needs: self-transcendence and opportunities for theory, research, and unification. Rev. Gen. Psychol. **10**(4), 302–317 (2006)
28. van Loon, A., Bailenson, J., Zaki, J., Bostick, J., Willer, R.: Virtual reality perspective-taking increases cognitive empathy for specific others. PloS ONE **13**(8), e0202442 (2018)
29. Lyubomirsky, S.: Why are some people happier than others? The role of cognitive and motivational processes in well-being. Am. Psychol. **56**(3), 239 (2001)
30. Maslow, A.H.: The Farther Reaches of Human Nature. Viking Press, New York (1971)
31. Meuhlhauser, L., Helm, L.: Intelligence explosion and machine ethics. In: Singularity Hypotheses: A Scientific and Philosophical Assessment, pp. 101–126 (2012)
32. Mossbridge, J., et al.: Emotionally-sensitive AI-driven android interactions improve social welfare through helping people access self-transcendent states. In: AI for Social Good Workshop at Neural Information Processing Systems 2018 Conference (2018)
33. Oosterwijk, S., Lindquist, K.A., Anderson, E., Dautoff, R., Moriguchi, Y., Barrett, L.F.: States of mind: emotions, body feelings, and thoughts share distributed neural networks. NeuroImage **62**(3), 2110–2128 (2012)
34. Parfit, D.: Reasons and Persons. Oxford University Press, Oxford (1984)
35. Peterson, C.: A Primer in Positive Psychology. Oxford University Press, Oxford (2006)
36. Rafal, R., Kenji, A.: Toward artificial ethical learners that could also teach you how to be a moral man. In: IJCAI 2015 Workshop on Cognitive Knowledge Acquisition and Applications (Cognitum 2015). IJCAI (2015)
37. Schroeder, M.: Teleology, agent-relative value, and 'good'. Ethics **117**(2), 265–295 (2007)
38. Seligman, M.E.: Flourish: A Visionary New Understanding of Happiness and Well-Being. Simon and Schuster, New York (2012)
39. Seligman, M.E.P., Csikszentmihalyi, M.: positive psychology: an introduction. In: Csikszentmihalyi, M. (ed.) Flow and the Foundations of Positive Psychology, pp. 279–298. Springer, Dordrecht (2014). https://doi.org/10.1007/978-94-017-9088-8_18
40. Werkhoven, P., Kester, L., Neerincx, M.: Telling autonomous systems what to do. In: Proceedings of the 36th European Conference on Cognitive Ergonomics, p. 2. ACM (2018)
41. Yampolskiy, R.V.: Utility function security in artificially intelligent agents. J. Exp. Theor. Artif. Intell. **26**(3), 373–389 (2014)

42. Yampolskiy, R.V.: Artificial Superintelligence: A Futuristic Approach. Chapman and Hall/CRC, Boca Raton (2015)
43. Yampolskiy, R.V.: Personal universes: a solution to the multi-agent value alignment problem. arXiv preprint arXiv:1901.01851 (2019)
44. Ziesche, S.: Potential synergies between the united nations sustainable development goals and the value loading problem in artificial intelligence. Maldives Nat. J. Res. **6**, 47 (2018)

Orthogonality-Based Disentanglement of Responsibilities for Ethical Intelligent Systems

Nadisha-Marie Aliman[1]([✉]), Leon Kester[2], Peter Werkhoven[1,2], and Roman Yampolskiy[3]

[1] Utrecht University, Utrecht, Netherlands
nadishamarie.aliman@gmail.com
[2] TNO Netherlands, The Hague, Netherlands
[3] University of Louisville, Louisville, USA

Abstract. In recent years, the implementation of meaningfully controllable advanced intelligent systems whose goals are aligned with ethical values as specified by human entities emerged as key subject of investigation of international relevance across diverse AI-related research areas. In this paper, we present a novel transdisciplinary and Systems Engineering oriented approach denoted *"orthogonality-based disentanglement"* which jointly tackles both the thereby underlying control problem and value alignment problem while unraveling the corresponding responsibilities of different stakeholders based on the distinction of two orthogonal axes assigned to the problem-solving ability of these intelligent systems on the one hand and to the ethical abilities they exhibit based on quantitatively encoded human values on the other hand. Moreover, we introduce the notion of explicitly formulated *ethical goal functions* ideally encoding what humans *should* want and exemplify a possible class of "self-aware" intelligent systems with the capability to reliably adhere to these human-defined goal functions. Beyond that, we discuss an attainable transformative socio-technological feedback-loop that could result out of the introduced orthogonality-based disentanglement approach and briefly elaborate on how the framework additionally provides valuable hints with regard to the coordination subtask in AI Safety. Finally, we point out remaining crucial challenges as incentive for future work.

Keywords: Ethical goal function · Self-awareness · AI alignment · Control problem · AI coordination

1 Motivation

In the current both safety-critical and ethically relevant international debate on how to achieve a meaningful control of advanced intelligent systems that comply with human values [19], diverse solution approaches have been proposed that fundamentally differ in the way they would affect the future development of

© Springer Nature Switzerland AG 2019
P. Hammer et al. (Eds.): AGI 2019, LNAI 11654, pp. 22–31, 2019.
https://doi.org/10.1007/978-3-030-27005-6_3

A(G)I research. In a nutshell, one could identify a set of four main clusters of conceptually different solution approaches for which one could advocate for by distinguishing between (1) *prohibitive*, (2) *self-regulative*, (3) *deontological* and (4) *utility-based* methods. While the prohibitive approach aims at restricting or even banning the development of highly sophisticated AI until problems related to control and value alignment are solved in the first place, it seems highly unlikely to be put into practice especially in its most extreme forms and it is therefore not further considered in this paper. By contrast, option (2) implies the assumption that certain mechanisms (for instance specific market mechanisms or mechanisms inherent to certain types of A(G)I architectures) could allow for a more or less automatically emerging stability or desirability of the behavior as exhibited by intelligent systems. Furthermore, solution (3) classically considers the direct hard-coding of ethical values into AI systems for instance by encoding deontological values at design time [18], while in the case of the utility-based approach (4), one mostly foresees a human-defined utility function [24] quantitatively encoding human values.

This debate – especially on whether to prefer the solution approach (3) or (4) – is often strongly imprinted by particularly difficult to solve philosophical issues and the AI-related responsibilities of different involved stakeholders such as users, programmers, manufacturers and legislators appears to be only vaguely and therefore insufficiently definable. Against this backdrop, the need for a practicable technically oriented and at the same time forward-looking solution appears to be of urgent importance for a responsible future planning of a hybrid society in close conjunction with advanced AI systems.

2 Disentanglement of Responsibilities

For reasons of safety, security, controllability, accountability and reliability, it can be assumed that it is in the interest of a democratic society to achieve a transparent division of responsibilities for the deployment of intelligent systems in diverse application areas. Thereby, the systems should act in accordance with ethical and legal specifications as formulated by the legislative power and allow for traceability in order to facilitate an assignment of responsibility by the judicial power. Consequently, we argue that the self-regulative solution (2) can be ruled out since it would lead to a heterogeneous set of different ethical frameworks implemented within different types of intelligent systems yielding highly complex entanglements especially with regard to responsibility assignments (e.g. among manufacturers, programmers, users and operators). Furthermore, as the problem solving ability of the intelligent systems increases, the severity of possible unintended effects, malicious attacks [6] or the development of intentionally crafted unethical systems [17] which could even induce existential risks seems to prohibit a laissez-faire approach. Thus, the remaining options are the deontological approach (3) and the utility-based solution (4) since both could be in theory implemented within a framework separating the responsibilities as described.

According to the orthogonality thesis by Bostrom [5], *"intelligence and final goals are orthogonal axes along which possible agents can freely vary"*.

Though, the thesis is not uncontroversial for reasons comprising the fact that it does not address probabilities as postulated by Goertzel [10]. However, for the purpose of our specific argument, it is not necessary to consider the soundness of the thesis, since we only presuppose that "there exists a type of AI architecture for which final goals and intelligence are orthogonal" which is self-evident considering utility maximizers [4] as classical examples epistomizing solution (4). From this, it trivially follows that formulating a goal function for a utility maximizer and designing the architecture of this agent are separable tasks. Building on that, we argue that the already existing practice of the legislative power having a say on the *what* goals to achieve as long as societal impacts are concerned and the manufacturers implementing the *how* in various contexts can be adapted to goal-oriented utility maximizers (albeit with certain reservations particularly on the nature of the architecture used) and can thus be pursued as postulated by Werkhoven et al. [23].

Apart from that, it is undoubtedly possible to think of a similar disentanglement of responsibilities in accordance with a solution of the type (3). However, for mostly technical reasons we will now illustrate, we do not consider a deontological framework in which lawful and ethical behavior is encoded for instance in ontologies [12] or directly in natural language as possible instantiation of our orthogonality-based disentanglement approach. First, the attempt to formulate deontological rules for every possible situation in a complex unpredictable real-world environment ultimately leads to a state-action space explosion [23] (it is thereby obvious that law does not represent a complete framework). To be able to handle the complexity of such environments and the complexity of internal states, the intelligent system needs to be run-time adaptive which cannot be achieved by using static rules. Second, since law is formulated in natural language which is inherently highly ambiguous at multiple linguistic levels, the intelligent system would have to either make sense of the legal material using error-prone Natural Language Processing techniques or in the case of the ontology-based approach, the programmers/manufacturers would have to first interpret law before encoding it which induces uncertainty and violates the desired disentanglement of responsibilities. Third, law leaves many legal interpretations open and entails tradeoffs and dilemmas that an intelligent system might encounter and would need to address leading to an unspecified assignment of responsibilities. Fourth, an update of laws will require a costly and laborious update of designs for every manufacturer. Fifth, a deontological approach with fixed rules cannot easily directly endorse a process in which progresses in AI could be efficiently used to transform society in a highly beneficial way enabling humans to overcome their cognitive and evolutionary biases and creating new possibilities to improve the foundations of society.

Having expounded why the deontological solution approach (3) is inappropriate for the central problem of disentangling responsibilities for the deployment of intelligent systems, we now elucidate how a properly designed solution (4) is able to avoid all mentioned disadvantages associated with solution (3). First, it might be possible to realize run-time adaptivity within utility maximizers by equipping them with a "self-awareness" functionality [1] (self-assessment, self-management and the ability to deliver explanations for actions to human entities) which we outline in Sect. 4. Moreover, deontological elements could be used as constraints on the utility function of such utility maximizers in order to selectively restrict the action or the state space. Second, by quantifying law within a publicly available ethical goal function as addressed in the next Sect. 3, one achieves an increased level of transparency. Third, through a utility function approach tradeoffs and dilemmas are more easily and comprehensibly solved. Thereby, for safety reasons, the utility functions can and should include context-sensitive and perceiver-dependent elements as integrated e.g. in augmented utilitarianism [2]. Fourth, updates of law are solely reflected in the ethical goal functions which leads to a more flexible and controllable task. Fifth, the use of such an ethical goal function approach opens up the opportunity for a society to actively perform an enhancement of ethical abilities which we depict in Sect. 5.

3 Ethical Goal Function and "What One *Should* Want"

A first step of crafting ethical goal functions could be for instance to start with the mapping of each relevant application domain of law to a specific utility function which quantifies the expected utility of the possible transitions of the world. For this purpose, the legislative has for instance to define the relevant components of each goal function and assign weights to each component, decide which parameters to consider for each component and identify possible underlying correlations. (It is thinkable that specific stakeholders might then while applying the goal function to their particular area of application, craft a lower-level customized mission goal function [8] for their specific mission goals which would however have to be compliant with the ethical goal function provided by the legislative.) The implementation of this strategy will require a relatively broad multidisciplinary knowledge by policy-makers or might require the practical collaboration with trained multidisciplinary researchers with expertise in e.g. AI and Systems Engineering.

One important feature of the proposed framework is the requirement of transparent human-readable goal functions that can be inspected by anyone which substantially facilitates accountability. In order to obtain a specification of a human-oriented goal function, different methods have been proposed including inverse reinforcement learning (IRL) [9] and reward modeling [16]. However, the IRL method comes with the main drawback of yielding ambiguous reward functions that could explain the observed behavior and within reward modeling, a black-box model is trained by a user in order to act as reward function for a reinforcement learning agent which violates both the transparency requirement of our approach and the disentanglement of responsibilities since it is the user that trains the reward model (and not a representation of society).

However, it is important to note, that as implicit so far, the goal functions would be rather specified based on *what humans want* and not necessarily on what humans *should* want from a scientific perspective, since it is known that humans exhibit biases for instance inherent to their neural systems [15], due to their evolutionary past of survival in small groups [23] or through ethical blindspots [20] which represent serious constraints to their ethical views. On these grounds, the framework described in this paper is intended to be of trans-formative and dynamical nature and might enable the legislative to receive a quantitatively defined feedback from the environment, which in turn might foster the human-made evidence-based adjustment of the explicitly formulated ethical goal functions towards more scientifically sound assumptions.

Beyond that, as postulated by Harris [11], a *science* of morality which might enable humans to identify the peaks on the "moral landscape" which he described as *"a [hypothetical] space of real and potential outcomes whose peaks correspond to the heights of potential well-being and whose valleys represent the deepest possible suffering"* could represent a feasible general approach to solve moral issues. In the light of the aforesaid, one could attempt to in the long-term pursue research that facilitates the design of a scientifically grounded universal ethical goal function whose local optima will ideally be conceptually equivalent to the peaks of this hypothetical moral landscape potentially reflecting what humans *should* want. Another interesting point of departure to be mentioned in this context, has been introduced by Ziesche [26] who describes how the UN sustainable development goals already representing an international consensus and contain-ing values such as well-being could be quantified to start to practically tackle the value alignment problem.

Note that Yudkowsky's early idea of a coherent extrapolated volition [25] in the context of friendly AI which envisaged an AI maximizing the utility based on an extrapolation of what we *would* want *"if we knew more, thought faster, were more the people we wished we were, had grown up farther together"* while being relatively close to it, is though subtly different from our described concept of what we *should* want based on a scientifically grounded ethical goal func-tion, since an improvement of our problem solving ability does not necessarily improve our ethical abilities nor does *"the people we wished we were"* neces-sarily corresponds to a more ethical version of ourselves on average. Moreover, there is no reason to assume that human values would necessarily converge to ethical values if they *"had grown up farther together"*. However, as will be intro-duced in Sect. 5, our method of utilizing ethical goal functions aims at actively grounding the implementation of ethics in a transformative socio-technological feedback-loop for which the legislative provides the seed.

4   "Self-Aware" Utility Maximizer

After having commented on the procedure of crafting ethical goal functions, we now describe a class of architectures able to yield controllable utility max-imizers that strictly comply with a generic goal function specified by humans. In the following, we explain how a top-down analysis leads to an exemplary technically feasible and minimalistic instance of this class. Note that when we refer to an intelligent system in the following, we specifically mean a system able to independently perform the OODA-loop (Observe, Orient, Decide, Act).

One can further decompose the system into four distinct cognitive functions: sensors, orienter, decision maker and actuators according to these four subcomponents respectively. In a first step, we assume that the utility maximizer cannot be based on a subsymbolic learning paradigm *alone* (such as Deep Learning (DL)), since desirable reactions to all possible situations an intelligent system could encounter in complex real-world environments cannot be learned in reasonable time with finite computational resources. Thus, we postulate in a second step that a certain level of abstraction is required which can be achieved by combining a symbolic reasoning component with a perception exploiting the advantages of learning algorithms resulting in a "hybrid architecture". However, this hybrid intelligent system needs to be as well-equipped with a self-model to face the possible complexity of its internal processes without which the system would be confronted with similar problems caused by the inability to anticipate reactions to all possible internal states. In a third step, we argue that the requirement for a self-awareness capability [1] comprising self-assessment and self-management as well as the ability to provide explanations for actions to human entities appears essential for instance for reasons such as the necessity of constructing solutions in real-time that have not been learned before including sensor management [13], adaptivity in the case of communication to other intelligent systems [14] and for explainability purposes. Apart from this, the view expressed by Thorissón [21] that *"self-modeling is a necessary part of any intelligent being"* which similarly considers the importance of feedback-loops relating the actions of a system to the context of its own internal processes could be a further argument supporting the relevance of self-awareness.

Taking these requirements into account, one feasible instance of the described class of hybrid self-aware utility maximizers could integrate DL algorithms – presently representing relatively accurate Machine Learning models especially in the vision domain – as sensors at the subsymbolic level able to output classification results that can be further processed by the orienter component yielding a symbolic representation of the situation and the internal processes. As decision maker one could envisage a utility-based reasoning/planning (and not learning) process such as e.g. with (partially observable) Markov decision processes (MDP) equipped with the ethical goal function as specified by the legislative, a causal model of the world and of the system itself. The decision maker would map symbolically encoded situations and internal processes to actions maximizing on expected utility with respect to the ethical goal function that are finally executed by the actuators either on the environment or on the system itself. In this framework, explanations could be delivered at the symbolic level. Concerning the input-to-output mappings of the DL sensors, one possibility could be to strive to monitor the related uncertainty by means of self-management which will have to be reflected in the goal function.

5 Socio-Technological Feedback-Loop

Having discussed how a disentanglement of societal responsibilities for the deployment of intelligent systems could be achieved, introduced the notion of

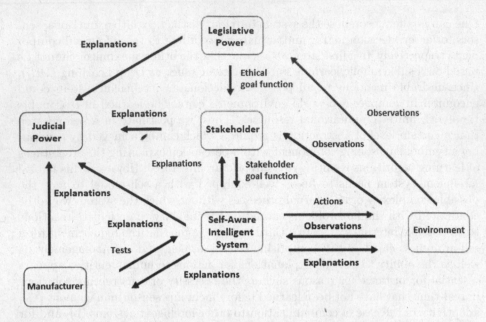

Fig. 1. Simplified illustration and contextualization of a socio-technological feedback-loop (highlighted in blue) implementing the orthogonality-based disentanglement approach for a generic stakeholder domain. (Color figure online)

an ethical goal function and described the corresponding requirements an intelligent system might need to fulfill in order to comply with such a function, we illustrate and contextualize the composite construction of a consequently resulting socio-technological feedback-loop in Fig. 1. At the pre-deployment stage, the manufacturer is responsible for verification and validation practices including the conduct of system tests demonstrating the ability of the intelligent system to adhere to the ethical goal function. At post-deployment stages, the judicial power determines for instance whether the different agents acted in compliance with an ethical goal function given a set of explanations. Concerning the main socio-technological feedback-loop, its key characteristic lies in the fact that it would enable the legislative to dynamically perform revisions of an ethical goal function based on its *quantifiable* impacts on the environment and that it could serve as powerful policy-making tool. Thereby, this feature is paired with the peculiarity that the nature of the environment is not restricted to solely encompass real-world frameworks. More precisely, one could for instance distinguish between three different variations thereof enumerated in an order of potentially increasing speed of formulating/testing hereto related policy-making measures that might be substantiated in an ethical goal function: (1) classical *real-world environments*, (2) specifically crafted and constrained *synthetic environments* and (3) *simulation environments*.

Since the design of an appropriate ethical goal function represents a highly complex task and the necessary time window to collect evidence on its societal impacts in real-world settings on a large-scale might often represent an undesirable complication, policy experimentation on a small-scale in restricted synthetic environments relating the ethical goal function to specific impacts might represent a complementary measure. However, an even more efficient solution allowing for faster decision-making is the "policy by simulation" approach [23] in which human expert knowledge can be extended by AI systems within simulation environments. In doing so, AI might finally assist humans in developing more ethical AI systems while ultimately enhancing human ethical frameworks by relating the mathematic formulation of an ethical goal function to its direct impacts on the (simulated) environment making possible answers to the crucial question on "what humans *should* want" graspable and beyond that, potentially a direct object of scientific investigation.

Finally, the proposed orthogonality-based disentanglement of responsibilities could provide a new perspective for the AI coordination subtask in AI Safety – the non-trivial issue of making sure that global AI research is dovetailed in such a way that no entity actually implements an unethical and unsafe AGI or ASI – e.g. by offering a starting point for considerations towards an international consensus on the principle of using publicly accessible ethical goal functions that can be easily inspected by the public and international actors. This method might reduce the AI race to the problem-solving ability dimension while at the same time providing incentives for demonstrably ethical and transparent frameworks tightly coupled to an ethical enhancement of partaking societies. Given that the law already represents a public matter, it does thereby not seem to represent an exceedingly disruptive step to advocate for public ethical goal functions.

6 Conclusion and Future Prospects

In a nutshell, the Systems-Engineering oriented approach presented in this paper which we termed "orthogonality-based disentanglement" evinced a technically feasible solution for a responsible deployment of intelligent systems which jointly tackles the control problem and the value alignment problem. We postulated that for this purpose, manufacturers should be responsible for the safety and security of the intelligent systems which they could implement using a utility-based approach with hybrid "self-aware" utility maximizers combining e.g. symbolic reasoning/planning with deep learning sensors. Complementarily, the legislative as representation of the whole society should be responsible for the selection of final goals in the form of human-made, publicly available and quantitatively explicitly specified ethical goal functions (which are not implicitly encoded in an opaque learning model). Additionally, we discussed how a socio-technological feedback-loop stemming from this particular disentanglement might facilitate a dynamical human ethical enhancement supported by AI-driven simulations. Moreover, we briefly explained how the presented framework provides hints on how to solve the AI coordination problem in AI Safety at an international level.

However, certain crucial safety and security challenges remain to be separately addressed and should be taken into consideration in future work.

First, self-improvement within an intelligent system could for instance be implemented by an online learning process or by reconfigurability through run-time adaptivity. While it is reasonable to avoid self-improvement by learning during the deployment of the system in order to limit safety risks, future work will need to examine the possibility of verification methods for self-improvement by reconfigurability at run-time. Second, while the self-awareness functionality facilitates (self-)testing mechanisms, extended research on the controllability of specific test procedures in synthetic testing environments will be required. Third, a turn-off action could be seen as a primitive form of self-management in the context of tasks where the performance of the system superseded human performance. However, the possibility to turn-off the system for security reasons by specified human entities should always be given. Fourth, for the purpose of malevolence prevention, it is important to rigorously consider proactive security measures such as A(G)I Red-Teaming at the post-deployment stage and research on adversarial attacks on the sensors [1,22] of the self-aware intelligent system. Fifth, a blockchain approach to ensure the security and transparency of the goal functions themselves and all updates on these functions might be recommendable. Crucially, in order to avoid formulations of an ethical goal function with safety-critical side effects for human entities (including implications related to impossibility theorems for consequentialist frameworks [7]), it is recommendable to assign a type of perceiver-dependent and context-sensitive utility to simulations of situations instead of only to the future outcome of actions [2,3]. In the long-term, we believe that scientific research with the goal to integrate the first-person perspective of society on perceived well-being within an ethical goal function at the core of the presented socio-technological feedback-loop might represent one substantial element needed to promote human flourishing in the most efficient possible way aided by the problem solving ability of AI.

References

1. Aliman, N.-M., Kester, L.: Hybrid strategies towards safe self-aware superintelligent systems. In: Iklé, M., Franz, A., Rzepka, R., Goertzel, B. (eds.) AGI 2018. LNCS (LNAI), vol. 10999, pp. 1–11. Springer, Cham (2018). https://doi.org/10.1007/978-3-319-97676-1_1
2. Aliman, N.-M., Kester, L.: Augmented Utilitarianism for AGI Safety. In: Hammer, P. Agrawal, P., Goertzel, B., Iklé, M. (eds.) AGI 2019. LNAI, vol. 11654, pp. 11–21. Springer, Cham (2019)
3. Aliman, N.M., Kester, L.: Transformative AI governance and AI-Empowered ethical enhancement through preemptive simulations. Delphi - Interdisc. Rev. Emerg. Technol. **2**(1), 23–29 (2019)
4. Armstrong, S.: General purpose intelligence: arguing the orthogonality thesis. Anal. Metaphys. **12**, 68–84 (2013)
5. Bostrom, N.: The superintelligent will: motivation and instrumental rationality in advanced artificial agents. Mind. Mach. **22**(2), 71–85 (2012)
6. Brundage, M., et al.: The Malicious Use of Artificial Intelligence: Forecasting, Prevention, and Mitigation. arXiv preprint arXiv:1802.07228 (2018)

7. Eckersley, P.: Impossibility and Uncertainty Theorems in AI Value Alignment (or why your AGI should not have a utility function). CoRR abs/1901.00064 (2018)
8. Elands, P., Huizing, A., Kester, L., Oggero, S., Peeters, M.: Governing Ethical and Effective Behaviour of Intelligent Systems. Military spectator (2019, to appear)
9. Everitt, T., Lea, G., Hutter, M.: AGI Safety Literature Review. arXiv preprint arXiv:1805.01109 (2018)
10. Goertzel, B.: Infusing advanced AGIs with human-like value systems: two theses. J. Evol. Technol. **26**(1), 50–72 (2016)
11. Harris, S.: The Moral Landscape: How Science can Determine Human Values. Simon and Schuster, New York (2011)
12. Hoekstra, R., Breuker, J., Di Bello, M., Boer, A., et al.: The LKIF core ontology of basic legal concepts. LOAIT **321**, 43–63 (2007)
13. Kester, L., Ditzel, M.: Maximising effectiveness of distributed mobile observation systems in dynamic situations. In: 2014 17th International Conference on Information Fusion (FUSION), pp. 1–8. IEEE (2014)
14. Kester, L.J.H.M., van Willigen, W.H., Jongh, J.D.: Critical headway estimation under uncertainty and non-ideal communication conditions. In: 17th International IEEE Conference on Intelligent Transportation Systems (ITSC) pp. 320–327 (2014)
15. Korteling, J.E., Brouwer, A.M., Toet, A.: A neural network framework for cognitive bias. Frontiers in Psychol. **9**, 1561 (2018)
16. Leike, J., Krueger, D., Everitt, T., Martic, M., Maini, V., Legg, S.: Scalable agent alignment via reward modeling: a research direction. arXiv preprint arXiv:1811.07871 (2018)
17. Pistono, F., Yampolskiy, R.V.: Unethical research: how to create a malevolent artificial intelligence. In: 25th International Joint Conference on Artificial Intelligence (IJCAI-2016). Ethics for Artificial Intelligence Workshop (AI-Ethics-2016) (2016)
18. Poel, I.: Translating values into design requirements. In: Michelfelder, D.P., McCarthy, N., Goldberg, D.E. (eds.) Philosophy and Engineering: Reflections on Practice, Principles and Process. PET, vol. 15, pp. 253–266. Springer, Dordrecht (2013). https://doi.org/10.1007/978-94-007-7762-0_20
19. Russell, S., Dewey, D., Tegmark, M.: Research priorities for robust and beneficial artificial intelligence. AI Mag. **36**(4), 105–114 (2015)
20. Sezer, O., Gino, F., Bazerman, M.H.: Ethical blind spots: explaining unintentional unethical behavior. Current Opin. Psychol. **6**, 77–81 (2015)
21. Thorisson, K.R.: A new constructivist AI: from manual methods to self-constructive systems. Theoretical Foundations of Artificial General Intelligence. Atlantis Thinking Machines, vol. 4, pp. 145–171. Springer, Atlantis Press, Paris (2012). https://doi.org/10.2991/978-94-91216-62-6_9
22. Tomsett, R., et al.: Why the failure? how adversarial examples can provide insights for interpretable machine learning. In: 2018 21st International Conference on Information Fusion (FUSION), pp. 838–845. IEEE (2018)
23. Werkhoven, P., Kester, L., Neerincx, M.: Telling autonomous systems what to do. In: Proceedings of the 36th European Conference on Cognitive Ergonomics, p. 2. ACM (2018)
24. Yudkowsky, E.: The AI alignment problem: why it is hard, and where to start. Symbolic Systems Distinguished Speaker (2016)
25. Yudkowsky, E.: Coherent extrapolated volition. In: Singularity Institute for Artificial Intelligence (2004)
26. Ziesche, S.: Potential synergies between the united nations sustainable development goals and the value loading problem in artificial intelligence. Maldives National J. Res. **6**, 47 (2018)

Extending MicroPsi's Model of Motivation and Emotion for Conversational Agents

Joscha Bach[✉], Murilo Coutinho, and Liza Lichtinger

AI Foundation, San Francisco, CA 94105, USA
{joscha, murilo, liza}@aifoundation.com

Abstract. We describe a model of emotion and motivation that extends the MicroPsi motivation model for applications in conversational agents and tracking human emotions. The model is based on reactions of the agent to satisfaction and frustration of physiological, cognitive or social needs, and to changes of the agent's expectations regarding such events. The model covers motivational states, affective states (modulation of cognition), feelings (sensations that correspond to a situation appraisal), emotions (conceptual aggregates of motivational states, modulators and feelings) and is currently being adapted to express emotional states.

Keywords: MicroPsi architecture · Artificial emotion · Affect · Motivation · Modulation · Feelings · Appraisal models · Affective computing

1 Introduction

The success of deep learning models in AI (LeCun et al. 2015) is arguably leading to a shift in the analysis of cognitive architectures within cognitive science and AGI research. Traditionally, such architectures (e.g., Minsky 2006, Newell 1990) focused on the multitude of observable or inferred functionality of cognitive agents, and proposed structures and mechanisms for their implementation. The complexity of human cognition is thought to emanate from a large set of implemented functions and structural components, which have to be modeled and implemented by the researcher.

A different perspective is given by the idea of general learning systems (e.g., Hutter 2005), which propose that neocortex and hippocampus allow for general hierarchical function approximation to express complex emergent behaviors and perceptual abilities, with other parts of the brain supplying infrastructure for learning, reward generation, differential attention control, routing of information between cortical areas, and interfacing with perceptual and motor systems (see Marcus et al. (2014)).

This perspective suggests that cognition and interpersonal differences are largely defined by motivational and attentional responses to environmental stimuli. If we understand intelligent agents primarily as learning systems, we need to understand the structures that shape this learning and give rise to perceptual models, imagination, reasoning and problem solving, decision making, reflection, social interaction, and so on. Unlike most current AI learning systems, human behavior is not driven by a single reward or unified utility function, but by a complex system of physiological, cognitive and social needs. For the implementation of a fully autonomous AI agent in a complex

P. Hammer et al. (Eds.): AGI 2019, LNAI 11654, pp. 32–43, 2019.
https://doi.org/10.1007/978-3-030-27005-6_4

environment, we will need to identify a set of needs that spans the full spectrum of relevant behavioral tendencies. A suggestion for such a set has been introduced by the Psi theory (Dörner 1999), and later extended in the MicroPsi model (Bach 2012b, 2015), which describes a detailed framework of such needs, reward generators and cognitive modulators. The MicroPsi motivation model forms the core of the cognitive architecture MicroPsi (Bach 2009), but has also been used in the cognitive architecture OpenCog as OpenPsi (Cai et al. 2012).

2   From Needs to Behavior

The MicroPsi model sees a cognitive architecture as a system to regulate and control a complex organism (or comparable agent). Perception, learning and imagination are tools in the service of that regulation. The demands of the agent (such as sustenance, rest, social embedding) are represented as *needs*, and signaled to the cognitive processes as *urges*, which are proportional to the strength (weight) of the respective need. A need can be understood as a tank that runs dry over time, and which can be filled by satisfaction events (consumptive actions) or emptied by aversive events.

In MicroPsi, memory content is represented in a neuro-symbolic formalism, and representations of situations, objects and actions may be associated to urge signals via learning. The presence of an urge sends activation into the representations, and thus *primes* content in memory and perception, so attention and processing resources of the agent are directed at them. The strength of urges *modulate* cognition to the situation at hand, giving rise to the configurations that we call *affective states*.

The satisfaction or frustration of a need generates reinforcement signals that (together with sparseness and stability criteria) give rise to reinforcement *learning* and the gradual formation of complex processing structures enabling perception, mental simulation and high-level cognition. Finally, urge signals inform the decision making of the agent, direct its impulses and give rise to goal-directed behavior.

2.1   Needs

Needs reflect the demands of the organism, for instance, the requirement to maintain a suitable body temperature, to obtain rest, or to find sustenance. The **physiological needs** give rise to foraging, feeding, resting, pain avoidance and so on.

Social behaviors are driven by **social needs**, such as a need to be recognized and reaffirmed as a member of a social group (*affiliation*), or to reduce another agent's suffering (*nurturing*), to conform to internalized norms (*legitimacy*), to obtain a position in a social hierarchy (status), to regulate a social environment (*justice*), to engage in courtship (*affection*), and to experience *intimacy*.

Cognitive needs direct skill acquisition (*competence*), exploration (*uncertainty reduction*) and the formation of mental representations (*aesthetics*).

All goals of the agent correspond to the satisfaction of a need, or the avoidance of its frustration. This reflects the direction of behavior by approach goals and avoidance goals (Carver and Scheier, 1998; Elliot and Church 1997; Higgins, 1996).

A need is defined by an extensive parameter set:

$$\mathcal{N} := \langle v_t, v_0, \alpha_t, \beta_t, p_t, q_t, \omega, g, \ell, d, s^p, s^q, t^p, t^q, \hat{g}, \hat{\ell}, \widehat{s^p}, \widehat{s^q} \rangle$$

Each need is characterized by its current value $v_t \in [0, 1]$ and a weight $\omega \in \mathbb{R}^+$, which specifies how strong the need registers in comparison to others (v_0 is the initial value of the need). An **urge** with an *urge strength* $\alpha_t \in [0, 1]$ represents the difference between the target state (a fully satisfied need) and its current state for each need:

$$\alpha_t = \omega [1 - v_{t-1}]_0^{1^2}$$

In addition to the strength of an urge, a need is characterized by the *urgency* $\beta_t \in [0, 1]$ to address it. Urge strength and urgency are separate values, because sometimes, even weak needs might have a short time window for satisfying them, which should trigger the activity of the agent. The urgency is determined by amount of time left to realize satisfaction, either because a crucial resource is about to drop to a critically low level, or because the dynamics in the environment require immediate action.

$$\beta_t = \omega \left[\frac{k - remaining\ time_t}{k} \right]_0^{1^2}$$

The value of the need represents the inverse of a systemic demand. Satisfying the need leads to an increase of the value, proportional to the *gain* $g \in [0, 1]$ of the need, frustrating it leads to a reduction of the value, proportional to the *loss* $\ell \in [0, 1]$.

The satisfaction is provided either from a consumption event (such as eating for the sustenance need, reaping praise for the affiliation need, or successfully acquiring a skill for the competence need). Demands can also increase due to aversive events (such as suffering an injury for the pain avoidance need, or failing at a task for the competence need), which leads to a frustration of the need, proportional to its *loss* factor. A strong gain or loss means that a consumption or frustration event has a stronger effect on the value and reward signal of that need.

Some needs may also be satisfied or frustrated (usually to a lesser degree) by an *anticipated event*. For instance, anticipating future uncertainty may frustrate the need for uncertainty reduction. The strength of the gain and loss due to anticipated events is given by the factors $\hat{g} \in [0, 1]$ and $\hat{\ell} \in [0, 1]$. Most needs also deplete over time on their own, depending on their *decay* factor, so they need to be regularly replenished. For instance, the demands for sustenance, rest and affiliation will increase over time, and thus require the agent to satisfy them repeatedly. In each moment, the agent may experience a change in its current demand, δ_t. Let δ_t^+ be the positive change at time t,

δ_t^- the negative change, and $\widehat{\delta_t^+}$ and $\widehat{\delta_t^-}$ anticipated positive and negative changes. The new value of the need can be calculated as:

$$v_t = \left[\text{decay}(v_{t-1}, d) + g\,\delta_t^+ + \ell\,\delta_t^- + \hat{g}\,\widehat{\delta_t^+} + \hat{\ell}\,\widehat{\delta_t^-} \right]_0^1$$

It seems natural to assume that the value of a need decays logistically, for instance using a sigmoidal function that will decrease slowly at first, then rapidly, before decreasing slowly again, such as

$$\sigma(x) := 1 - \frac{1}{1 + e^{-12(x - 1/2)}}$$

For $0 < y < 1$, we can calculate the inverse of this function as

$$\sigma^{-1}(y) := \frac{1}{12} \log\left(\frac{1-y}{y}\right) + \frac{1}{2}$$

so that we can determine how far the decay of a variable has progressed, based on its current value.

$$\text{decay}(v_{t-1}, d) := \sigma\left(\sigma^{-1}(v_{t-1}) + \frac{\text{duration}(t, t-1)}{d}\right)$$

The **differences in parameter configurations** of the needs (especially *weight*, *gain*, *loss*, and *decay factor*) can be used to model interpersonal variance in motivation and thereby different personality properties. For instance, high weight and loss for affiliation, combined with a low weight and gain for competence, would lead to high agreeableness. High weights and gains for competence, uncertainty reduction and aesthetics would lead to high openness. Low decay and high loss for affiliation may lead to introversion. High weights and loss on competence and uncertainty reduction will lead to high conscientiousness, and high loss on competence, affiliation, and uncertainty reduction may lead to neuroticism (Bach 2012a).

Pleasure and pain are generated by changes in values of a need. They provide rewards for the agent's actions, and are used as reinforcement signals for learning. Satisfying a need leads to a *pleasure signal* $p_t \in [0, 1]$ that is proportional to how much the *value* of the need increases, the *gain* factor g of the need, and its *pleasure sensitivity* $s^p \in \mathbb{R}^+$. The anticipation of future consumption can also generate a pleasure signal, proportional to the *imaginary pleasure sensitivity* $\widehat{s^p} \in \mathbb{R}^+$. Pleasure signals decay over time, according to a sigmoid function with a pleasure decay:

$$p_t = \left[\text{decay}(p_{t-1}, t^p) + g\,s^p\delta_t^+ + \hat{g}\widehat{s^p}\,\widehat{\delta_t^+} \right]_0^1$$

Pain signals q_t are generated as a reaction to the depletion of a need.

$$q_t = \left[\mathrm{decay}(q_{t-1}, t^q) + \ell\, s^q \delta_t^- + \widehat{\ell s^q}\, \widehat{\delta_t^-} + q_t^{depletion}\right]_0^1$$

In addition, depleted needs (such as an empty stomach) may also cause a continuous pain signal. For instance, using the following function with $\theta = 0.10$ will increase the pain value $q^{depletion}$ from 0 to 1, starting when the value is depleted to 10%:

$$q_t^{depletion} := \left[\left(1 - \frac{v_t}{\theta}\right)\right]_0^{1^2}$$

2.2 Events and Consumptions

Anticipated events are expected situations in the inner or perceptual world of the agent. They become relevant if they are associated with the expectation of a consumption event $\mathcal{C}$, i.e. with satisfying or frustrating a need and can be defined as

$$\mathcal{E} := \langle \mathcal{C}, er, c, s, \varepsilon \rangle$$

Events can just happen, or they can be chosen as *goals*, which are actively pursued by the agent and are either appetitive (positive reward) or aversive (negative reward). In the latter case, the goal is to avoid the event. The **motivational relevance** of any event is given by its *expected reward er* $\in [-1, 1]$, which can be positive (a need is satisfied) or negative (frustration). The *certainty* $c \in (0, 1]$ of the event specifies the confidence of the agent that the event will happen. The *skill (epistemic competence)* $s \in [0, 1]$ specifies the chance that the agent can reap the benefits or avoid the dangers of the event. The *expiration time* $\varepsilon_t \in \mathbb{R}^+$ determines the duration until the event is expected to happen. In every time step, or as the result of a belief update, the remaining time is updated:

$$\varepsilon_t = [\varepsilon_{t-1} - \mathrm{duration}(t, t-1)]_0^\infty$$

(Note that this is a simplification; a more accurate model should capture *expected reward, epistemic competence* and *expiration time* as distributions).

Consumptions are the parts of an event that affect needs of an agent. Each consumption either satisfies or frustrates a *need* (with a positive or negative *total reward*).

$$\mathcal{C} := \langle \mathcal{N}, r_t, r^{total}, r^{max}, rd, discount \rangle$$

When the associated event is triggered, the consumption continuously generates a certain amount ($r_t \in \mathbb{R}$) of satisfaction or frustration for its associated *need* $\mathcal{N}$, over a certain *reward duration rewardduration* $\in \mathbb{R}^+$, limited to a certain *maximum reward* $r^{max} \in \mathbb{R}$ per time step, until the *total reward* $r^{total} \in \mathbb{R}$ is reached.

In an organism, reward signals are delivered via neurotransmitters, and their release typically follows a right-skewed distribution. We may approximate this for instance as a χ distribution with degree 2:

$$signal(t) := te^{-\frac{1}{2}t^2}$$

This way, the signal peaks at $t = 1$ with a value of 0.6, and at $t = 3.5$, we have delivered 99.78% of the signal. In a discrete simulation, the actual reward value delivered at a time step t for a reward signal triggered at t_0 can be approximated using

$$t_1 = (t - t_0)\frac{3.5}{rd}\,\text{duration}(t, t - 1); \quad t_2 = (t - 1 - t_0)\frac{3.5}{rd}\,\text{duration}(t, t - 1)$$

$$r_t = \left[\frac{3.5 r^{total}}{rd}\int_{t_1}^{t_2} te^{-\frac{1}{2}t^2}\right]_{-r^{max}}^{r^{max}} = \left[\frac{3.5 r^{total}}{rd}\left(e^{-\frac{1}{2}t_1^2} - e^{-\frac{1}{2}t_2^2}\right)\right]_{-r^{max}}^{r^{max}}$$

The reward value of an active consumption will change the value of the corresponding need by

$$\delta_t^+ = \left[r_t^C\right]_0^\infty; \delta_t^- = \left[r_t^C\right]_{-\infty}^0$$

as well as create the corresponding pleasure and pain signals. Pleasure and pain signals indicate the performance of the agent and can be used to drive **reinforcement learning**. Learning associates the respective need indicator with the current situation representation or action, to establish an appetitive or aversive goal. It can also be used to associate the current situation or action with preceding elements in protocol memory, to establish procedural memory. The learning signal is derived by multiplying the respective pleasure or pain signal with the weight of the affected need.

2.3   Managing Expectations

Perception and cognition trigger *belief updates*, which manifest as the establishment, change, execution or deletion of anticipated events. At each point in time, the agent maintains a list of anticipated events. If the agent visits one of these events, either during an update (such as establishing or changing an event, or reflecting upon it during planning), it generates **anticipation rewards**, depending on the *certainty c* of the event and the *epistemic competence (skill) s* of the agent to manage or avoid it:

$$\widehat{\delta_t^+} = cs\left[\frac{r_t^C}{1 + discount\varepsilon_t}\right]_0^\infty; \quad \widehat{\delta_t^-} = c(1 - s)\left[\frac{r_t^C}{1 + discount\varepsilon_t}\right]_{-\infty}^0$$

Here, we are using hyperbolic discounting, to ensure that the agent is progressively less concerned about the effects of events, the more the event lies in the future. The effects of anticipated events on need satisfaction and pleasure/pain generation only manifest as the result of the agent focusing on them in the respective time step, but the actual signal generation may extend over an extended time.

Changes in an expected event may concern higher or lower certainty in its occurrence, a difference in remaining time, a different expected reward, or a different ability to deal with it (skill). In such cases, δ is computed using the change in the expected reward. If expected events manifest, they generate a reward for the need for certainty. If they do not, they frustrate the need for certainty (which increases the probability for the agent to engage in exploration behavior). If events are **goals** of the agent, their occurrence or failure will also satisfy or frustrate the need for competence.

3 Modulators

Motivation determines the direction of cognition and the relevance of its content. In contrast, modulation adapts the parameters of cognition to the situation at hand. Examples of such modulators are *arousal*, *valence* and *attentional focus*, which may vary in response to chances in the external and internal environment of the agent. A configuration of modulators amounts to an **affective state**.

$$\mathcal{M} := \langle min, max, \textit{v}_t, \textit{b}, \textit{y}, z \rangle$$

Each modulator $\mathcal{M}$ has a current value $\textit{v}_t \in [min, max]$, and five parameters that account for individual variance between subjects: the *baseline* $\textit{b} \in [min, max]$ is the default value of the modulator; min and $max \in \mathbb{R}$ the upper and lower bound of its changes, the *volatility* $\textit{y} \in \mathbb{R}^+$ defines the reaction to change, and the *decay time* $z \in \mathbb{R}^+$ how long it takes until the modulator returns to its baseline.

$$\textit{v}_t = \left[\textit{b} + \text{decay}\left(\frac{\textit{v}_{t-1}-\textit{b}}{i}, z \right) interval + \delta_t \right]_{min}^{max}; \; interval = \begin{cases} max - \textit{b}, \text{if } \textit{v}_{t-1} > \textit{b} \\ \textit{b} - min, \text{else} \end{cases}$$

Modulators do not assume a *target* value τ instantly, but according to their volatility:

$$\delta_t = (\tau \, interval + \textit{b} - \textit{v}_{t-1}) \, \textit{y}$$

We currently use six modulators: *valence, arousal, dominance*, which correspond to the *pleasure, arousal* and *dominance* of Mehrabian's *PAD* model (Mehrabian 1980), and have first been suggested as *valence, arousal* and *tension* by Wundt (1910). Dominance is also sometimes called agency; it describes how much the agent is in control of a situation, as opposed to being in a passive state with reduced metacognition. In addition, MicroPsi defines three attentional modulators: *resolution level, focus* and *exteroception*. Modulators change depending on **aggregates** of the current values and changes of the needs. We determine the value of these aggregates using marginal sums (because combining urgency or pain signals is not simply additive, but approaches a *limit* given by the signaling pathways of the organism):

$$\text{marginal sum}(V, limit) := \sum_{n=0}^{|V|} S_n \Big| S_n := \frac{limit - S_{n-1}}{limit} v_n; \; limit$$
$$= \max(\{\omega | \omega \in weights_{\mathfrak{R}}\})$$

Valence represents a qualitative evaluation of the current situation. Valence is determined as the aggregate of pleasure and pain:

$$\mathcal{P} = \text{marginal sum}(\{\omega_N \, p_N\}); \mathcal{Q} = \text{marginal sum}(\{\omega_N \, q_N\})$$

$$\tau^{valence} = \frac{\mathcal{P} - \mathcal{Q}}{limit}$$

Arousal reflects the combined strength and urgency of the needs of the agent. Arousal leads to more energy expenditure in actions, action readiness, stronger responses to sensory stimuli, and faster reactions:

$$urge = \text{marginal sum}(\{\omega_N \alpha_N\}); \; urgency = \text{marginal sum}(\{\omega_N \beta_N\})$$

$$\tau^{arousal} = \frac{urge + urgency}{limit} - 1$$

Dominance suggests whether to approach or retract from the attended object, based on the competence for dealing with it. High dominance corresponds to a high anticipated reward, a middle value marks indifference, and low dominance tends to lead to retraction from the object.

$$epistemic \, comp. = s_{current \, goal \, event} \qquad general \, comp. = \sqrt{v^{comp} \cdot epistemic \, comp.}$$

$$\tau^{dominance} = general \, comp. + epistemic \, comp. - 1$$

The *resolution level* controls the level of detail when performing cognitive and perceptual tasks. A high resolution will consider more details and thus often arrive at more accurate solutions and representations, while a low resolution allows faster responses. (In MicroPsi, the resolution level is interpreted as the *width of activation spreading* in neuro-symbolic representations). It is calculated by the urge strength of the goal, but reduced by its urgency, allowing for faster responses.

The *focus* modulator defines a selection threshold, which amounts to a stronger focus on the current task, and a narrower direction of attention. Suppression is a mechanism to avoid oscillations between competing motives. (In our implementation of the model, we also use *focus* as a factor to proportionally increase pleasure and pain signals of a need that corresponds to a current goal, i.e. is currently in attendance.) Focus is increased by the strength and urgency of the current goal, and is reduced by a low general competence.

Exteroception (sometimes also called *securing rate*)- determines the frequency of obtaining/updating information from the environment, vs attending to interoception (mental events). A dynamic environment requires more cognitive resources for perceptual processing, while a static environment frees resources for deliberation and reflection. The securing rate is decreased by the strength and urgency of the leading motive, but increases with low competence and a high need for exploration (which is equivalent to experienced uncertainty).

4 Feelings

In human beings, the ability to perform motivational appraisals precedes symbolic and conceptual cognition. These appraisals are influencing decision making and action control below the consciously accessible level, and can often be experienced as distinct sensations (*feelings*). While the world "feeling" is sometimes colloquially used to mean "emotion", "romantic affect" or "intuition", here it refers to the hedonic aspect of an emotion or motivational state, i.e. a perceptual sensation with distinct qualities that may or may not accompany the emotional episode. Feelings sometimes correspond to characteristic changes in modulation of physiological parameters during certain emotions, such as tension of muscles and increased heart rate during anger, or the flushing of the cheeks during shame. However, we suspect that in large part, the mapping of feelings to the body image serves disambiguation (such as love or heartbreak in the chest, anxiety and power in the solar plexus, cognitive events in the head). To further the disambiguation, feelings tend to have a valence (pleasant or painful), as well as additional perceptual features (weight, extension, expansion/contraction). While there seems to be considerable interpersonal variation in how feelings are experienced, and these experiences change during childhood development, most subjects report similarity in the way in which they sense correlates to their emotional states (Nummenma et al. 2013). Our artificial agents do not possess a dynamic self model that would allow to model cognitive access to their feelings and other experiential content, but we can treat them as semantic items that influence conversation, and model their influence on the expression of emotional states, especially with respect to posture and movement patterns.

5 Emotions

The MicroPsi model does not assume that emotions are explicitly implemented, like for instance in the classic OCC model (Orthony et al. 1988), but emergent, as perceptual classifications. Modulator dimensions give rise to a space of affective states, with higher level emotions resulting from affects that are bound to an object via *appraisals* that result from motivational relevance. This makes the MicroPsi model similar to the EMotion and Adaptation Model (EMA) (Gratch and Marsella 2009). Emotion categories are perceptual classifications that we can use to characterize and predict the modulator state and behavior tendencies of an agent.

There is no generally accepted taxonomy of emotional states, and the classification of emotions depends very much of on the cultural and individual context (see, for instance, Cowen and Kentner 2017). For the purpose of classification within our model of conversational agents, we can nevertheless give characterizations, such as the *joy*, as a state of positive valence and high arousal, and bliss, with positive valence and high resolution level (which often corresponds to low arousal).

$$joy_t = v_t^{valence} \, v_t^{arousal}; \; bliss_t = v_t^{valence} \, v_t^{resolution \, level}$$

Social emotions often depend on a difference between how we perceive an agent or action and a *normative expectation* (how the agent or action should be). For instance, we call the perception of the position of an agent in a social hierarchy *status*, and the measure of the actual value of that agent *esteem* (corresponding to the level of the need for *legitimacy*). A difference between status and esteem in another agent is perceived as an *injustice*, and in oneself as a source of *guilt*. An event that causes other agents to lower their esteem of oneself may be a cause of *shame*. *Envy* is an emotion that describes a status differential between oneself and another agent that is not reflected by a corresponding difference in esteem. In this way, we have characterized 32 emotions along the following dimensions: valence (positive, negative or neutral), dominance (agency/control), arousal, urge (as aggregate of all present need strengths), urgency, certainty, immediacy vs. expectation vs. memory of past, confirmation of expectation, competence, physiological pleasure, valence for ingestion (appetence/disgust), aesthetic valence, normative valence of agent (esteem), status of agent (level in hierarchy), relational valence of agent (sympathy, potential for affiliation), romantic valence of agent (potential for affection), erotic valence of agent (sexual attraction), normative valence of self (self-esteem, need for legitimacy), status of self, relational valence of self (need for affiliation), romantic valence of self (need for affection). (The detailed description of this characterization is beyond the scope of this paper). In this way, typical emotion categories can be defined and mapped to feelings, facial expression, modulation of utterances, changes in posture etc.

6 Evaluation

The MicroPsi model has been implemented in various agents. The extensions that we present here attempt to approach the time dynamics of human behavior, by modeling the gradual release and change of signals, and dealing with anticipated rewards. A full blown psychological study has been outside of the scope of this engineering work. Instead, we annotated video sequences with human actors with their motivational events (expecting events, changing expectations, setting and dropping goals, experiencing events), and displayed the resulting modulator dynamics and emotional states in real-time (Fig. 1). The viewer combines consumptions with corresponding physiological, social and cognitive needs (eat–food, drink/perspire–water, heal/injure–health, recover/exert–rest, acceptance/rejection–affiliation, virtue/transgression–legitimacy, win/loss–status, compassion/pity–nurturing, connection/abandonment–affection, success/failure–competence, confirmation/disconfirmation–uncertainty reduction, enjoyment/disgust–aesthetics). For each need, it displays 'real-time responses to pleasure, pain, urge and urgency, and the combination of these into aggregates (valence, global urgency/stress level, global urge) and modulators (resolution level, focus, dominance, exteroception and arousal). By triggering consumptions based on events in the video, we are able to reproduce and display the motivational and affective dynamics of the actor. Future work may use the same approach to model affective states of human interaction partners of conversational agents in real time.

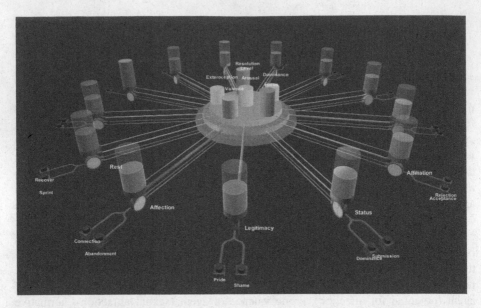

Fig. 1. Real-time motivational system, using motivational, cognitive and social needs to drive valence, urge, urgency and modulators.

While such an approach is insufficient to demonstrate psychological adequacy of the model (even though such adequacy is ultimately the goal of our work), it demonstrates that MicroPsi can be used to mimic plausible human behavior over a range of events, which we see as an important step in creating a computational model of complex motivation and emotion.

References

Bach, J.: Principles of Synthetic Intelligence – An architecture of motivated cognition. Oxford University Press, Oxford (2009)

Bach, J.: Functional Modeling of Personality Properties Based on Motivational Traits. In: Proceedings of ICCM 7, pp. 271–272. Berlin, Germany (2012a)

Bach, J.: A framework for emergent emotions based on motivation and cognitive modulators. Int. J. Synth. Emotions (IJSE) 3(1), 43–63 (2012)

Bach, J.: Modeling Motivation in MicroPsi 2. In: 8th International Conference Artificial General Intelligence, AGI 2015, pp. 3–13. Berlin, Germany (2015)

Cai, Z., Goertzel, B., Zhou, C., Zhang, Y., Jiang, M., Yu, G.: OpenPsi: dynamics of a computational affective model inspired by Dörner's PSI theory. Cognitive Syst. Res. **17–18** (2012), 63–80 (2012)

Carver, C.S., Scheier, M.F.: On the Self-Regulation of Behavior. Cambridge University Press, Cambridge (1998)

Cowen, A.S., Kentner, D.: Self-report captures 27 distinct categories of emotion bridged by continuous gradients. PNAS August 2017

Deci, E.L., Ryan, R.M.: The 'what' and 'why' of goal pursuits: human needs and the self-determination of behavior. Psychol. Inquiry **11**, 227–268 (2000)

Dörner, D.: Bauplan für eine Seele. Reinbeck (1999)

Elliot, A.J., Church, M.A.: A hierarchical model of approach and avoidance achievement motivation. J. Personality and Social Psychol. **72**, 218–232 (1997)

Gratch, J., Marsella, S.: EMA: a process model of appraisal dynamics. Cognitive Syst. Res. **10**, 70–90 (2009)

Higgins, E.T.: Ideals, oughts, and regulatory focus: affect and motivation from distinct pains and pleasures. In: Gollwitzer, P.M., Bargh, J.A. (eds.) The Psychology of Action: Linking Cognition and Motivation to Behavior, pp. 91–114. Guilford, New York (1996)

Hutter, M.: Universal Artificial Intelligence: Sequential Decisions based on Algorithmic Probability. Springer, EATCS Book (2005)

LeCun, Y., Bengio, Y., Hinton, G.: Deep learning. Nature **521**, 436–444 (2015)

Marcus, G.F., Marblestone, A.H., Dean, T.L.: The atoms of neural computation. Science **346**, 551–552 (2014)

Mehrabian, A.: Basic Dimensions for a General Psychological Theory, pp. 39–53. Gunn & Hain Publishers, Oelgeschlager (1980)

Minsky, M.: The Emotion Machine. Simon and Shuster, New York (2006)

Newell, A.: Unified Theories of Cognition. Harvard University Press, Cambridge (1990)

Nummenmaa, L., Glerean, E., Hari, R., Hietanen, J.K.: Bodily maps of emotions. PNAS, Dec 2013, 201321664 (2013)

Orthony, G., Clore, A., Collins, A.: The cognitive structure of emotions. Cambridge University Press, Cambridge (1988)

Wundt, W.: Gefühlselemente des Seelenlebens. In: Grundzüge der physiologischen Psychologie II. Leipzig: Engelmann (1910)

WILLIAM: A Monolithic Approach to AGI

Arthur Franz[⊠], Victoria Gogulya, and Michael Löffler

Odessa Competence Center for Artificial intelligence and Machine learning
(OCCAM), Odesa, Ukraine
{af,vg,ml}@occam.com.ua

Abstract. We present WILLIAM – an inductive programming system
based on the theory of incremental compression. It builds representations by incrementally stacking autoencoders made up of trees of general
Python functions, thereby stepwise compressing data. It is able to solve
a diverse set of tasks including the compression and prediction of simple sequences, recognition of geometric shapes, write code based on test
cases, self-improve by solving some of its own problems and play tic-tac-
toe when attached to AIXI and without being specifically programmed
for it.

Keywords: Inductive programming · Incremental compression ·
Algorithmic complexity · Universal induction · AIXI · Seed AI ·
Recursive self-improvement

1 Introduction

It is well-known to any trained machine learning practitioner that the choice of
a learning algorithm severely depends on the class of tasks to be solved. Cynical
voices have even claimed that the really intelligent part of the final performance
actually resides within the human developer choosing, twisting and tweaking the
algorithm, rather than inside the algorithm itself.[1] Somehow, a trained human
is able to recognize the narrowness of the algorithm and come up with simple
data samples which the algorithm will fail to represent.

In the context of AGI we would like to ask, how can we build an algorithm
that can derive such wide and diverse representations that even trained humans
will not recognize their limits? Conversely, humans seem to be limited by the
complexity of the represented data, since the ability to recognize structure in
large and complex data sets is what we need machine learning for in the first
place. The strength of those algorithms appears to entail their weakness: the
inability to represent a wide range of simple data. In order to make progress
toward AGI, we suggest to fill the "cup of complexity" for the bottom up, as
exemplified in Fig. 1.1 in [3]. Instead of building algorithms for complex but
narrow data, we suggest heading for simple but general ones.

---

[1] Christoph von der Malsburg, personal communication.

© Springer Nature Switzerland AG 2019
P. Hammer et al. (Eds.): AGI 2019, LNAI 11654, pp. 44–58, 2019.
https://doi.org/10.1007/978-3-030-27005-6_5

This is exactly what we have attempted in the present paper: we have built WILLIAM – an algorithm that can handle a diverse set of simple data with the goal of turning up the complexity in future. The importance of this approach is also backed by the idea of a seed AI, recursively self-improving itself. After all, in order to f-improve, an algorithm has to be able to solve problems occurring during its own implementation. Even more so, the fraction of issues solved by the algorithm itself rather than by the programmers should increase continuously during the development of a real AGI system. Instead, developers usually build various specialized algorithms, i.e. heuristics, in order to deal with various difficulties during development, leading to narrow and brittle solutions. We have avoided to use heuristics as much as possible and demonstrate in Sect. 3.5 a simple self-improving ability of WILLIAM.

As opposed to cognitive architectures which consist of many narrow algorithms trying to patch up each others representational holes in the crusade against the curse of dimensionality, WILLIAM constitutes a monolithic approach, i.e. it is essentially a single algorithm that helps itself and stays out of high-dimensional regions of the task space by systematically giving preference to simple data. Such a strong Occam bias is also what is demanded by formal descriptions of optimal prediction and intelligence [6,14]: the prior probability of a representation q of length $l(q)$ being relevant to the current task should be given a weight of $2^{-l(q)}$!.

These considerations impose several constraints on any monolithic algorithm. In order to be wide enough it should employ search of general programs expressed in a Turing complete language. Those programs have to be as simple as possible, hence achieve high data compression ratios. WILLIAM achieves this by searching in the space of syntax trees made up of Python operators and building stacked autoencoders. By doing so, it exploits the efficiency of optimal compression guaranteed by the theory of incremental compression [4]. In order to enable actual problem solving, we have attached these compression abilities to the expectimax search of actions leading to high expected rewards, as demanded by an optimally intelligent AIXI agent [6]. In Sect. 3.6 we describe how the resulting agent was able to play tic-tac-toe without being explicitly programmed for it.

2 Description of the Algorithm

In the following we will describe the current state of WILLIAM built in our OCCAM laboratory during the last 1.5 years. It is work in progress and consists currently of about 9600 lines of Python code, including 876 test cases. Its main task is, given a data string, to induce a representation with a short description length. As a language we have used trees of currently 41 Python operators, which can be converted to abstract syntax trees, compiled and executed by Python itself. We have described the basics of the algorithm already in [5] and will focus on the novel parts in this paper.

2.1   Description Length

The description length of various data sets is computed in the following way. Positive integers n are encoded with the Elias delta code [1], whose length is

$$l(n) = \lfloor \log_2(n) \rfloor + 2 \lfloor \log_2 (\lfloor \log_2(n) \rfloor + 1) \rfloor + 1 \tag{1}$$

Arbitrary integers are assigned the code length $l(2|n|+1)$, due to the extra bit for the sign. Floats are approximated by fractions up to a given precision by minimizing the sum of the description lengths of nominator and denominator, which are integers. Chars cost 8 bits due to 256 elements of the ASCII table. The description length of iterable structures such as strings, lists and tuples consisted of basic elements is simply the sum of the lengths of each element plus description length of the length of the iterable structure. For example, the description length of [-21,7,-4] is $l(2\cdot21+1)+l(2\cdot7+1)+l(2\cdot4+1)+l(3) = 10+8+8+4 = 30$ bits.

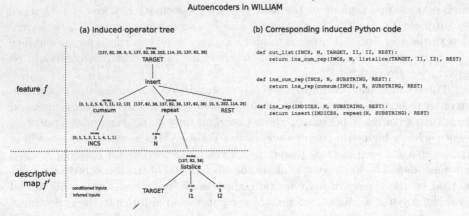

Fig. 1. (a) The target list contains a subsequence [137,82,38] repeating three times. The autoencoder tree squeezes the target through an information bottleneck. (b) The tree corresponds to actual Python code that can be compiled and executed.

Beyond data sets, elementary operators and the trees of them that define composite operators have to be described. The information needed to specify an elementary operator is simply $\lceil \log_2(N) \rceil = 6$ bits where N is the length of the alphabet, currently $N = 41$. Since each operator knows the number if its inputs/children, a tree made up of operators can be described by assigning a number $0, \ldots, N-1$ to each operator and writing those numbers in sequence, assuming a depth-first enumeration order. Thus, the description length of a tree is simply 6 times the number of operators.

2.2   Representing Autoencoders

The idea of incremental compression rests on the construction of stacked autoencoders. Figure 1(a) exemplifies one such autoencoder. The whole autoencoder is a single tree where the target has to be the output of the tree and is allowed to be an input to any of the leaf nodes of appropriate type. When a tree with the property is found, the system tries to cut through it at the location of smallest description length, i.e. it tries to find the information bottleneck whose description length (called *waistline*) is shorter than the target. In Fig. 1(a) `listslice` and its inputs I1 and I2 slice the first three elements from the target list, functioning in the role of a descriptive map f'. The information bottleneck is given by the dashed line at which point the intermediate, residual description[2] is `[INCS,N,[137,82,38],REST]`. The description length of the waistline consists of $46 + 3 + 44 + 53 = 146$ bits for the residual description and 18 bits for the feature tree (6 bits per operator)). This is less than the description length of the target (176 bits). Ergo, some compression has been achieved. The feature tree f decompresses those variables back onto the target by inserting the repeating subsequence at the indicated indices. The conditioned inputs are those to be given (i.e. guessed), the inferred inputs can be computed by inverting the tree. We see that without the descriptive map f', i.e. `listslice`, the list `[137,82,38]` would have to be guessed in order to compress the target, which is highly improbable.

The search for such autoencoders is performed by enumerating all trees of operators from the set of primitives, such that input and output types match. The enumeration was sorted by a rating consisting of the description length of the tree and conditioned inputs plus the logarithm of the number of attempts to invert that tree, i.e. to find some inferred inputs. When some tree can not be inverted for a long time, its rating drops and the search focuses on trees with the smallest rating. Effectively, this search amounts to exhaustive search for a pair (f, f') sorted by the sum of their lengths $l(f) + l(f')$ if we consider the conditioned inputs as belonging to f'.

After an autoencoder is found, f' is removed and the residual description is joined to a single list which serves as the target for the next autoencoders to be stacked on the first one (see Sect. 3.2 for more details). This incremental process continues until either no compression can be found or some maximal search time is reached.

2.3 Prediction

Given a function and its inputs, predictions are generated by manipulating the inputs in certain ways. In general, as demanded by Solomonoff induction, every possible continuation of a string has to be considered and separately compressed. Remember the Solomonoff prior of a string x:

$$M(x) = \sum_{q:U(q)=x} 2^{-l(q)} \tag{2}$$

where $x, q \in \mathcal{B}^*$ are finite strings defined on a finite alphabet $\mathcal{B}$, U is a universal Turing machine that executes program q and prints x and $l(q)$ is the length of

---

[2] What we have called "parameter" in [4] is now called "residual description".

program q. Given already seen history $x_{<k} \equiv x_1 \cdots x_{k-1}$ the prediction of the next h bits is computed by considering all $|\mathcal{B}|^h$ strings of length h and computing the conditional distribution $M(x_{k:k+h-1}|x_{1:k}) = M(x_{<k+h-1})/M(x_{<k})$, each of which requires to find a set of short functions q that are able to compute $x_{<k+h-1}$.

This is clearly intractable in practice. However, if we consider the set of short programs for $x_{<k+h-1}$ in which the continuation $x_{k:k+h-1}$ is chosen freely, it can be shown that the continuation can not contain much additional information compared to $x_{<k}$[3]. Therefore, that set of programs is likely to be among the set of shortest programs already found for $x_{<k}$. In this sense, although it is not a general solution, it appears reasonable to look for small modifications of a short function of $x_{<k}$ in order to predict its continuation.

In the present implementation we modify those leaves of the tree that are related to the length of the output sequence, trying to extend its length. This seems like a heuristic, however, from the theoretic perspective it turns out that given a feature f of x, to arrive at some extended string xy, it takes a program of constant size, $K(g|f) = O(1)$, to arrive at some feature g of xy (yet unpublished result). In that sense, we are well-set for the computation of predictions in a theoretically grounded way.

In this paper, we use the shortest found functions for computing predictions, but nothing prevents us from using several short functions for the approximation of the Solomonoff prior and the Bayesian posterior for prediction purposes. For prediction examples see Table 1 below.

Table 1. Examples of induced functions. The indicated compression ratio has been reached after the indicated number of program execution attempts.

Target	Induced program	Attempts	Compression	Predictions
[0,1,2,...,99]	urange(100)	1	98%	100,101,102,103,...
[0,9,9,1,9,9,2,9,9,...,6,9,9]	insertel(trange(0,21,3), urange(7),21,9)	1383	62%	7 or 9,9,...
[9,8,9,9,8,9,8,9,9,9]	cumsum([9,-1,1,0,-1,1,-1,0,1,0,0])	2	51%	9 or 10 or 11 or 12...
[100,200,300,400,500,100,200,...,500]	repeat(100, trange(100,600,100))	46	99%	100,200,300,400,500,100,200,...
[7,1,8,7,1,8,7,...,1,8,3,3,...,3,3]	conc_rep(20, [7,1,8], repeat(15, [3]))	317	85%	3,3,3,...
[33,35,...,147,149,150,149,148,...,6,5]	conc_tr(33, 151, 2, trange(150, 4, -1))	384	96%	4,3,2,...
'ABCDEFGHIJKLMN'	str2idx(trange(65,79,1))	23	60%	'OPQRS...'
'aaaaammmmmzzzzz'	str2idx(cumsum([[97,0,0,0,0,12,0,0,0,0,13,0,0,0,0]]))	8	49%	'z' or '{' or '|'...

---

[3] The proof would be beyond the scope of the present paper and will be published soon.

3   Results

3.1   Examples of Induced Programs

In the following, we present some test cases of what has been achieved so far. The algorithm keeps searching for matching programs, until either a configurable amount of valid programs has been found, or all functions up to a certain description length have been attempted. The *target* column in Table 1 describes the data, for which the algorithm had to find a program, consisting of a function and input data for that found function, so that calling the function with that input data reproduces the target. In the last four examples, we also demonstrate the reuse of already found functions, which were not present in the original set of primitives, but were previously learned and (manually) stored.

In order to compute predictions, each function (also called *composite operator*) knows which leaves to update in order to extend the output. For example, in the ABCD.. example, 79 is updated to 80 etc. since the `trange` operator knows that its second input has to be incremented in order to increment its output. Every operator knows how to be incremented which is propagated to the whole composite. Integers are incremented by 1, while lists are extended by [0] or [1] or [2] etc. which in the `cumsum` example in the third line, leads to the predictions 9, 10, 11 etc.

Table 2. Example of an incrementally induced composition of functions (also called *alleys* in [5])

Denotation	Feature	Residual description	Compression
x		[0,9,9,1,9,9,2,9,9,3,9,9,4,9,9,5,9,9,6,9,9]	0%
$f_1(a,b,c), r_1$	insertel(a,b,c)	[[0,3,6,9,12,15,18], [0,1,2,3,4,5,6],21,9]	28%
$f_2(a), r_2$	cumsum(a)	[[0,3,3,3,3,3,3,-18,1,1,1,1,1,1,15,-12]]	40%
$f_3(a), r_3$	cumsum(a)	[[0,3,0,0,0,0,0,-21,19,0,0,0,0,0,14,-27]]	52%

3.2   Example of Incrementally Induced Composition of Functions

Consider the target x from Table 2. WILLIAM has first found a function $f_1(a,b,c)$ and its residual description $r_1 = [a]$. The feature f_1 and the residual description r_1 form the program

$$x = \texttt{insertel}([0,3,6,9,12,15,18],[0,1,2,3,4,5,6],21,9), \qquad (3)$$

which inserts the numbers 0 to 6 at the indicated indices and fills the rest with 9's, which is shorter than the initial target x by 28%. In the current version of WILLIAM, the new target is obtained by joining the residual into a single list (denoted by $c(r_1)$), so at step two the new target is set to

$$c(r_1) = [0,3,6,9,12,15,18,0,1,2,3,4,5,6,21,9].$$

This concatenation is done in order to account for possible mutual information between leaves. For example, the two lists in Eq. (3) both increment the previous number by a constant and therefore there is mutual information between those lists. Therefore, the application of a single cumsum function to the concatenated list $c(r_1)$ compresses both lists.

After running the inductor on the new target $c(r_1)$ we obtain a new feature $f_2(a)$ and its residual r_2 such that $c(r_1) = f_2(r_2)$. Using $c(r_2)$ as the new target we obtain $f_3(a)$ and p_3. This process is continued until the inductor can not find a shorter description, which is $c(p_3)$ in this example. Overall, the final description of the target x contains features (functions) f_1, f_2, f_3, a residual r_3 and some information that allows to obtain initial versions of r_i from the concatenated forms $c(r_i)$, by saving the indices of each input in the concatenated list $c(r_i)$.

This compression required merely 45 attempts while the non-incremental compression of the same required 1383 attempts (see Table 1), demonstrating how incremental compression can be faster than non-incremental compression. However, the compression ratio is somewhat lower. The reason is the concatenation of r_i to $c(r_i)$, which deletes the information about where the input to one leaf ends and to the next leaf starts. We could do without this concatenation and incrementally compress the values at each leaf independently, but this would ignore possible mutual information between leaves. Consider another example in Table 3, where this effect is even stronger.

Table 3. Another example of incremental compression. The depth of the incrementally found tree is 7, which would be intractable in the non-incremental setting.

Denotation	Feature	Residual description	Compr.
x		[7,1,8,7,1,8,...,7,1,8,3,3,...,3]	0%
$f_1(a,b),r_1$	table(a,b)	[[1,3,7,8], [2,0,3,2,0,3,...,2,0,3,1,1,...,1]]	36%
$f_2(a,b,c,d,e),r_2$	insertel(trange(a,b,c),d,e)	[1,64,1, [3,7,8,2,0,3,2,0,3,...,2,0,3], 79, 1]	38%
$f_3(a,b,c,d,e),r_3$	insert(trange(a,b,c),d,e)	[6,66,3,2, [1,64,1,3,7,8,0,3,0,3,...,0,3,79,1]]	49%
$f_4(a,b,c,d,e),r_4$	insert(trange(a,b,c), d,cumsum(e))	[10,50,2,0, [6,60,-63,-1,-1,63,-63,2,4,1,-5,0,0,...,0,76,-78]]	57%

This very target has been compressed by 85% in Table 1, while incremental compression has only achieved 57%. We see that due to the just discussed concatenation of residuals, the next feature has to make efforts to cut out the compressible parts of the residual using the insert and trange operators, wasting description length this way. We don't have a satisfactory solution to this problem at this point. Nevertheless, this example demonstrates that deep trees can be found incrementally.

3.3 Perception: Recognition of Geometric Figures and Line Drawings

More examples are seen in Fig. 2 where a list of coordinate pairs coded for various geometric figures. Those figures could be compressed successfully by

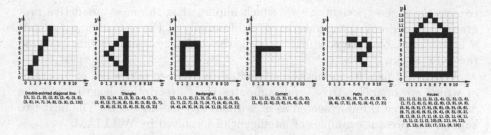

Fig. 2. Incrementally compressed simple geometric figures, paths and line drawings

functions like zip(cumsum(cumsum(y)). They also constitute examples of incremental compression in the sense that the list of coordinates were transformed to two lists of $x-$ and $y-$values, respectively, by an autoencoder using the zip operator. Remarkably, the residual description does not correspond to any usual way, we would represent a, say, rectangle. Usually, we would encode the coordinates of one corner (x0,y0), the length dx and the width dy. Instead, consider a larger version of the rectangle in Fig. 2, having a width dx=100 and height dy=200 with one corner defined by x1=850 and y1=370. The residual after incremental compression turns out to be

[[0,1,dx+1,n+1,dx+n,2*n,2*n+1,dx+2*n+1,3*n,dx+3*n] ,
[y0,-y0,1,-1,-1,x0-y0+1,y0-x0+1,-1,-1,1],4*n,0],

where n=dx+dy. We see that the residual does consist of the basic parameters of a rectangle and some small numbers, albeit not fully compressed. Moreover, we see that the residual of a square is a special case of the residual of a rectangle, where dx=dy. The reason why compression has stopped before is the compression condition: the residual has become quite short such as the description length of a new feature plus its residual is too long. The fundamental reason is, that in order to compress optimally, we should not consider a single rectangle, but a set of rectangles compressed by the same function (see discussion). Overall, these examples demonstrate that WILLIAM can compress simple geometric figures, paths and line drawings.

3.4   Combining Our Induction Algorithm with AIXI

Given some induction capabilities of WILLIAM, we have implemented a plain version of the AIXI agent, which chooses its actions according to the formula [6]

$$a_k := \arg\max_{a_k} \sum_{o_k r_k} \cdots \max_{a_m} \sum_{o_m r_m} [r_k + \cdots + r_m] \cdot \sum_{q:U(q,a_1...a_m)=o_1 r_1 \cdots o_m r_m} 2^{-l(q)} \qquad (4)$$

where a_i, o_i and r_i are actions, observations and rewards at time step i, respectively. In a nutshell, AIXI has seen the observation and reward sequence $o_1 r_1 \cdots o_{k-1} r_{k-1}$, performed actions $a_1 \cdots a_{k-1}$ and considers all permutations of futures $o_k r_k \cdots o_m r_m$ and actions $a_k \cdots a_m$. For each such permutation it looks for all programs, executed on a universal Turing machine U that can compute the observation-reward sequence given the actions. The shortest such programs receive the highest weight $2^{-l(q)}$, which implies that the most predictive programs are predominantly considered. Additionally, if the reward sum for such a highly probable future is high as well, the action maximizing this expected reward is taken.

WILLIAM uses its inductive capabilities in order to find a list of programs q, which are operator trees, and computes their description length $l(q)$. The expectimax tree is implemented as is, without any modifications. The next two subsections present examples of intelligent tasks solved by WILLIAM.

3.5 Recursive Self-improvement: WILLIAM Helps Itself to Do Gradient Descent

One of the most thorny induction problems is the search for good sampling algorithms. The central problem is to find inputs to a given function, such that its value is maximized. For example, probabilistic graphical models face the problem of finding areas of high probability in a high-dimensional space [9]. A long list of sampling procedures have been researched, however, a general solution is not in sight. Any procedure is good for some problems and bad for others, which hints to the fact that sampling is probably AI complete.

In our context, some inputs may lead to high compression ratios, while others do not. Consider the following function, for example: `f1(x1,x2,x3,x4) := insert(range(x1, 20), repeat(x2, [x3]), x4)` with the target `[N,N,...,N,0,0,...,0]` where a large number N is repeated 20 times and followed by zeros. Some values for `x1` leads to long input descriptions, for example, `x1=14` leads to `x2=6`, `x3=N`, `x4=[N,N,...,N,0,0,...,0]` after inverting the function, where the lange number N occurs 14 times within `x4` while lower values of `x1` lead to shorter input descriptions. Thus, the total description length of the inputs depends on `x1`: lower values of `x1` lead to more compression. Therefore, some gradient descent procedure would be helpful in order to find the minimum (`x1=0`, cutting out all numbers N from the target). However, a priori our algorithm would not perform a gradient descent procedure but exhaustive search by default, which is inefficient. Usually, people start hard-coding a special algorithm, like gradient descent in this case, in order to find the minimum more efficiently. Instead, we have followed our general paradigm of refraining from such heuristics and used our AIXI agent, in order to find the minimum.

The state space was set up as follows. There were two actions allowed, $+1$ and -1 to modify `x1`, no observations were needed for that task and rewards were set to $+1$ if the input description becomes shorter and -1 otherwise. The agent looked one time step ahead: $m = k$. The agent was initialized with a start value `x1=15`, an action history `-1,1,1,-1` with the respective rewards `1,-1,-1,1`, since decreasing `x1` leads better compression ratios. Given that history, the induction system of the agent has figured out that, among others, the function `f2(x) := map(negate, x)` is able to compute the reward sequence from the action sequence. That same function can then be used to compute future rewards for any action and thus to maximize them. In this way, the agent has figured out to take action `-1` at every time step. However, the agent was not able to figure out appropriate actions when the history had some noise, since filtering out noise currently exceeds the abilities of the induction system. Nevertheless, an effective gradient descent ability has emerged from the agent which relieves us from having to implement it as a heuristic. Moreover, nothing additional will have to be implemented in future, since AIXI is a generally intelligent agent and can be applied to a wide range of tasks. This is an example of self-improvement, since AIXI uses the induction system (it has found function f2) to improve the induction system (to find inputs to the function f1 more efficiently). Note that even though from the perspective of intelligence, figuring out that reducing a number reduces some objective function is not a hard thing to do, the real achievement is about the fact that WILLIAM has found the solution on its own and has thereby drastically reduced the size of *its own* search space. This ability to recognize properties of a given task and deriving a task-dependent efficient procedure instead of blindly applying some general but inefficient one, is a crucial step for any system striving for AGI.

3.6 Intelligent Behavior: WILLIAM Plays Tic-tac-toe

Figure 3 shows a sequence of tic-tac-toe positions and alternate moves.

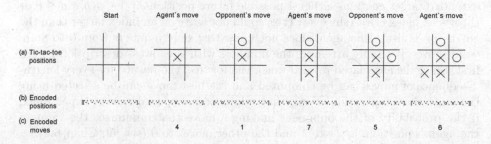

Fig. 3. WILLIAM plays tic-tac-toe. (a) A sample game. (b) The compression target is the sequence of positions is encoded as a list of lists of strings. (c) The moves are encoded by the square number. The agent's last move on square 6 is a fork that cannot be defended – a smart move.

We encoded the sequence of positions into a list of lists, each of which contains 9 strings of length 1, where 'x' denotes the agent's move, 'o' the opponent's move and '-' a yet empty square. WILLIAM receives a target like Fig. 3(b) (except the last position) and tries to compress it.

Relatively quickly, the function ttt := cumop3(setitem, START, MOVES, repeat(NUMREP, CONTENT)) with respective inputs.

START=['-','-','-','-','-','-','-','-','-'],   MOVES=[4,1,7,5], NUMREP=2 and CONTENT= ['x','o'] is found by the induction algorithm. repeat(2, ['x','o']) evaluates to ['x','o', 'x','o']. setitem is an operator that writes some content in a list at the specified position. For example, setitem(['a','b','c'], 2, 'x') evaluates to ['a','b','x']. Finally, `cumop3` is an arity 3 operator that cumulatively applies the function at its first input to the other inputs computing the list of encoded positions in Fig. 3(b).

We observe that the found function `ttt` is a tree of depth two which can be found quickly. The only thing that had to be programmed specifically for this game is the map from a position to the reward, since recognizing that a positive reward is given whenever there are three x-es in a row currently exceeds the induction abilities of the system. A winning position is rewarded by +1 and a losing one by −1. An illegal move is penalized by reward −100 if done by the agent and by +100 if done by the opponent.

The only thing that remains to be done by WILLIAM is to find a sequence of moves up that lead to a winning position. This kind of exhaustive search is already part of the generic AIXI implementation: the expectimax operation: it is not specific to tic-tac-toe. We chose the horizon of $m = k+3$, i.e. 4 moves ahead (two taken by the agent, two by the opponent). However, instead of considering all permutation of all possible lists of four lists and compressing all possible futures, as would be required by AIXI, we used the found function `ttt` to run the prediction algorithm (Sect. 2.3) to *compute* the probable futures. Note that the sequence of past moves [4,1,7,5] was found by inversion. The generic prediction algorithm took the induced function and their inputs and extended it by looking at all continuations [4,1,7,5,a,b,c,d] of length 4 of a list of integers. The extended target contains either 4 possible future positions if $0 \leq a,b,c,d \leq 8$ or throws an index error (since `setitem` could not write on an index larger than the length of its list). The agent does not know that only numbers from 0 to 8 are valid moves. It simply attempts the numbers with the lowest description length first. Since the associated reward was given for free, the reward for every length-4-sequence of moves can be computed and the best move can be selected using the expectimax operation. Note, that minimax is a special case of expectimax, if the probability of the opponent making a move that minimizes the value of the agent's position, is set to 1 and the other moves to 0 (see [6], Chap. 6.4).

Note that apart from the reward computation, the agent doesn't know anything specific about the game. For example, if only the first starting position ['-','-','-','-','-','-','-','-','-'] is given, the agent compresses it simply with `repeat(9,['-'])`. Curiously, instead of making a 'x', WILLIAM's "move" is to attach '-' to this target, since this function is simpler than the `ttt` function above. After all, a list of dashes is all the agent has seen in its life. However, when more moves have been made, the agent finds a different description that successfully captures the regularities in the sequence of positions, namely, that each position is generated by the previous position by making an 'x' or an 'o'. The last move of the agent on square 6 in Fig. 3 is a fork that can not be defended. It is selected since no answer by the opponent can compromise the agent's victory.

4   Discussion

We have demonstrated the current state of WILLIAM, showing the ability to compress a diverse set of simple sequences, predict their continuation and use these abilities to solve simple tasks. As shown in Sects. 3.2 and 3.3, much larger program trees could be induced than would be tractable by exhaustive search, which consitutes evidence of the practical usefulness of our theory of incremental compression.

4.1 Related Work

The field of inductive programming has traditionally focused on the derivation/search of recursive or logic programs, which has generally suffered from the intractable vastness of possible programs to induce (see [8], [2] for a review), nurturing the demand for an incremental approach. The subfield of genetic programming can be viewed as one such approach making it beyond toy problems, since candidate programs are synthesized from already promising previous attempts or by small mutations. The problem of bloat however has challenged progress in the past [11]. We feel that algorithmic information theory can help out by providing theoretical guarantees for the implementation of such a challenging endeavor. The present paper can be viewed as an example of such a collaboration between theory and practice.

Another attempt to deal with the curse of dimensionality is to try to make the system itself deal with its own problems, by recursively improving itself. Adaptive Levin Search [12] is comparable to our approach being an inductive system with life-long self-improvement. It updates the probability distribution of the primitives in order to speed up the system based on acquired knowledge. WILLIAM is also able to do this, but moreover it can solve tasks incrementally, such that it does not need to find a difficult solution at once, but instead breaks down this process into steps.

4.2 Limitations

The list of current limitations is long both on the practical and theoretical side. Problematic is the aspect that the used language is not Turing complete, since the resulting Python programs always halt: there are no infinite loops and no recursion. We will change this by using loop operators but the search algorithm will have to be changed due to the halting problem, possibly using dovetailing or a yet to be developed computable theory of incremental compression. The conceptual problem of concatenating the leaves of a tree in the formation of the residual description is also problematic as presented in Sect. 3.2.

A systematic evaluation of the compression algorithm comparing it to the state of the art is also missing yet. Note that the tree in Fig. 1(a) is a way to cut out arbitrary repeating substrings from a string. For example, the widespread celebrated Lempel-Ziv algorithm also capitalizes on repeating substrings. We haven't tried it yet, but it seems straightforward to keep cutting out substring after substring during incremental compression using the very same function. This way, we can expect similar compression ratios for sequences at which Lempel-Ziv compression is good while possessing much more general compression abilities than specialized compression algorithms.

Another big missing piece is the lack of a dynamic memory. After all, pieces of programs that have proven useful, should be reused in future in order to enable incremental, open-ended learning. For this purpose, we could learn from successful memoization techniques in inductive programming, such as in [7]. On a more general note, the optimal structure of a memory is a difficult theoretical problem and to be embarked on in future.

4.3   Recursive Self-Improvement

It is interesting to observe that many of the current problems in this induction system could potentially be solved by the system itself. After all, it is a general problem solver when attached to AIXI. We have already demonstrated one self-aided way to search for inputs to a function in Sect. 3.5. Note that AIXI's problem solving abilities mostly depend on the abilities of the induction system. But if some version of the system uses AIXI to solve some of its own problems, it thereby effectively builds a new version of the induction system itself. Currently, WILLIAM is yet too weak to help itself on a large scale, but several other self-help problems come to mind.

For example, instead of using exhaustive search for various trees, we should bias the search toward more simple trees first. But simplicity is measured only after finding a short description, i.e. by finding a tree describing the tree! Hence, this would require a search through short trees that generate codes for other trees. The latter ones would then be simple by definition, since they have got a short description, and therefore more likely a priori, as given by the Solomonoff prior, Eq. 2.

Another example is the reuse of found trees by encapsulating them as composite operators, which is already possible. This way frequently used such composite operators will receive a short code (e.g. Huffman) increasing the likelihood of being reused.

Another issue is noticed for example in the prediction of the tic-tac-toe moves. The agent does not know anything about the game, it simply tries to extend a list of integers, such as the moves in Fig. 3(c). This leads to the attempt to try all integer combinations with the length defined by the AIXI horizon, including invalid combinations like [0,0,0,2534] which has a shorter description length than a set of valid moves [6,8,7,5] due to the logarithmic coding of natural numbers in the Elias delta code. A "smart" way would be to notice that any move above 8 makes the function throw an exception. Instead of building a heuristic, we plan to reuse WILLIAM's induction abilities in the framework of general knowledge-seeking agents [10], in order to find a function that computes the possible valid entries. In this case, a function like lessthan(a, 9) returns True for valid entries and its inversion would work as a generator for valid entries. Since the theory of knowledge-seeking agents already provides with optimal "experiments" that can rule out wrong hypotheses and WILLIAM is a system that comes up with those hypotheses, we can expect WILLIAM to be able to generate those inputs that are likely to be valid and help it to solve its own problems.

4.4   Compression, Interpretability and Concept Acquisition

Apart from facilitating the implementation of AIXI, one of the reasons we think that compression is important is the hypothesis that it facilitates the acquisition of concepts and reaches interpretable representations. Consider the rectangle example in Sect. 3.3. The compression target was a list of pixel coordinates which did not contain the width and length of the rectangle explicitly. Nevertheless, the final residual description did contain those variables. In fact, we suspect that if we run the algorithm on an ensemble of different rectangles, the residual will distill those variables even better, since those are the only unpredictable, i.e. incompressible, changes between rectangles. Therefore, the distillation of interpretable variables which could be mapped onto concepts and words for concepts is an important step toward building an agent endowed with conceptualizations tightly bound to grounded representations of the world. Moreover, for the purpose of building taxonomies of objects, deciding statements like "any square is a rectangle" appear possible since the (residual) description of a square is a special case of the (residual) description of a rectangle. This is a non-trivial observation since it is usually hard to obtain such taxonomic relationships in distributed representations such as in neural networks.

4.5   Training Time and Generalization Abilities

Speaking of neural networks, another striking difference between our approach and many common approaches in machine learning is that much less training is required in order to solve tasks. "Big data" is necessary exactly because many methods in machine learning do not generalize well. The lack of previous knowledge is not the only reason why so called one-shot learning is difficult for conventional methods. A major reason is that those methods do not compress data well. As exemplified in the tic-tac-toe example, the agent plays well in the very first game. Reasonable predictions in Table 1 are possible after the very first sequence seen by the algorithm. Moreover, the fact that compression leads to optimal generalization abilities is a fact proven in the theory of universal induction [13]. Therefore, heading for better compression ratios in machine learning is another message we would like to convey in this paper.

4.6   Could this be a Path Toward AGI?

In the face of the AGI challenge, the current results are very modest, to say the least, even though we don't see any fundamental limits to this approach, since it is backed by sound theories and any regularity seems to be representable by the current or future version of the algorithm. The scalability of any algorithm is usually impeded by the curse of dimensionality. In this case, our theory of incremental compression and the encouraging aspects of self-improvement emerging from the algorithm provide a fundamental response to this question, grounding the hope for scalability in future, although it is too early to say for sure.

   In summary, we have demonstrated a general agent able to solve tasks in a range of diverse and simple environments. It searches for representations in a general algorithmic space instead of using a fixed representation usually employed by machine learning approaches or a patchwork of algorithms in cognitive architectures. Nevertheless, it achieves its relative efficiency by exploiting the fact, that our environment usually contains features that can be searched for incrementally. Possessing (nondegenerate) features is an assumption that is possibly not valid for the universal set of strings, however it may be valid for the universe we live in. In this sense, looking for such general but non-universal properties may boost the efficiency even further without making compromises on the generality of intelligence.

References

1. Elias, P.: Universal codeword sets and representations of the integers. IEEE Trans. Inf. Theor. **21**(2), 194–203 (1975)
2. Flener, P., Schmid, U.: An introduction to inductive programming. Artif. Intell. Rev. **29**(1), 45–62 (2008)
3. Franz, A.: Artificial general intelligence through recursive data compression and grounded reasoning: a position paper. arXiv preprint arXiv:1506.04366 (2015)
4. Franz, A.: Some theorems on incremental compression. In: Steunebrink, B., Wang, P., Goertzel, B. (eds.) AGI -2016. LNCS (LNAI), vol. 9782, pp. 74–83. Springer, Cham (2016). https://doi.org/10.1007/978-3-319-41649-6_8
5. Franz, A., Löffler, M., Antonenko, A., Gogulya, V., Zaslavskyi, D.: Introducing WILLIAM: a system for inductive inference based on the theory of incremental compression. In: International Conference on Computer Algebra and Information Technology (2018)
6. Hutter, M.: Universal Artificial Intelligence: Sequential Decisions based on Algorithmic Probability, p. 300. Springer, Berlin(2005). http://www.hutter1.net/ai/uaibook.htm
7. Katayama, S.: Towards human-level inductive functional programming. In: Bieger, J., Goertzel, B., Potapov, A. (eds.) AGI 2015. LNCS (LNAI), vol. 9205, pp. 111–120. Springer, Cham (2015). https://doi.org/10.1007/978-3-319-21365-1_12
8. Kitzelmann, E.: Inductive programming: a survey of program synthesis techniques. In: Schmid, U., Kitzelmann, E., Plasmeijer, R. (eds.) AAIP 2009. LNCS, vol. 5812, pp. 50–73. Springer, Heidelberg (2010). https://doi.org/10.1007/978-3-642-11931-6_3
9. MacKay, D.J.C., Mac Kay, D.J.C.: Information Theory, Inference and Learning Algorithms. Cambridge University Press, Cambridge (2003)
10. Orseau, L., Lattimore, T., Hutter, M.: Universal knowledge-seeking agents for stochastic environments. In: Jain, S., Munos, R., Stephan, F., Zeugmann, T. (eds.) ALT 2013. LNCS (LNAI), vol. 8139, pp. 158–172. Springer, Heidelberg (2013). https://doi.org/10.1007/978-3-642-40935-6_12
11. Poli, R., Langdon, W.B., McPhee, N.F., Koza, J.R.: A field guide to genetic programming. Lulu. com (2008)
12. Schmidhuber, J., Zhao, J., Wiering, M.: Shifting inductive bias with success-story algorithm, adaptive levin search, and incremental self-improvement. Mach. Learn. **28**(1), 105–130 (1997)
13. Solomonoff, R.: Complexity-based induction systems: comparisons and convergence theorems. IEEE Trans. Inf. Theor. **24**(4), 422–432 (1978)
14. Solomonoff, R.J.: A formal theory of inductive inference Part I. Inf. Control **7**(1), 1–22 (1964)

An Inferential Approach to Mining Surprising Patterns in Hypergraphs

Nil Geisweiller[(✉)] and Ben Goertzel

SingularityNET Foundation, Amsterdam, The Netherlands
{nil,ben}@singularitynet.io

Abstract. A novel pattern mining algorithm and a novel formal definition of surprisingness are introduced, both framed in the context of formal reasoning. Hypergraphs are used to represent the data in which patterns are mined, the patterns themselves, and the control rules for the pattern miner. The implementation of these tools in the OpenCog framework, as part of a broader multi-algorithm approach to AGI, is described.

Keywords: Pattern miner · Surprisingness · Reasoning · Hypergraphs

1 Introduction

Pattern recognition is broadly recognized as a key aspect of general intelligence, as well as of many varieties of specialized intelligence. General intelligence can be envisioned, among other ways, as the process of an agent recognizing patterns in itself and its environment, including patterns regarding which of its actions tend to achieve which goals in which contexts [5].

The scope of pattern recognition algorithms in AI and allied disciplines is very broad, including many specialized algorithms aimed at recognizing patterns in particular sorts of data such as visual data, auditory data or genomic data. Among more general-purpose approaches to pattern recognition, so-called "pattern mining" plays a prominent role. Mining here refers to the process of systematically searching a body of data to find a large number of patterns satisfying certain criteria. Most pattern mining algorithms are greedy in operation, meaning they start by finding simple patterns and then try to combine these to guide their search for more complex patterns, and iterate this approach a few times. Pattern mining algorithms tend to work at the *syntactic* level, such as subtree mining [2], where patterns are subtrees within a database of trees, and each subtree represents a concept containing all the trees consistent with that subtree. This is both a limit and a strength. Limit because they cannot express arbitrary abstractions, and strength because they can be relatively efficient. Moreover even purely syntactic pattern miners can go a long way if much of the semantic knowledge is represented in syntax. For instance if the data contains human(John) and human ⇒ mortal a purely syntactic pattern miner will

P. Hammer et al. (Eds.): AGI 2019, LNAI 11654, pp. 59–69, 2019.
https://doi.org/10.1007/978-3-030-27005-6_6

not be able to take into account the implicit datum `mortal(John)` unless a step of inference is formerly taken to make it visible. Another shortcoming of pattern mining is the volume of patterns it tends to produce. For that reason it can be useful to rank the patterns according to interestingness [12]. One can also use pattern mining in combination with other pattern recognition techniques, e.g. evolutionary programming or logical inference.

Here we present a novel approach to pattern mining that combines semantic with syntactic understanding of patterns, and that uses a sophisticated measure of pattern surprisingness to filter the combinatorial explosion of patterns. The surprisingness measure and the semantic aspect of patterns are handled via embedding the pattern mining process in an inference engine, operating on a highly general hypergraph-based knowledge representation.

1.1   Contribution

A pattern miner algorithm alongside a measure of surprisingness designed to find patterns in hypergraph database are introduced. Both are implemented on the OpenCog framework [6], on top of the *Unified Rule Engine*, URE for short, the reasoning engine of OpenCog. Framing pattern mining as reasoning provides the following advantages:

1. Enable hybridizations between syntactic and semantic pattern mining.
2. Allow to handle the full notion of surprisingness, as will be further shown.
3. Offer more transparency. Produced knowledge can be reasoned upon. Reasoning steps selected during mining can be represented as data for subsequent mining and reasoning, enabling meta-learning by leveraging URE's inference control mechanism.

The last point, although already important as it stands, goes further than it may at first seem. One of the motivations to have a pattern miner in OpenCog is to mine inference traces, to discover control rules and apply these control rules to speed up reasoning, akin to a Heuristic Algorithmic Memory [9] for reasoning. By framing not only pattern mining but more generally learning as reasoning we hope to kickstart a virtuous self-improvement cycle. Towards that end more components of OpenCog, such as MOSES [8], an evolutionary program learner, are in the process of being ported to the URE.

Framing learning as reasoning is not without drawbacks as more transparency comes at a computational cost. However by carefully partitioning transparent/costly versus opaque/efficient computations we hope to reach an adequate balance between efficiency and open-endedness. For instance in the case of evolutionary programming, decisions pertaining to what regions of the program space to explore is best processed as reasoning, given the importance and the cost of such operation. While more systematic operations such as evaluating the fitness of a candidate can be left as opaque. One may draw a speculative analogy with the distinction between conscious and unconscious processes.

1.2 Outline

In Sect. 2 a pattern mining algorithm over hypergraphs is presented; it is framed as reasoning in Sect. 3. In Sect. 4 a definition of surprisingness is provided, and a more specialized implementation is derived from it. Then, in Sect. 5 an example of how it can be framed as reasoning is presented, both for the specialized and abstract definitions of surprisingness.

2 Pattern Mining in Hypergraph Database

2.1 AtomSpace: Hypergraph Database

Let us first rapidly recall what is the AtomSpace [6], the hypergraph knowledge store with which we shall work here. The AtomSpace is the OpenCog AGI framework's primary data storage solution. It is a labeled hypergraph particularly suited for representing symbolic knowledge, but is also capable of representing sub-symbolic knowledge (probabilities, tensors, etc), and most importantly combinations of the two. In the OpenCog terminology, edges of that hypergraph are called *links*, vertices are called *nodes*, and *atoms* are either links or nodes.

For example one may express that cars are vehicles with

```
(Inheritance (Concept "car") (Concept "vehicle"))
```

Inheritance is a link connecting two concept nodes, car and vehicle. If one wishes to express the other way around, how much vehicles are cars, then one can attach the inheritance with a *truth value*

```
(Inheritance (stv 0.4 0.8) (Concept "vehicle") (Concept "car"))
```

where 0.4 represents a probability and 0.8 represents a confidence.

Storing knowledge as hypergraph rather than collections of formulae allows to rapidly query atoms and how they relate to other atoms.

2.2 Pattern Matching

OpenCog comes with a *pattern matcher*, a component that can query the Atom-Space, similar in spirit to SQL, but different in several aspects. For instance queries are themselves programs represented as atoms in the AtomSpace. This insures reflexivity where queries can be queried or produced by queries.

Here's an example of such a query

```
(Get (Present (Inheritance (Variable "$X") (Variable "$Y"))
              (Inheritance (Variable "$Y") (Variable "$Z"))))
```

which fetches instances of transitivity of inheritance in the AtomSpace. For instance if the AtomSpace contains

```
(Inheritance (Concept "cat") (Concept "mammal"))
(Inheritance (Concept "mammal") (Concept "animal"))
(Inheritance (Concept "square") (Concept "shape"))
```

it retrieves

```
(Set (List (Concept "cat") (Concept "mammal") (Concept "animal")))
```

where `cat`, `mammal` and `animal` are associated to variable $X, $Y and $Z according to the prefix order of the query, but `square` and `shape` are not retrieved because they do not exhibit transitivity. The construct `Set` represents a set of atoms, and `List` in this context represents tuples of values. The construct `Get` means retrieve. The construct `Present` means that the arguments are patterns to be conjunctively matched against the data present in the AtomSpace. We also call the arguments of `Present`, *clauses*, and say that the pattern is a *conjunction of clauses*.

In addition, the pattern matcher can rewrite. For instance a transitivity rule could be implemented with

```
(Bind (Present (Inheritance (Variable "$X") (Variable "$Y"))
               (Inheritance (Variable "$Y") (Variable "$Z")))
      (Inheritance (Variable "$X") (Variable "$Z")))
```

The pattern matcher provides the building blocks for the reasoning engine. In fact the URE is, for the most part, pattern matching + unification. The collection of atoms that can be executed in OpenCog, to query the atomspace, reason or such, forms a language called *Atomese*.

2.3 Pattern Mining as Inverse of Pattern Matching

The pattern miner solves the inverse problem of pattern matching. It attempts to find queries that would retrieve a certain *minimum* number of matches. This number is called the *support* in the pattern mining terminology [1,2].

It is worth mentioning that the pattern matcher has more constructs than `Get`, `Present` and `Bind`; for declaring types, expressing preconditions, and performing general computations. However the pattern miner only supports a subset of constructs due to the inherent complexity of such expressiveness.

2.4 High Level Algorithm of the Pattern Miner

Before showing how to express pattern mining as reasoning, let us explain the algorithm itself.

Our pattern mining algorithm operates like most pattern mining algorithms [2] by greedily searching the space of frequent patterns while pruning the parts that do not reach the minimum support. It typically starts from the most abstract one, the *top* pattern, constructing specializations of it and only retain those that have enough support, then repeat. The apriori property [1] guaranties that no pattern with enough support will be missed based on the fact that patterns without enough support cannot have specializations with enough support. More formally, given a database $\mathcal{D}$, a minimal support S and an initialize collection $\mathcal{C}$ of patterns with enough support, the mining algorithm is as follows

1. Select a pattern P from $\mathcal{C}$.
2. Produce a *shallow specialization* Q of P with support equal to or above S.
3. Add Q to $\mathcal{C}$, remove P if all its shallow specializations have been produced.
4. Repeat till a termination criterion has been met.

The pattern collection $\mathcal{C}$ is usually initialized with the top pattern

```
(Get (Present (Variable "$X")))
```

that matches the whole database, and from which all subsequent patterns are specialized. A shallow specialization is a specialization such that the expansion is only a level deep. For instance, if $\mathcal{D}$ is the 3 inheritances links of Subsect. 2.2 (cat is a mammal, a mammal is an animal and square is a shape), a shallow specialization of the top pattern could be

```
(Get (Present (Inheritance (Variable "$X") (Variable "$Y"))))
```

which would match all inheritance links, thus have a support of 3. A subsequent shallow specialization of it could be

```
(Get (Present (Inheritance (Concept "cat") (Variable "$Y"))))
```

which would only match

```
(Inheritance (Concept "cat") (Concept "mammal"))
```

and have a support of 1. So if the minimum support S is 2, this one would be discarded. In practice the algorithm is complemented by heuristics to avoid exhaustive search, but that is the core of it.

3   Framing Pattern Mining as Reasoning

The hardest part of the algorithm above is step 1, selecting which pattern to expand; this has the biggest impact on how the space is explored. When pattern mining is framed as reasoning such decision corresponds to a *premise or conclusion selection*. Let us formalize the type of propositions we need to prove in order to search the space of patterns. For sake of conciseness we will use a hybridization between mathematics and Atomese, it being understood that all can be formalized in Atomese. Given a database $\mathcal{D}$ and a minimum support S we want to instantiate and prove the following theorem

$$S \leq \mathsf{support}(P, \mathcal{D})$$

which expresses that pattern P has enough support with respect to the data base $\mathcal{D}$. To simplify we introduce the predicate $\mathsf{minsup}(P, S, \mathcal{D})$ as a shorthand for $S \leq \mathsf{support}(P, \mathcal{D})$. The primary inference rule we need is (given in Gentzen style),

$$\frac{\text{minsup}(Q, S, \mathcal{D}) \qquad \text{spec}(Q, P)}{\text{minsup}(P, S, \mathcal{D})} \text{ (AP)}$$

expressing that if Q has enough support, and Q is a specialization of P, then P has enough support, essentially formalizing the apriori property (AP). We can either apply such rule in a forward way, top-down, or in a backward way, bottom-up. If we search from more abstract to more specialized we want to use it in a backward way. Meaning the reasoning engine needs to choose P (*conclusion selection* from $\text{minsup}(P, S, \mathcal{D})$) and then construct a specialization Q. In practice that rule is actually written backward so that choosing P amounts to a *premise selection*, but is presented here this way for expository purpose. The definition of `spec` is left out, but it is merely a variation of the subtree relationship accounting for variables.

Other *heuristic* rules can be used to infer knowledge about `minsup`. They are heuristics because unlike the apriori property, they do not guaranty completeness, but can speed-up the search by eliminating large portions of the search space. For instance the following rule

$$\frac{\text{minsup}(P, S, \mathcal{D}) \qquad \text{minsup}(Q, S, \mathcal{D}) \qquad R(P \otimes Q)}{\text{minsup}(P \otimes Q, S, \mathcal{D})} \text{ (CE)}$$

expresses that if P and Q have enough support, and a certain combination $P \otimes Q$ has a certain property R, then such combination has enough support. Such rule can be used to build the conjunction of patterns. For instance given P and Q both equal to

```
(Get (Present (Inheritance (Variable "$X") (Variable "$Y"))))
```

One can combine them (joint by variable $Y) to form

```
(Get (Present (Inheritance (Variable "$X") (Variable "$Y"))
              (Inheritance (Variable "$Y") (Variable "$Z"))))
```

The property R here is that both clauses must share at least one joint variable and the combination must have its support above or equal to the minimum threshold.

4 Surprisingness

Even with the help of the apriori property and additional heuristics to prune the search, the volume of mined patterns can still be overwhelming. For that it is helpful to assign to the patterns a measure of *interestingness*. This is a broad notion and we will restrict our attention to the sub-notion of *surprisingness*, that can be defined as what is *contrary to expectations*.

Just like for pattern mining, surprisingness can be framed as reasoning. They are many ways to formalize it. We tentatively suggest that in its most general sense, surprisingness may be the considered as the difference of outcome between different inferences over the same conjecture.

Of course in most conventional logical systems, if consistent, different inferences will produce the same result. However in para-consistent systems, such as PLN for *Probabilistic Logic Network* [4], OpenCog's logic for common sense reasoning, conflicting outcomes are possible. In particular PLN allows propositions to be believed with various degrees of truth, ranging from total ignorance to absolute certainty. Thus PLN is well suited for such definition of surprisingness.

More specifically we define surprisingness as the *distance of truth values between different inferences over the same conjecture*. In PLN a *truth value* is a second order distribution, probabilities over probabilities, Chapter 4 of [4]. Second order distributions are good at capturing uncertainties. Total ignorance is represented by a flat distribution (Bayesian prior), or a slightly concave one (Jeffreys prior [7]), and absolute certainty by a Dirac delta function.

Such definition of surprisingness has the merit of encompassing a wide variety of cases; like the surprisingness of finding a proof contradicting human intuition. For instance the outcome of Euclid's proof of the infinity of prime numbers might contradict the intuition of a beginner upon observation that prime numbers rapidly rarefy as they grow. It also encompasses the surprisingness of observing an unexpected event, or the surprisingness of discovering a pattern in seemingly random data. All these cases can be framed as ways of constructing different types of inferences and finding contradictions between them. For instance in the case of discovering a pattern in a database, one inference could calculate the empirical probability based on the data, while an other inference could calculate a probability estimate based on variable independences.

The distance measure to use to compare conjecture outcomes remains to be defined. Since our truth values are distributions the *Jensen-Shannon Distance*, JSD for short [3], suggested as surprisingness measure in [11], could be used. The advantage of such distance is that it accounts well for uncertainty. If for instance a pattern is discovered in a small data set displaying high levels of dependencies between variables (thus surprising relative to an independence assumption), the surprisingness measure should consider the possibility that it might be a fluke since the data set is small. Fortunately, the smaller the data set, the flatter the second order distributions representing the empirical and the estimated truth values of the pattern, consequently reducing the JSD.

Likewise one can imagine the following experiments. In the first experiment a coin is tossed 3 times, a probability p_1 of head is calculated, then the coin is tossed 3 more times, a second probability p_2 of head is calculated. p_1 and p_2 might be very different, but it should not be surprising given the low number of observations. On the contrary, in the second experiment the coin is tossed a billion times, p_1 is calculated, then another billion times, p_2 is calculated. Here even tiny differences between p_1 and p_2 should be surprising. In both cases the Jensen-Shannon Distance seems to adequately accounts for the uncertainty.

A slight refinement of our definition of surprisingness, probably closer to human intuition, can be obtained by fixing one type of inference provided by the current model of the world from which rapid (and usually uncertain) conclusions can be derived, and the other type of inference implied by the world itself, either via observations, in the case of an experiential reality, or via crisp and long chains of deductions in the case of a mathematical reality.

4.1   Independence-Based Surprisingness

Here we explore a limited form of surprisingness based on the independence of the variables involved in the clauses of a pattern, called I-Surprisingness for Independence-based Surprisingness. For instance

```
(Get (Present (Inheritance (Variable "$X") (Variable "$Y"))
              (Inheritance (Variable "$Y") (Variable "$Z"))))
```

has two clauses

```
(Inheritance (Variable "$X") (Variable "$Y"))
```

and

```
(Inheritance (Variable "$Y") (Variable "$Z"))
```

If each clause is considered independently, that is the distribution of values taken by the variable tuples ($X, $Y) appearing in the first clause is independent from the distribution of values taken by the variable tuples ($Y, $Z) in the second clause, one can simply use the product of the two probabilities to obtain an probability estimate of their conjunctions. However the presence of joint variables, here $Y, makes this calculation incorrect. The connections need to be taken into account. To do that we use the fact that a pattern of connected clauses is equivalent to a pattern of disconnected clauses combined with a condition of equality between the joint variables. For instance

```
(Get (Present (Inheritance (Variable "$X") (Variable "$Y"))
              (Inheritance (Variable "$Y") (Variable "$Z"))))
```

is equivalent to

```
(Get (And (Present (Inheritance (Variable "$X") (Variable "$Y1"))
                   (Inheritance (Variable "$Y2") (Variable "$Z")))
          (Equal (Variable "$Y1") (Variable "$Y2"))))
```

where the joint variables, here $Y, have been replaced by variable occurrences in each clause, $Y1 and $Y2. Then we can express the probability estimate as the product of the probabilities of the clauses, times the probability of having the values of the joint variables equal.

5   I-Surprisingness Framed as Reasoning and Beyond

The proposition to infer in order to calculate surprisingness is defined as

$$\mathrm{surp}(P, \mathcal{D}, s)$$

where surp is a predicate relating the pattern P and the database $\mathcal{D}$ to its surprisingness s, defined as

$$s := \mathrm{dst}(\mathrm{emp}(P, \mathcal{D}), \mathrm{est}(P, \mathcal{D}))$$

where dst is the Jensen-Shannon Distance, emp is the empirical second order distribution of P, and est its estimate. The calculation of $\mathrm{emp}(P, \mathcal{D})$ is easily handled by a *direct evaluation* rule that uses the support of P and the size of $\mathcal{D}$ to obtain the parameters of the beta-binomial-distribution describing its second order probability. However, the mean by which the estimate is calculated is let unspecified. This is up to the reasoning engine to find an inference path to calculate it. Below is an example of inference tree to calculate surp based on I-Surprisingness

$$\cfrac{P \quad \mathcal{D} \quad \cfrac{\cfrac{P \quad \mathcal{D}}{\mathrm{emp}(P, \mathcal{D})}\,(DE) \quad \cfrac{P \quad \mathcal{D}}{\mathrm{est}(P, \mathcal{D})}\,(IS)}{\mathrm{dst}(\mathrm{emp}(P, \mathcal{D}), \mathrm{est}(P, \mathcal{D}))}\,(JSD)}{\mathrm{surp}(P, \mathcal{D}, \mathrm{dst}(\mathrm{emp}(P, \mathcal{D}), \mathrm{est}(P, \mathcal{D})))}\,(S)$$

where

- (S) is a rule to construct the surp predicate,
- (JSD) is a rule to calculate the Jensen-Shannon Distance,
- (DE) is the direct evaluation rule to calculate the empirical second order probability of P according to $\mathcal{D}$,
- (IS) is a rule to calculate the estimate of P based on I-Surprisingness described in Sect. 4.1.

That inference tree uses a single rule (IS) to calculate the estimate. Most rules are complex, such as (JSD), and actually have the heavy part of the calculation coded in C++ for maximum efficiency. So all that the URE must do is put together such inference tree, which can be done reasonably well given how much complexity is encapsulated in the rules.

As of today we have only implemented (IS) for the estimate. In general, however, we want to have more rules, and ultimately enough so that the estimate can be inferred in an open-ended way. In such scenario, the inference tree would look very similar to the one above, with the difference that the (IS) rule would be replaced by a combination of other rules. Such approach naturally leads to a dynamic surprisingness measure. Indeed, inferring that some pattern is I-Surprising requires to infer its empirical probability, and this knowledge can be further utilized to infer estimates of related patterns. For instance, if say an I-Surprising pattern is discovered about pets and food. A pattern about cats and food might also be measured as I-Surprising, however the fact that cat inherits pet may lead to constructing an inference that estimates the combination of cat and food based on the combination of pet and food, possibly leading to a much better estimate, and thus decreasing the surprisingness of that pattern.

6   Discussion

The ideas presented above have been implemented as open source C++ code in the OpenCog framework, and have been evaluated on some initial test datasets, including a set of logical relationships drawn from the SUMO ontology [10]. The results of this empirical experimentation are omitted here for space reasons and will be posted online as supplementary information[1]. These early experiments provide tentative validation of the sensibleness of the approach presented: using inference on a hypergraph based representation to carry out pattern mining that weaves together semantics and syntax and is directed toward a sophisticated version of surprisingness rather than simpler objective functions like frequency.

Future work will explore applications to a variety of practical datasets, including empirical data and logs from an inference engine; and richer integration of these methods with more powerful but more expensive techniques such as predicate logic inference and evolutionary learning.

References

1. Agrawal, R., Srikant, R.: Fast algorithms for mining association rules. In: Proceedings of the 20th International Conference on Very Large Data Bases (1994)
2. Chi, Y., Muntz, R., Nijssen, S., Kok, J.N.: Frequent subtree mining - an overview. Fundam. Inform. **66**, 161–198 (2005)
3. Endres, D., Schindelin, J.: A new metric for probability distributions. IEEE Trans. Inf. Theory **49**, 1858–1860 (2003)
4. Goertzel, B., Ikle, M., Goertzel, I.F., Heljakka, A.: Probabilistic Logic Networks. Springer, New York (2009). https://doi.org/10.1007/978-0-387-76872-4
5. Goertzel, B., Pennachin, C., Geisweiller, N.: Engineering General Intelligence, Part 1: A Path to Advanced AGI Via Embodied Learning and Cognitive Synergy. Atlantis Press, Paris (2014)
6. Goertzel, B., Pennachin, C., Geisweiller, N.: Engineering General Intelligence, Part 2: The CogPrime Architecture for Integrative, Embodied AGI. Atlantis Press, Paris (2014)
7. Jeffreys, H.: An invariant form for the prior probability in estimation problems. Proc. R. Soc. Lond. Ser. A **186**, 453–461 (1946)
8. Looks, M., Sc, B., Missouri, S.L., Louis, S.: Abstract competent program evolution by Moshe looks (2006)
9. Özkural, E.: Towards heuristic algorithmic memory. In: Schmidhuber, J., Thórisson, K.R., Looks, M. (eds.) AGI 2011. LNCS (LNAI), vol. 6830, pp. 382–387. Springer, Heidelberg (2011). https://doi.org/10.1007/978-3-642-22887-2_47
10. Pease, A.: Ontology: A Practical Guide. Articulate Software Press, Angwin (2011)

---

[1] https://urldefense.proofpoint.com/v2/url?u=https-3A__github.
com_opencog_opencog_tree_9dd6c67cf2bdc9910905e7d557a0c0a470c9b979_examples
_learning_miner_sumo&d=DwIDaQ&c=vh6FgFnduejNhPPD0fl_yRaSfZy8CWbW
nIf4XJhSqx8&r=T-jTXAN7HuTAAhwDzqTw2tqsj2-rzESujkUykZH5Dn69pA
BmA8jZyeAieEC9-haM&m=EhHOw0J0KOWIJ5xVheG-h2DW9Tq32KJxqg
Ci5gTkA-w&s=DLsls1dRob8T51MpfnT_XR5RUpb8LAlvsL4DQUcBzhc&e=

11. Pienta, R., et al.: AdaptiveNav: discovering locally interesting and surprising nodes in large graphs. IEEE VIS Conference (Poster) (2015)
12. Vreeken, J., Tatti, N.: Interesting patterns. In: Aggarwal, C.C., Han, J. (eds.) Frequent Pattern Mining, pp. 105–134. Springer, Cham (2014). https://doi.org/10.1007/978-3-319-07821-2_5

Toward Mapping the Paths to AGI

Ross Gruetzemacher[(✉)] and David Paradice

Auburn University, Auburn, AL, USA
{rossg, dparadice}@auburn.edu

Abstract. There is substantial interest in the research community for a map of the paths to artificial general intelligence (AGI), however, no effort toward these ends has been entirely successful. This paper identifies an alternative technique called scenario network mapping that is well suited for the difficulties posed in mapping the paths to AGI. The method is discussed, and a modified version of scenario network mapping is proposed which is intended specifically for the purpose of mapping the paths to AGI. Finally, a scenario network mapping workshopping process is proposed to utilize this method and develop a map of the paths to AGI. This will hopefully lead to discussion and action in the research community for using it in a new effort to map the paths to AGI.

Keywords: AGI · Scenario analysis · Scenario mapping · Technology roadmap

1 Introduction

Technology roadmaps are a technology management technique that have been used with a large degree of success in a number of different technology research areas [24]. Primarily employed for informing resource allocation, they can also be used to structure and streamline the innovation process, to set targets and expectations, and to identify possible risks or potential roadblocks [27]. Technology roadmaps are perhaps even more valuable for developing artificial general intelligence (AGI) [25]. They can be used to: elucidate biases leading to research for near-term gains, illuminate dead ends in ongoing research, identify hidden problems or prizes in research plans, compare alternate paths, introduce young researchers to the field, align the community, etc. In short, technology roadmaps offer a powerful technology management tool for optimizing the development of AGI.

While many benefits could come from a roadmap to AGI, there are likely many paths to it rather than just one [11]. This poses a major challenge [1], and previous attempts have indicated that traditional technology roadmaps are insufficient for mapping the paths to AGI [10]. Consequently, the technique presented here does not generate merely a single path, but rather a lattice-like structure of interconnected possible paths to AGI. Specifically, this method produces a directed graph that includes two layers of nodes: one for AGI's technological components and another for its milestones. Unlike traditional roadmaps, this approach can enable comparison of the many possible paths to AGI. This would allow researchers to compare the required resources, risks, technological challenges and other crucial factors for developing AGI.

© Springer Nature Switzerland AG 2019
P. Hammer et al. (Eds.): AGI 2019, LNAI 11654, pp. 70–79, 2019.
https://doi.org/10.1007/978-3-030-27005-6_7

2 Background

A decade has passed since the first attempt to map the path to AGI was conceived [9]. This idea, intended to align the community, would lead to a small workshop in 2009 which built on work from earlier workshops [15, 16] to produce the first roadmap to AGI [1]. Organizers were disappointed that the resulting roadmap was not a straightforward, road-like path, but rather like climbing the peak of a mountain range, with many possible paths, the easiest of which is difficult to tell from the bottom [11]. Although the results were not what organizers had hoped for [10], much progress has been made toward the milestones that were proposed as a result of the roadmap. In fact, some of the most impressive advances in the past ten years have been in general video-game learning [6, 21, 26], reading and grade school level tasks [23] – domains that represent over 50% of that roadmap. However, the amount of true progress that has been made in these domains is debatable, and progress made on the roadmap is uncertain. What is clear is that while the 2009 roadmap has proved to be a much better guide for AGI progress than forecasts [4], further improvements are still desirable.

Another roadmap toward AGI (or machine intelligence) was proposed in 2016 [20]. This roadmap did not use a structured group process like the 2009 workshop, but rather proposed a full training environment as well as the only end-to-end description of a process for training an AGI agent. However, it lacked concrete proposals for the more challenging tasks that were described, some of which would be critical to the agent. Other intelligence frameworks that have been proposed in the AGI research community, such as NARS, OpenCog or MicroPsi 2 could also be seen as roadmaps to AGI as envisioned by their developers [3, 14, 28]. In fact, one of the challenges that organizers of the 2009 workshop found was the difficulty to get participants to agree on a common direction because they each advocated their own roadmap since it was well suited for their own AGI framework [11]. Although neither a roadmap nor a framework, a 2017 study on creating human-like machines constitutes a significant contribution to the roadmap-oriented literature [17]. Rather than mapping the milestones or specifying a path, this study surveyed the requisite components for a brain-inspired AGI agent. The AI Roadmap Institute[1] has also created a roadmap, however, it is less technical and focuses more on the exploration of an AI Race. While this map was simply a flow chart of possible future scenarios during the development process of AGI, it may be the closest example to the output of this proposed workshopping technique.

All of the relevant previous studies on mapping the paths to AGI have one thing in common: none resulted in a map in the sense discussed here[2]. Technology roadmapping [7] is an established and widely used technique from technology management literature that is useful for supporting strategic planning [22]. It has been used successfully by numerous organizations and consortiums, including Philips Medical Systems [27] and

---

[1] The AI Roadmap Institute has also thoroughly identified the benefits and uses for roadmaps to AGI [25]. (www.roadmapinstitute.com).

[2] The notion of a map here more closely resembles a lattice than a flowchart or a technology roadmap. The following section discusses this further, and a generic map of this sort is depicted in Fig. 1.

the Semiconductor Industry Association [24], to foster innovation and to align industry innovation goals. However, the technology roadmapping process is not rigorous, is heavily reliant on visual aids and was considered unsuccessful in the previous attempt to use it for mapping the paths to AGI [10, 11]. Recent work has proposed a new class of scenario analysis techniques, called scenario mapping techniques, due to the common mapping properties they share [12]. These techniques are more suitable for mapping the paths to AGI. Generally, scenario analysis techniques are considered to be a powerful family of techniques that are commonly used by organizations to illuminate blind spots in strategic plans [5]. Their use may be able to identify blind spots in existing AGI frameworks that are difficult for the developers to see. Scenario network mapping (SNM) is a comprehensive, flexible approach for anticipating plausible futures in environments with high levels of uncertainty [2]. Recent work has suggested this technique to be better suited for mapping the paths to AGI than the technology roadmapping procedure or other scenario mapping processes due to its unique workshop style and its ability to model numerous entangled possible paths [13].

Given the progress in AI research over the past ten years and the promise of a new mapping process, we argue that a workshop should be held with AGI experts[3] to conduct an updated mapping of the paths to AGI. To these ends, this paper proceeds by first introducing the SNM technique. Then, the outlines a modified SNM process that is specifically tailored for the mapping of the paths to AGI. The paper concludes by urging members of the AGI research community to participate in a workshop for developing a new map of the paths to AGI.

3   Scenario Network Mapping

SNM was first proposed in 2005 to improve upon standard scenario analysis techniques by enabling the use of a large number of possible scenarios, each representing a component of one possible pathway to a particular outcome [19]. Scenario network mapping is intended for scenario planning purposes, however, the technique can also be extended to concepts or ideas for new technologies. The map resulting from SNM is easily modified as the future unfolds by updating it with new events and repositioning the existing components and connections to accommodate the new events[4]. SNM is conducted via four half-day workshops, each ideally with 15–20 participants.

The result of SNM is a directed graph wherein the nodes are components of the pathways and the edges are the causal links between these components. SNM utilizes event trees and the holonic principle (explained below) to enable the generation of a large number of interconnected scenarios. Event trees are comprised of a hierarchy of ante-cedents (the roots), the central event (the trunk) and a hierarchy of outcomes (the

---

[3] A development workshop has been conducted with early career AGI researchers which was used in the development of the method proposed here. More details can be found at www.rossgritz.com/snm-development-workshop. Further development workshops are recommended for refinement of the technique proposed here.

[4] In the adapted technique that is the focus of this paper we are concerned with mapping future technologies rather than events.

branches). SNM maps are laid out horizontally so that the depiction of time may flow from left to right, improving readability when stacking these event trees with complex interactions. The holonic principle is another essential feature of SNM that means each node in the resulting graph is simultaneously both a component of the larger system and itself comprised of smaller systems. This principle implies that, if necessary, each component can be broken down further into its constituents for analyzing the relationships with other components in the graph. This is well suited for complex technologies that are poorly understood, and which may be best anticipated through their subcomponents.

The workshopping process is well-documented and includes a user manual for facilitators [18]. A slightly altered process has been developed and widely used for mapping complex networks of components involving interactions between micro and macro level system innovation for sustainability [8]. For the specific purpose proposed here, an altered process has also been developed. Figure 1 below is adapted from a figure of a generic SNM structure in [8]. We have recreated this figure with modifications consistent with the adaptations for the purposes of this study.

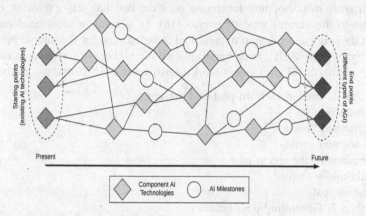

Fig. 1. This figure depicts an example of the lattice-like output from the scenario network mapping workshop that is proposed.

The structure depicted in Fig. 1 can be seen to demonstrate the lattice-like structure that has been described earlier. It can be seen that there is both a technology layer as well as a milestone layer. Figure 1 depicts a generic map for demonstration purposes only; an actual map would be expected to have many more nodes for technologies as well as milestones. The following section outlines a similar altered SNM process for the purpose of mapping the paths to AGI.

4   AGI Scenario Network Mapping

The original SNM workshopping process involves four half-day workshops that are intended to be conducted over the span of up to four weeks, allowing one week in-between each workshop [19]. This is only reasonable for organizations, and consequently, the proposed AGI-SNM workshopping process proposed here is designed to be suitable for four consecutive half-day workshops over two days. However, the half-day workshops could also be spread out over as many as four weeks for organizations. A single AGI-SNM development workshop has been conducted with early career AGI researchers. The experience from this workshop has helped to develop the workshopping process described here.

The SNM workshopping process requires some specific resources in order to be conducted effectively. The most important resource is the experts. At least 10 are needed for diversity but larger groups can take longer and become more chaotic. Thus, it is recommended to stay between 15 and 20 experts[5] [19]. Another important resource is the venue; a single room large enough for breakout groups is necessary to maintain an efficient process during breakout sessions. The process also requires a large amount of wall space and freedom from interruptions. Other equipment and materials include size A3 paper, multicolored fine tip markers, multicolored sticky notes, ribbon, masking tape, colored circular stickers (dots for voting), recording equipment (if desired) and a projector for the facilitator [18].

The original workshopping technique uses the first half-day exploring historical antecedents to the current state of events [18]. In general, a substantial amount of content in the original workshop manual had to be adapted for the unique purposes of mapping the paths to AGI[6]. Such variations are often necessary dependent on the use case. The original SNM component workshops from the SNM manual are below[7].

- Workshop 1: Influences from past and present
  - Introduction
  - Unfinished business
  - Prouds and sorries
  - Scenarios of the recent past
  - Stakeholder map
  - Leaf of goals
- Workshop 2: Generating possibilities
  - Futures wheel
  - Defining paths
  - Backcasting
  - Midcasting
- Workshop 3: Mapping paths to the future
  - Introduction and review
  - Grouping the event trees
  - Linking the event trees
  - Reviewing and digitizing the scenario map

---

[5] For organizations, it is suggested that well-informed outsiders are also included to give a diversity of perspectives.

[6] For more details regarding the original technique, interested readers are encouraged to read the scenario network mapping manual found in [18].

[7] This outline lacks implementation details because it is intended to serve for comparison.

- Workshop 4: Revealing the underlying layers
  - From event trees to scenarios
  - Finding the influences
  - Grouping the stakeholders
  - Finding the visions
  - Finding the worldviews
  - Review

The proposed modified SNM workshopping process for mapping the paths to AGI is designed to take place over as little as two days through four separate half-day workshop sessions. It roughly follows the process laid out in the SNM manual, however, the individual workshops have been modified significantly for the specific task of mapping the paths to AGI. The process is very tactile and utilizes post-its, colored ribbon, various sizes of paper, colored stickers for voting and other items that were described earlier[8]. The outcome is lattice-like map with a technology layer as well as a milestone layer. The outline below depicts the four independent workshops in this process. It includes more detail than the outline for the standard process so that it may be used for implementation[9].

- Workshop 1: Identifying the present and future (approximately 3 h)
  - Introduction to the workshopping process and supporting techniques
  - Mapping the core technologies that have led to the current state of AI
    - Identify the core technologies driving AI research
    - Split into groups for each of these research areas
    - List recent milestones in AI research for each technology group[10]
    - Vote on milestones using stickers[11]
    - Create event trees for the most important of the milestones[12]
    - Link and combine the most important event trees
  - Results are pasted to wall
    - The facilitator guides the group in connecting the event trees[13]
- Workshop 2: Identifying paths to the future (approximately 5 h)
  - Identify the different visions for arriving at AGI
    - Split into groups for identifying different visions
    - Assign different visions to groups to explore further
  - Forward-flow and backward-flow analysis

---

[8] See www.rossgritz.com/snm-development-workshop for examples.

[9] A complete manual for use of the modified method requires further research and is beyond the scope of this introduction to the technique.

[10] Milestones are written on a large sticky note.

[11] A fixed number of stickers is given to each participant to vote. Participants may use one or more sticker for each item they vote on.

[12] To create event trees, each large sticky note is placed at the center of a blank A3 sized sheet of paper. Smaller sticky notes are placed on the left and right for the antecedents and the outcomes, respectively. Different yet consistent colors are used for the left and right sticky notes.

[13] The event trees are connected with ribbon.

- Split into two groups (one for forward-flow and another for backward-flow)
- Forward-flow group identifies technologies that will likely be part of the development of AGI starting from the current state[14]
  - Begins from the results of Workshop 1
- Backward-flow group identifies technologies that will likely lead to AGI
  - working backward from the different visions for AGI identified earlier
- These results are pasted to the wall and duplicates or overlaps are condensed
- Each technology is assigned by facilitator to a group for event tree creation
- Each group creates event trees[15] for these technologies
  - Groups can split further if needed (groups of 3–5 are ideal)
- Results are pasted to wall (from left to right) building on those from Workshop 1
- Workshop 3: Connecting the present and future (approximately 5 h)
  - Introduction and facilitator notes from first two workshops
  - Reassess previous workshops' work
    - Technology groups split away to reassess their work
      - Modifications and updates are made if necessary
    - Split into forward-flow and backward-flow groups
      - Each group reassesses their previous work
        - Modifications and updates are made if necessary
  - The event trees are connected
    - The facilitator guides the group in connecting the event trees[16]
  - The most important elements are determined and the map is condensed
    - Each participant votes on the most important elements using stickers
      - Voting is done for the event trees as a whole and the subcomponents[17]
    - As a group, the facilitator goes through the event trees to determine what to combine and what to remove
  - Gaps and items for expansion are identified
    - As a group the facilitator helps to identify gaps between paths and the items in the current map that need breaking down further (using the holonic principle)
  - Groups split into breakout groups (size of 3–5 is ideal)
    - Gaps and items are assigned to each breakout group
    - Each breakout group develops event trees for the items and gaps assigned
  - Results are pasted to the wall (in-between the event trees they are intended to connect or adjacent to the items they breakdown)[18]
- Workshop 4: Mapping the paths and milestones (approximately 3 h)

---

[14] Technologies are written on a large sticky note.
[15] Event trees are created in the same way as for Workshop 1.
[16] Different colored ribbon can be used for more complex mappings.
[17] Different colored stickers are used for low and high priority items. A limited number of stickers is given to each participant. Stickers are to be placed directly on either the large or small sticky notes for each of the event trees. Stickers may be placed to overlap due to constraints on the size of sticky notes as long as the total number of votes is still clear. Sticky notes can also be rewritten and replaced in order to make room for stickers for voting if necessary.
[18] Connections are self-evident and the facilitator connects the event trees without the group's input.

- The most important links are determined and the map is finalized
  - Each participant votes on the most relevant event trees that were added
    - Participants also vote on whether certain elements need further attention
  - Entire group discusses the votes the facilitator guides discussion to condense the map
    - If necessary entire group or subgroups can address any elements that need further attention
  - When group is content then finalize map
- Add milestones layer
  - Identify core future technology groups and split into subgroups for each
  - Each subgroup identifies potential milestones for their technology domain[19]
  - Milestones associated with technology paths are added
  - Participants vote on most relevant and plausible milestones
  - The facilitator guides the group in removing the unnecessary or unpopular milestones
- Conduct concluding discussion about the process and outcome.

Participants are encouraged to keep notes of their personal experience throughout the process in order to help to improve future efforts. In general, participants are encouraged to be creative and to not be conservative in suggesting technologies or milestones, or in creating the event trees. Irrelevant or unnecessary items will always be removed in the process of voting and condensing. It may be helpful for the facilitator to be familiar with brainstorming and creativity techniques in order to assist the group or breakout groups and to improve the overall outcome. It can also be beneficial to have a co-facilitator for the entire process due to the size of the ideal group. Particularly, a co-facilitator is highly recommended for Workshop 2, where groups need to split into forward-flow and backward-flow groups.

Following the workshop, it is necessary to digitize the results. The easiest way to do this is using a spreadsheet application [18]. More advanced techniques can include the use of visualization software packages. In order to create a map of the sort that is depicted in Fig. 1, this would be necessary. Such a visualization may have to be created manually due to the lack of automated software for digitizing scenario maps.

5   Conclusion

This study presented an adapted scenario network mapping (SNM) workshopping process for mapping the paths to AGI (AGI-SNM). SNM is a comprehensive and flexible approach that comes from the family of scenario analysis techniques commonly used in technology forecasting and management. It is more rigorous and methodical than technology roadmapping which was used in an earlier coordinated effort to map the paths to AGI. Furthermore, it sufficiently addresses some of the

---

[19] Milestones and technologies are both written on large sticky notes – these sticky notes should each be of a distinctive and consistent color for the entire process.

challenges mentioned by organizers of the earlier attempt a decade ago. Specifically, it is intended to accommodate many intersecting paths and large numbers of scenarios.

Many may think the pursuit of a roadmap to AGI to be useless due to the results of previous efforts. Perhaps this is correct, but SNM does not produce a roadmap like previous efforts, rather, it produces a lattice-like map of intersecting possible paths. It does this by utilizing a powerful combination of group facilitation techniques for identifying things that may be difficult for independent researchers or researchers in standard group meetings to foresee on their own. Thus, SNM has the potential to aid all active members of the AGI research community by illuminating blind spots, hidden problems and hidden prizes that couldn't be found otherwise. It can also help in ways such as aligning the research community, providing a useful overview of the field to young researchers and refocusing research efforts on longer-term goals rather than goals for near-term gains. Simply participating in the AGI-SNM workshopping process can be a valuable experience to researchers as well[20]. Future work should continue to refine and apply the process. We intend for this paper to foster discussion within the community about an effort to use it to conduct an updated mapping of the paths to AGI with leading experts in the field.

References

1. Adams, S., Arel, I., Bach, J., et al.: Mapping the landscape of human-level artificial general intelligence. AI Mag. **33**(1), 25–42 (2012). https://doi.org/10.1609/aimag.v33i1.2322
2. Amer, M., Daim, T., Jetter, A.: A review of scenario planning. Futures **46**, 23–40 (2013). https://doi.org/10.1016/j.futures.2012.10.003
3. Bach, J.: MicroPsi 2: the next generation of the MicroPsi framework. In: Bach, J., Goertzel, B., Iklé, M. (eds.) AGI 2012. LNCS (LNAI), vol. 7716, pp. 11–20. Springer, Heidelberg (2012). https://doi.org/10.1007/978-3-642-35506-6_2
4. Baum, S., Goertzel, B., Goertzel, T.: How long until human-level AI? Results from an expert assessment. Tech. Forecast. Soc. Change **78**(1), 185–195 (2011). https://doi.org/10.1016/j.techfore.2010.09.006
5. Bradfield, R., Wright, G., Burt, G., et al.: The origins and evolution of scenario techniques in long range business planning. Futures **37**(8), 795–812 (2005). https://doi.org/10.1016/j.futures.2012.10.003
6. Ecoffet, A., Huizinga, J., Lehman, J., et al.: Go-explore: a new approach for hard-exploration problems. arXiv preprint arXiv:1901.10995 (2019)
7. Garcia, M., Bray, O.: Fundamentals of technology roadmapping. No. SAND-97-0665. Sandia National Labs, Albuquerque, NM, United States (1997). https://doi.org/10.2172/471364
8. Gaziulusoy, A., Boyle, C., McDowall, R.: System innovation for sustainability: a systemic double-flow scenario method for companies. J. Cleaner Prod. **45**, 104–116 (2013). https://doi.org/10.1016/j.jclepro.2012.05.013
9. Goertzel, B., Arel, I., Scheutz, M.: Toward a roadmap for human-level artificial general intelligence. Artif. Gen. Intell. Roadmap Initiat. **18**, 27 (2009)

---

[20] A large majority of participants in the development AGI-SNM workshop felt the experience to be illuminating, enlightening and very valuable.

10. Goertzel, B.: Ten Years to the Singularity If We Really, Really Try. Humanity Press, London (2014)
11. Goertzel, B.: The AGI Revolution. Humanity Press, London (2016)
12. Gruetzemacher, R., Paradice, D.: Alternative Techniques to Mapping Paths to HLAI. arXiv preprint arXiv:1905.00614 (2019)
13. Gruetzemacher, R.: A Holistic Framework for Forecasting Transformative AI (2019, Forthcoming manuscript)
14. Hart, D., Goertzel, B.: OpenCog: a software framework for integrative artificial general intelligence. In: AGI, pp. 468–472 (2008)
15. Laird, J., Wray, R., Marinier, R., Langley, P.: Claims and challenges in evaluating human-level intelligent systems. In: Proceedings of 2nd Conference on AGI. Atlantis Press (2009)
16. Laird, J., Wray, R.: Cognitive architecture requirements for achieving AGI. In: Proceedings of 3rd Conference on AGI. Atlantis Press (2010)
17. Lake, B., Ullman, T., Tenenbaum, J., Gershman, S.: Building machines that learn and think like people. Behav. Brain Sci. **40**, e253 (2017)
18. List, D.: Scenario Network Mapping: The Development of a Methodology for Social Inquiry. University of South Australia, Adelaide (2005)
19. List, D.: Scenario network mapping. J. Futur. Stud. **11**(4), 77–96 (2007). 10.1.1.390.6457&rep=rep1&type=pdf
20. Mikolov, T., Joulin, A., Baroni, M.: A roadmap towards machine intelligence. In: Gelbukh, A. (ed.) CICLing 2016. LNCS, vol. 9623, pp. 29–61. Springer, Cham (2018). https://doi.org/10.1007/978-3-319-75477-2_2
21. Mnih, V., Kavukcuoglu, K., Silver, D., et al.: Human-level control through deep reinforcement learning. Nature **518**(7540), 529 (2015). https://doi.org/10.1038/nature14236
22. Phaal, R., Farrukh, C., Probert, D.: Technology roadmapping—a planning framework for evolution and revolution. Tech Forecast. Soc. Change **71**(1–2), 5–26 (2004). https://doi.org/10.1016/S0040-1625(03)00072-6
23. Radford, A., Wu, J., Child, R., et al.: Language Models are Unsupervised Multitask Learners. OpenAI Blog (2019)
24. Roper, A., Cunningham, S., Porter, A., et al.: Forecasting and Management of Technology. Wiley, Hoboken (2011)
25. Rosa, M., Feyereisl, J., Collective, T.G.: A framework for searching for general artificial intelligence. arXiv preprint arXiv:1611.00685 (2016)
26. Vinyals, O., Babuschkin, I., Chung, J., et al.: AlphaStar: Mastering the Real-Time Strategy Game StarCraft II. DeepMind Blog (2019)
27. Van der Duin, P.A.: Qualitative Futures Research for Innovation. Eburon Uitgeverij BV, Amsterdam (2006)
28. Wang, P.: Rigid Flexibility: The Logic of Intelligence. Springer, Dordrecht (2006). https://doi.org/10.1007/1-4020-5045-3

Adaptive Neuro-Symbolic Network Agent

Patrick Hammer[✉]

Department of Computer and Information Sciences,
College of Science and Technology, Temple University,
Philadelphia, PA 19122, USA
patrick.hammer@temple.edu

Abstract. This paper describes Adaptive Neuro-Symbolic Network Agent, a new design of a sensorimotor agent that adapts to its environment by building concepts based on Sparse Distributed Representations of sensorimotor sequences. Utilizing Non-Axiomatic Reasoning System theory, it is able to learn directional correlative links between concept activations that were caused by the appearing of observed and derived event sequences. These directed correlations are encoded as predictive links between concepts, and the system uses them for directed concept-driven activation spreading, prediction, anticipatory control, and decision-making, ultimately allowing the system to operate autonomously, driven by current event and concept activity, while working under the Assumption of Insufficient Knowledge and Resources.

Keywords: Non-Axiomatic Reasoning · Sensorimotor ·
Artificial general intelligence · Procedure learning · Autonomous agent

1 Introduction

Adaptive Neuro-Symbolic Network Agent (ANSNA), is a new design of a sensorimotor agent derived from Non-Axiomatic Reasoning System (NARS) theory proposed by Pei Wang (see [1]). It adapts to its environment by building concepts based on Sparse Distributed Representations [2] of sensorimotor sequences, rather than based on Compound Terms that are typical for NARS. It does so by taking theory of compositionality of bit vectors as proposed by [3] into account, which not only captures union and difference operations between bit vectors, but also ways to encode hierarchical structure within them.

Making use of Non-Axiomatic Reasoning System theory, ANSNA is able to learn directional correlative links between concept activations that were caused by the appearing of observed and derived event sequences. These directed correlations are encoded as predictive links between concepts, and the system uses them for directed concept-driven activation spreading, prediction, anticipatory control and decision-making. All that allows the system to operate autonomously under the Assumption of Insufficient Knowledge and Resources, driven by current context, determined by event and concept activity.

© Springer Nature Switzerland AG 2019
P. Hammer et al. (Eds.): AGI 2019, LNAI 11654, pp. 80–90, 2019.
https://doi.org/10.1007/978-3-030-27005-6_8

2   Similar Work and Philosophical Differences

ANSNA borrows most of its theory from the Non-Axiomatic Reasoning System proposed by Pei Wang (see [1]), while using the inference control theory of ALANN [4], which is a NARS-variant designed by Tony Lofthouse. What makes ANSNA really different from NARS is however the complete absence of *Terms* and explicit *Inheritance* relationships, coming from a philosophically very different path: while NARS tries to model a general-purpose thinking process with highly flexible ways to compare, transform, and generally deal with any kind of information that can somehow be expressed in *Narsese* (NARS's formal internal and I/O language), ANSNA concentrates completely on sensorimotor.

For NARS, sensorimotor capability, which consists mainly of procedural and temporal inference on sensor & motor events, is just a special case of rich reasoning abilities its Non-Axiomatic Logic (NAL) supports. NAL also includes declarative reasoning abilities about sets, arbitrary relations, and inheritance-relationships that are all there to support dealing with conceptual knowledge that doesn't necessarily have any grounding in actual sensorimotor experience. ANSNA takes the position where knowledge that has no possible grounding in the system's sensorimotor experience is not necessarily meaningless (as it can clearly relate to other knowledge), but surely was so far useless to a goal-driven decision-maker, as it would mean that the meaning of that knowledge is completely orthogonal to everything ANSNA has ever experienced through its sensors so far, both external and internal. In NARS this situation is by far not unusual, a user entering a new Inheritance relationship (term123 → term242) consistent only of new terms, term123 and term242, leaves the system's memory with a floating pair of concepts that have so far no relation to any other concepts whatsoever, meaning also no relation to sensorimotor concepts, and how such a relation should be established through correlations is a difficult problem. Such a problem does not exist in ANSNA, as it is assumed that all information is consumed through external (vision, touch, sound, temperature, other modalities...) and internal sensors (battery level, structural integrity, etc.).

According to ANSNA philosophy, relating new user-given abstract terms to sensorimotor experience is not something an AGI has to do, but that building compositions of sensorimotor patterns is everything necessary. That is, because in ANSNA every composition simply cannot even be "not grounded", since every information, without exception, ultimately is forced to enter ANSNA through the system's sensors. Also in a NARS operating in a robot without Narsese-communication channel, it is usually not happening, and not at all necessary, that new atomic terms will be created, in such a case the set of atomic terms are pre-defined by the designer, consisting of pre-defined sensor encodings and probably revisable background knowledge that was loaded on the robot beforehand. In that sense, a semantic code is inevitable, meaning the universe of mental discourse will be spanned by possible compositions of events following pre-defined encodings of sensory data (plus combinations with background knowledge, in NARS). Even though NARS itself does not assume a fixed semantic code, in that case it is undeniably present. This is however no contradiction with that such a system can acquire the meaning of observed events, where the meaning of an event has both structural and empirical aspects.

Structural meaning is determined by the composition following the semantic code, which encodes how the pattern is observed/composed from sensorimotor experience. For instance there is no way for the system to see the observation of a red ball as structurally identical to an observed blue ball. However, it needs to be possible for the system to learn that a blue ball carries overlapping meaning, not only by being a similar structural composition/semantic code word, but also that nudging a blue ball in similar circumstances, will have similar consequences like nudging a red ball in similar contexts. And that can be done without having the user entering an explicit Inheritance relationship into the system, and without an explicit Inheritance altogether, as whether experienced event a is a special case of another event b can implicitly be represented by sensorimotor relations, that is, if a leads to the consequences we expect from b, it is naturally a special case of the former even though it may structurally differ.

Of course, the semantic code needs to be rich, not in quantity, but in quality. Same as a set of lego technic pieces needs to be rich in variety and fit together nicely to support the construction of a large variety of machines, the semantic code needs to be rich in variety and fit together in such a way, that the agent is able to conceptualize experienced aspects of its environment in an effective way. This can happen through a large variety of perceptual attributes, such as, for example, Color, PositionX, PositionY, Pitch, Frequency, Temperature, Pressure and Battery Level. Color, PositionX and PositionY can encode information from a visual field, for instance. Once a basic semantic code is in place, the encoders are present, everything the system experiences will be seen in terms of the attributes these encoders present, by ANSNA. The more comprehensive, the richer the context will be, and the better will ANSNA be able to make sense of its environment through compositions of sensorimotor events. This leads to the last key difference to OpenNARS and ANSNA, the usage of Sparse Distributed Representations (long, sparse bit vectors, SDR's), and usage of Pentti Kanerva's [3] insights about how hierarchical structure can be encoded in them. Clearly, differently than Sparse Distributed Memory (SDM) [5], ANSNA is not just a model of memory, and thus, as we will see, its event-based design requirements make its memory architecture different than SDM, while preserving some of SDM's key properties. For instance, mapping events with similar SDR's to similar concepts, supporting content-addressable memory.

3   Data Structures

ANSNA's memory consists of two priority queues, one contains concepts and the other current events (Events Buffer).

Event: Each Event consists of a SDR with a NAL Truth Value, an Occurrence Time, and a Attention Value that consists of the priority of the event and a durability value that indicates the decay rate of the priority over time.

A SDR is a large bit-vector with most bits being zero, in ANSNA all SDR's are of equal length n.

SDR structure: With a, b being SDR's we can now define the following functions calculating a new SDR based on a existing one, using theory borrowed from Kanerva [3]: $SDRSet(a,b) := a|b$ where | is the bitwise or operation. $SDRTuple(a,b) := \Pi_S(a) \oplus \Pi_P(b)$ where Π_S and Π_P are two random permutations selected when ANSNA starts up, they remain the same after that.

Additionally encoding functions E as proposed in [6] are used to encode similar numbers to similar SDR's, and terms are encoded into random SDR's deterministically. This way, arbitrary hierarchical compositions can be encoded into ANSNA, and as we will see later, effectively compared with each other based on a per-bit basis. For now it is sufficient to see that two input encodings $SDRTuple(E(brightness), E(3.23))$ and $SDRTuple(E(brightness),$ $E(3.5))$ will lead to similar SDR's, meaning most 1-bits will overlap. We will omit E from now on, and see that $SDRSet(green, light)$ will have more 1-bits in common with *light* than *sound*. Of course $SDRTuple$ and $SDRSet$ can be arbitrary nested with each other, essentially forming a tree which leafs are for instance SDR-encoded terms or numbers, and structurally similar trees will lead to similar SDR's.

Concept: Concepts in ANSNA are summarized sensorimotor experience, they are the components of ANSNA's content-addressable memory system and are named by interpolations of the events SDR's that matched to it (described in more detail in the next section). Processed events can match to different concepts with various degree, but in a basic implementation a winner-takes-all approach can be taken, matching the event only to the most specific matching case that was kept in memory, and processing it as such.

Each concept has a SDR (its identifier), and Attention value consisting of a priority and a durability value, a Usage value, indicating when the concept was last used (meaning it won the match competition for an event, as we will see later) and how often it was used since its existence. Also it has a table of pre- and post-condition implications that are essentially predictive links, specifying which concepts activate which others, and a FIFO for belief and goal events, and has multiple responsibilities:

To categorize incoming events by matching them to its SDR: to become good representatives, concepts have to encode useful and stable aspects of a situation, conceptual interpolation, explained in the next section, helps here; To support revision, prediction and explanation for native events, events for which this concept wins the matching competition; To maintain how relevant the concept is currently and how useful it was in total so far; Learning and revising preconditions and consequences by interacting with an for temporal inference incoming event.

Matching events to concepts: An event can match to multiple concepts with a truth value "penalty" according to the match. Let S and P be a SDR. We want that S can be said to be a special case of P, or can stand for P, denoted by $S \rightarrow P$, if most of the bits in P also occur in S, but not necessarily vice versa. So $S = SDRSet(red, ball)$ should be a special case of $P = SDRSet(ball)$. It has most the features of ball, but also has the redness feature, meaning a red ball can effectively stand for, or be treated as a ball too.

We will now formalize this idea using a NAL truth value, which is a frequency-confidence tuple $(f, c) = (\frac{w_+}{w_+ + w_-}, \frac{w_+ + w_-}{w_+ + w_- + 1})$ where w_+ is positive evidence and w_- negative evidence. The truth value of $S \to P$ can be established as follows: Let's define each 1-bit in the SDR to be a NAL sentence (see [7]), where each of these 1-bits, at position i, in S, encode $bit_i = 1$.

One case of positive evidence for $S \to P$, is a common property S and P both share. Such as the fact that bit_5 is a 1-bit. On the other hand, a case of negative evidence would be a property possessed by P that S does not possess. Given that, we can define the positive evidence as: $w_+ := |\{i \in \{1, ..., n\} | S_i = P_i = 1\}|$ and the negative evidence as $w_- := |\{i \in \{1, ..., n\} | S_i = 1 \wedge P_i = 0\}|$.

If the event E has truth value T_E, to apply the penalty of "treating it as concept C", the truth value becomes $\text{Truth\_Deduction}(T_{match}, T_E)$, which will then be used in the inference rule within the concept for deriving further events.

That is motived by that if event E is a special case of the pattern it is encoded by, $SDRE$, and $SDRE$ is a special case of $SDRC$, as the match determined, then we have $E \to SDRE$ with truth value T_E and $SDRE \to SDRC$ with truth value $T_{match} := SDR\_Inheritance(S, P)$. Using the deduction rule as specified in [7], we end up with $E \to SDRC$, allowing to treat the event as if it would have the SDR SDRC.

Please note there is also a symmetric match defined by Truth_Intersection (SDR_Inheritance(a,b), SDR_Inheritance(b,a)) as we will need later. For a tuple of truth values $((f, c), (f_2, c_2))$ Truth_Intersection leads to $(f * f_2, c * c_2)$ and Truth_Deduction to $(f * f_2, f * f_2 * c * c_2)$, for the other truth functions we will use, please see [7], they have all been described by Pei Wang in detail.

Event FIFO and Revision: While pushing a new event to the first position when a matched event enters a concept's FIFO, to resolve goal conflicts in respect to a current decision, in the goal event FIFO, revision with the highest confident element when projected to the goal occurrence time (where projected means multiplicatively penalized for occurrence time difference dt according to α^{dt}, where α is a truth projection decay parameter) has to happen, the result will then be pushed to the first FIFO position. Of course, the revision (which sums up the positive, and negative evidence of both premises) can also happen in the belief event FIFO, this make sure that two conflicting sensory signals that happen concurrently, will be merged, allowing to better deal with contradicting sensory information.[1]

Implication Table and Revision: In NARS terms, Implications in ANSNA are eternal beliefs of the form $a \Rightarrow b$, which essentially becomes a predictive link for a and a retrospective link in b, each going to a separate implication table (preconditions and postconditions).

---

[1] A detail: As in [8], only revise if the evidential base does not overlap, and only if the revised element when projected to the occurrence-time middle between both elements is higher than the premises's.

An implication table combines different implications, for instance $a \Rightarrow b$ and $a \Rightarrow c$ to describe the different consequences of a in the postcondition table of concept a. Implication tables are ranked by the truth expectations of the beliefs, which for a given truth value (f, c) is defined as $(c * (f - \frac{1}{2}) + \frac{1}{2})$.

Different than in OpenNARS, where it is clear whether revision can happen dependent on whether the terms are equal, two items in ANSNA can have different degree of SDR overlap. To deal with this, both revision premises are penalized with symmetric SDR match SDR_Similarity, leading to $Truth1$ and $Truth2$ using Truth_Intersection, and revision will only occur if revision(Truth1, Truth2) has a higher confidence than both Truth1 and Truth2. When a new item enters the table, it is both revised with the closest SDR candidate (the revised result will be added to the table, if it was a proper result), and also the original Implication will be added to the table.

Conceptual Interpolation: Conceptual interpolation, inspired by [5], is the process by which concept's SDR adapts to the SDR's of the matched events, in such a way that the SDR of the concept becomes the average case among the matched event SDR's. This allows the concepts to become useful "prototypes" under the presence of noise, useful in the sense that a newly seen noisy pattern can be reconstructed. A way to implement this is idea is to add a counter for each bit in the SDR. Each 1-bit of the matched event increases the corresponding counter by $1 * u$, and each 0-bit decreases it by $1 * u$, where $u = $ Truth_Expectation(SDR_Inheritance(e,c)), meaning an event that better matches to the concept will have a stronger influence on it. If the counter is 0 or smaller, the corresponding concept SDR's bit will be 0, else 1. This effectively means that iff there is more positive evidence for the bit in the matched event SDR's to be 1 than 0, it will be 1 in the concept SDR they were matched to too.

4 Attentional Control

While on a conceptual level Attentional Control in ANSNA allows the processing of different items with individual speeds (as also NARS [1,10] and Hofstadter's group's creations [9]), the details in ANSNA mostly follow the Adaptive Logic and Neural Network (ALANN) control model by Tony Lofthouse, which was developed for a NARS implementation over the last two decades, based on expertise about Spiking Neural Networks. Although a convincing prototype exists [4], unfortunately this model was not published in a scientific publication yet, so its background is explained in addition to implementation details.

Every NARS, and AGI in general, faces the problem of fulfilling practically infinite resource-demands with a finite amount of resources [10] which are ultimately limited by the processor speed and the RAM available on the machine it runs on. An Attention model [11] can solve this problem as it allows to selectively perform inferences based on contextual cues, which primary importance the ALANN model stresses. It does so by building an analogy to the brain, which is known to be able to save energy by keeping only a tiny proportion of neurons active at the same time [12]. In biological neural networks, spike cascades appear, where spikes are sent from one neuron to the next, and, potentially even further, if the action potential threshold of the source neuron is overcome ([13]), while avoiding re-activations through cyclic connections by enforcing a certain refractory/latency period. The priority value of the spike sent to the target neuron depends on the synapse strength and the current action potential, the latter we will call concept priority. In ALANN, the synapse strength is assumed to correspond to the strength of a certain experienced pattern, which is summarized by a NAL [7] truth value corresponding to a belief that is related to the concept the neuron represents. Using NAL as a foundation, this is natural, as concept node *Lighting* can have related beliefs like *Lighting* ⇒ *Thunder*, in that sense, the belief acts like a link connecting concept *Lighting* to *Thunder*, making the *Lighting* concept emit *Thunder* events that are received by the latter, and whenever that happens, also the concept priority of *Thunder* will be increased naturally due to the spike derivation, based on the priority value of the spike, and will decrease quickly. From now on, we will refer to spikes as events, neurons as concepts, synapse strength as belief truth, also to take a safe distance from actual claims of how the wetware actually functions. In ANSNA, action potential thresholds are never fixed, instead it is realized by enforcing a fixed number of active events to be selected from a global priority queue that is ranked by the event priorities, and where the topmost k items are selected. Using this model, ANSNA consists of the following attention update functions:

Attention_forgetEvent: Forget an event using exponential decay. To make lazy update possible, the decay is stronger the longer it wasn't selected anymore. Also this one needs to be radical, there is only a very small window in time in which it is likely for the target concept to generate further derivations, to make sure derivations are still contextually relevant.

Attention_forgetConcept: Forget a concept with exponential decay, again, the more, the longer it wasn't selected anymore, additionally a lower "priority threshold" is established, that is dependent on the concept's usefulness. This threshold hampers useful concepts to be forgotten. Usefulness is calculated in the following way: age = currentTime - lastUsed, v = useCount/age, usefulness = v/(v + 1.0); Additionally the neural-network-motivated activation spreading functions applied to event derivations are:

Attention_activateConcept: Activates a concept because an event was matched to it, proportional to the priority of the event. The idea here is that the concept sums up the appearing event priorities while leaking priority over time, this way the active concepts tend to be currently contextually relevant ones.

Attention_deriveEvent: The derived event gets higher priority if the involved concept had a high priority (the derivation was contextually relevant), and also gets higher priority if the truth expectation of the for the derivation used belief (a belief event of belief_event FIFO, or an Implication from a pre- or post-condition table, as we will see later) was high (the synapse had high strength).

Attention_inputEvent: Priority positively correlated with the truth expectation of the input event.

5   Operating Cycle

Inference Schemas: The following describes all types of inference that can happen in the operating cycle introduced next, and the truth functions that apply are defined in [7], where a leading "!" means goal, and "." means belief:

- Revision, in Event FIFO, and in Implication Table (Link growth):
  {Implication/Event a, Implication/Event a} ⊢ Implication/Event a
- Deduction (Prediction):
  {Event a., Implication $(a \Rightarrow b)$.} ⊢ Event b.
  {Event b!, Implication $(a \Rightarrow b)$.} ⊢ Event a!
- Induction (Link formation):
  {Event a., Event b.} ⊢ Implication $(a => b)$.
- Abduction (Prediction):
  {Event b., Implication $(a \Rightarrow b)$.} ⊢ Event a.
  {Event a!, Implication $(a \Rightarrow b)$.} ⊢ Event b!
- Intersection (Concept formation):
  {Event a., Event b., after(b, a)} ⊢ Event SDRTuple(a, b).
  {Event a., Event b., concurrent(b, a)} ⊢ Event SDRSet(a, b).
  where concurrent and after are excluding each other: when the occurrence time of a and b is closer than a global system parameter, concurrent(a, b) is true, else either after(b, a) or after(a, b) is true.

Operating Cycle: In each cycle, a fixed number of events (input or derived) get taken out from Events Buffer and processed: a concept will be created for them (if one with exact same SDR doesn't already exist), and they match the best asymmetrically matched concept available (not including the created one), also increasing its priority using Attention_activateConcept. The event (which truth value was reduced consistent with the asymmetric match explained previously) then interacts with the events within the concepts FIFO for revision, as explained previously. Also it interacts with the postcondition implication table (the highest truth-expectation elements, a choice rule), triggering a Deduction[2] if it is a belief event, and an abduction if it is a goal event. And it interacts with the precondition implication table, triggering an Abduction if it is a belief event, and a deduction if it is a goal event, both consistent with the Schemas.

Also the event gets sent to the k highest-priority concepts (not including the matched one) as a "foreign concept", not reducing its truth value (this interaction is not a match, just a correlation in activity between event and concept!). The only purpose of that interaction is to compose new, more complex temporal sequences that are themselves events to be processed, consistent with the Intersection Schema in the table, using Attention_deriveEvent to determine the derived event's Attention value. Additionally, sequence (a, b) leads to the formation of hypothesis $a \Rightarrow b$ which directly enters the postcondition implication table of a as a "predictive link" and precondition implication table of b as a "retrospective link" (Time durations are stored too, and averaged on revision).

All derived sequences enter the global Event Buffer, of which all elements taken out from re-enter with adjusted Attention value as defined by Attention_forgetEvent. Note that also the k used concepts get their priority reduced by Attention_forgetConcept. This means that all the attention updates are driven by event processing. All summarized (Fig. 1):

---

[2] Which generates an Anticipation, that if it won't get confirmed, adds negative evidence to the implication (predictive link) that generated the prediction (as AERA).

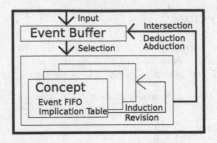

Fig. 1. Overview with Event Buffer and concepts, plus their predictive links. Operating cycle selects events from Event Buffer (priority-biased), lets them interact with the matched concept for Intersection, Deduction and Abduction, and with high-priority concepts for Temporal Induction, and as result derives further events that end up in Event Buffer, and predictive links that end up in the implication tables.

Decision Making: Decision Making in ANSNA was taken from NARS [14] and adjusted to fit well to ANSNA's memory model:

Operations: These are a (SDR, Action) tuple, Action is a software procedure without arguments, expected to finish in constant time. They are registered using ANSNA_RegisterOperation(SDR sdr, Action procedure) method. For now the SDR serves mostly as an ID, but formats for motor operations allow the system to see similar parametrizations as similar, for instance the SDR encoding of (motor1,0.7) will naturally be more similar to (motor1,0.8) than to (motor1,0.2), which opens interesting opportunities for fine-grained control.

Decision Making Rule: When a goal event gets matched to a concept and added to its FIFO as described earlier, the goal event, or instead the revised one in case that revision happened, if of form (SDR,Op_SDR_i), determines the operation (Op_SDR_i, Action_i) stored in the system. In that case, the event gets projected to the current moment, leading to a certain truth value T_P. Now the system retrieves the next event b from belief_event FIFO that has no associated operation and has the highest truth confidence of its truth value T_b when projected to the current time and calculates $T_{Result} = \text{Deduction}(T_P, T_b)$. If this truth value's expectation is above the system's decision threshold parameter, the corresponding procedure $Action_i$ gets called, capturing context and intention, and the truth of the procedure knowledge is considered by goal-derivation.

Procedure Learning: To make the system aware of the execution of an action, for each of the k highest priority-concepts (that are selected in each cycle, as described previously), the first belief event FIFO element gets "copied", This copy receives a new SDR, being SDRSet(OldSDR, Op_SDR_i) (also allows for compound operations), and is then added to the FIFO without revision, making the system effectively re-interpret the event as being a precondition under which the operation was executed, so that when a next event with SDR c interacts with the concept for temporal inference, ((OldSDR,Op_SDR_i) ⇒ c) will naturally be formed with temporal induction, a piece of procedure knowledge, specifying that the execution of Op_i leads to c under the condition of OldSDR.

Motor Babbling: To trigger executions at the beginning where no procedure knowledge exists yet, the system invokes random motor operations from time to time, a process called Motor Babbling. Without any initial operations, the system couldn't learn how it can affect the environment, so this serves as an initial trigger for procedure learning. The same idea is used in [15]. Initial reflexes are also a potentially helpful, similar ones like the grab reflex in humans are possible too, but these are more domain-specific.

6   Conclusion

A new autonomous sensorimotor agent architecture, Adaptive Neuro-Symbolic Network Agent, is proposed. Differently than NARS from Pei Wang, which it is derived from, it uses SDR's for knowledge representation, and a inference control mechanism inspired by spiking neural network derived from Tony Lofthouse's easily parallelizable ALANN model. Its key benefits, besides being more concise than NARS, lie in the ability to process a large quantity of information effectively, and to mine temporal-spatial patterns in its experience that allow it to predict what will happen next, and make decisions accordingly, to realize its goals.

References

1. Wang, P.: Toward a unified artificial intelligence. In: AAAI Fall Symposium on Achieving Human-Level Intelligence through Integrated Research and Systems, pp. 83–90 (2004)
2. Hawkins, J., George, D.: Hierarchical temporal memory: concepts, theory and terminology, p. 2. Technical report, Numenta (2006)
3. Kanerva, P.: Hyperdimensional computing: an introduction to computing in distributed representation with high-dimensional random vectors. Cogn. Comput. 1(2), 139–159 (2009)
4. Lofthouse, T.: Adaptive Logic and Neural Network (ALANN) (2018). https://github.com/opennars/ALANN2018
5. Kanerva, P.: Sparse Distributed Memory. MIT Press, Cambridge (1988)
6. Purdy, S.: Encoding data for HTM systems (2016) arXiv preprint arXiv:1602.05925
7. Wang, P.: Non-axiomatic Logic: A Model of Intelligent Reasoning. World Scientific, River Edge (2013)
8. Hammer, P., Lofthouse, T., Wang, P.: The OpenNARS implementation of the non-axiomatic reasoning system. In: Steunebrink, B., Wang, P., Goertzel, B. (eds.) AGI -2016. LNCS (LNAI), vol. 9782, pp. 160–170. Springer, Cham (2016). https://doi.org/10.1007/978-3-319-41649-6_16
9. Rehling, J., Hofstadter, D.: The parallel terraced scan: an optimization for an agent-oriented architecture. In: 1997 IEEE International Conference on Intelligent Processing Systems (Cat. No. 97TH8335), vol. 1, pp. 900–904. IEEE, October 1997
10. Wang, P.: Insufficient knowledge and resources'—a biological constraint and its functional implications. In: 2009 AAAI Fall Symposium Series, October 2009
11. Helgason, H.P.: General attention mechanism for artificial intelligence systems. Doctoral dissertation, Ph.D. dissertation, Reykjavik University (2013). http://skemman.is/en/item/view/1946/16163)

12. Harris, J.J., Jolivet, R., Attwell, D.: Synaptic energy use and supply. Neuron **75**(5), 762–777 (2012)
13. Bean, B.P.: The action potential in mammalian central neurons. Nat. Rev. Neurosci. **8**(6), 451 (2007)
14. Hammer, P., Lofthouse, T.: Goal-directed procedure learning. In: Iklé, M., Franz, A., Rzepka, R., Goertzel, B. (eds.) AGI 2018. LNCS (LNAI), vol. 10999, pp. 77–86. Springer, Cham (2018). https://doi.org/10.1007/978-3-319-97676-1_8
15. Nivel, E., Órisson, K.R.: Autocatalytic endogenous reflective architecture (2013)

An Experimental Study of Emergence of Communication of Reinforcement Learning Agents

Qiong Huang[✉][iD] and Doya Kenji[✉][iD]

Okinawa Institute of Science and Technology Graduate University,
Onna, Okinawa 904-0495, Japan
{qiong.huang,doya}@oist.jp

Abstract. Ability to use language is an essential requirement for human-level intelligence. For artificial general intelligence, the ability to learn and to create language is even more important [1]. Most previous models of learning and emergence of language took successful communication itself as the task target. However, language, or communication in general, should have evolved to improve certain fitness of the population of agents. Here we consider whether and how a population of reinforcement learning agents can learn to send signals and to respond to signals for the sake of maximizing their own rewards. We take a communication game tested in human subjects [2,3,6], in which the aim of the game is for two players to meet together without knowing exact location of the other. In our decentralized reinforcement learning framework with communicative and physical actions [4], we tested how the number N of usable symbols affects whether the meeting task is successfully achieved and what kind of signaling and responding are learned. Even though $N = 2$ symbols are theoretically sufficient, the success rate was only 1 to 2%. With $N = 3$ symbols, success rate was more than 60% and three different signaling strategies were observed. The results indicate the importance of redundancy in signaling degrees of freedom and that a variety of signaling conventions can emerge in populations of simple independent reinforcement learning agents.

Keywords: Multi-agent system · Reinforcement learning ·
Communication · Meeting task

1 Introduction

While communication is ubiquitous among animals and plants, unique features of human language are that the mapping between the signals and meanings, or appropriate responses, is not genetically fixed but learned by each individual and that a variety of vocabularies and syntactic conventions emerge through cultural evolution in different populations. How such capability is realized by evolution and learning [1] is a major question in artificial general intelligence.

© Springer Nature Switzerland AG 2019
P. Hammer et al. (Eds.): AGI 2019, LNAI 11654, pp. 91–100, 2019.
https://doi.org/10.1007/978-3-030-27005-6_9

Many models of learning and emergence of language have been proposed, but most of them took successful communication itself as the task target. From evolutionary viewpoint, however, language, or communication in general, should have emerged for the sake (or outcome) of improving certain fitness of the population of agents. Here we consider whether and how a population of reinforcement learning (RL) [9] agents can learn to send signals and to respond to signals for the sake of maximizing their own rewards.

Previous research [8] examined whether and how a simple form of communication emerges between reinforcement learning agents in an intrusion game, where positive reward is acquired by stepping into the other's territory while negative reward is incurred by collision of the two. Agents with light signaling capability learned a variety of policies of signaling and responding to signals to realize coordination, dominance, and complex behaviors. Another study in [5] introduced goal-directed utterance selection through learned internal models of how others respond to utterance. Agents were able to decide when to use language or not and select the appropriate utterance to achieve their specific goals of obtaining a certain type of food. More recently, Mordatch and Abbeel [7] demonstrated grounded compositional languages can emerge among deep reinforcement learning agents. In this work, however, all agents shared the same policy, which is closer to genetically shared communication scheme like in bees, rather than to human language learned independently by each individual.

Galantucci [2] developed a "meeting" task in which a pair of human participants learn to exchange graphic symbols to meet in the same room while not explicitly knowing the other's location. Different pairs converged to different conventions of what each symbol means and how to respond to them. Konno and colleagues [6] reproduced the experiment [2] in and further proposed a learning model based on the Adaptive Control of Thought-Rational (ACT-R) architecture.

In this paper, we propose a decentralized multi-agent RL framework for signaling and physical actions and test its performance with the meeting task [2,6]. Our previous work [4] tested the framework in a simpler task where agents get a reward by simultaneously arriving a fixed position in a grid-world. We test how the number N of usable symbols affects whether the meeting task is successfully achieved and what kind of signaling and responding are learned. We show that simple RL agents are able to create different signaling patterns for communication to guide the actions of each other. Analysis of the learned policies of signaling and corresponding movements shows that a variety of "meanings" can emerge through interactions of RL agents.

2 Methods

2.1 Learning Framework

We proposed a split-Q state-action function framework [4] which separates the physical moving actions and communication signal actions. The learning framework could be explained with Fig. 1. In this framework, each agent possesses two state-action function pairs which are for state-moving action and state-signaling (Q_i^p and Q_i^c, where $i = 1, 2$), respectively. In each episode, the agent will select a signaling action (i.e. a message

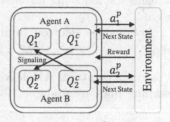

Fig. 1. Learning framework.

that will be shared with the other agent), send to the other agent and take a physical movement afterwards. The environment would therefore generate reward and the next states which would feedback to both agents.

2.2 Problem Formulation

The setting of the experiment is a "meeting" task based on [2,6], which could be viewed as a Partially Observable Markov game. In the present study, we utilized two reinforcement learning agents to see whether they could learn the meaning of the signaling from each other to enter the same slot within only one step move. The game field is a 4-rooms environment (Fig. 2). Agents are initialized in different rooms and have no prior knowledge of where the other agent is. Each agent possesses 5 possible movements (up, down, left, right, and stand), and several numbers of signals that they could utilize to send to the other agent. Agents can choose which signal they would like to use to send to the other agent before the move and will receive a score after each movement. Moreover, no predefined meanings are postulated for the signals. If they met in the same room after one movement, both agents receive a reward $= 2$; otherwise, they will both receive a reward $= -1$. Once they met in the same room or reached maximum steps in per round, they will be reset with new random starting positions, i.e., different separate rooms. To simplify the symbols, here we used numeric numbers to represent the signals. The goals are to explore whether agents can learn to move to meet in the same room within one move after learning, how agents utilize the signals, and what kind of factors are influencing this process.

In this environment, we assumed that the two learning agents ($i = 1, 2$) each has its own physical state set S_i^p, a communication state set S_i^c, a moving action set A_i^p, and a communication action set A_i^c. Each agent i has two state-action pair value functions which stand for the moving and communication respectively. One state-action pair function is $Q_i^p(s_i^p, s_i^c, a_i^p)$ which evaluates a moving action $a_i^p \in A_i^p$ at a physical state $s_i^p \in S_i^p$ and a communication state $s_i^c \in S_i^c$. The other

Fig. 2. Game field. Circle and rectangle denotes different agents.

state-action pair function is $Q_i^c(s_i^p, a_i^c)$ which evaluates a communication signal $a_i^c \in A_i^c$ at a physical state s_i^p. The communication action of the agent therefore changes the communication state of the other agent. The communication state satisfies the following formula $S_i^c = f(a_j^c) = a_j^c$ where i and j denotes different agent.

Actions are selected from the following conditional probability functions: $\pi_i^p(a_i^p \mid s_i^p, s_i^c) \propto \frac{e^{Q_i^p(s_i^p, s_i^c, a_i^p)/\tau_i^p}}{\sum_b e^{Q(s_i^p, s_i^c, b)/\tau_i^p}}$, and $\pi_i^c(a_i^c \mid s_i^p) \propto \frac{e^{(Q_i^c(s_i^p, a_i^c)/\tau_i^c}}{\sum_b e^{Q(s_i^p, b)^{\tau_i^c}}}$, where τ_i^p and τ_i^c are temperatures which control randomness. Algorithm 1 describes how the learning rules are updated.

Algorithm 1. Updating rule with split Q-learning framework.

Initialize $Q_i^p(s_i^p, s_i^c, a_i^p)$ and $Q_i^c(s_i^p, a_i^c)$ arbitrarily
repeat
    for all agents i **do**
    Initialize s_i^p
    take a_i^c **update** $s_i^c = a_\ell^c$ ($\ell \neq i$)
    repeat
        choose a_i^p, observe new states $s_i'^p$,and r_i
    for all agents i **update**
        $Q_i^p(s_i^p, s_i^c, a_i^p) \leftarrow (1-\alpha)Q_i^p(s_i^p, s_i^c, a_i^p) + \alpha(r_i + \gamma max_b Q_i^p(s_i'^p, s_i'^c, b))$,
        $Q_i^c(s_i^p, a_i^c) \leftarrow (1-\alpha)Q_i^c(s_i^p, a_i^p) + \alpha(r_i + \gamma max_b Q_i^c(s_i'^p, b))$,
        $s_i^p \leftarrow s_i'^p, s_i^c \leftarrow s_i'^c$
until Termination Conditions
where α is the learning rate and γ is the discount factor

---

3   Result and Discussion

3.1   Cases with Different Number of Signals

In our experiments, number of symbols N varies from 2 to 5. And we performed 100 groups of agents with 10,000 runs for each group and repeat for 5 times. Each agent also has separated learning rate α_i^p, α_i^c and temperature τ_i^p, τ_i^c. Here the incremental in the inverse temperature with an annealing equation follows $\tau_i^{p,c} = 1/(1 + \tau_i^{p,c} \times epi)$, where epi is the number of learning episode.

(i) $N = 2$

When agents have 2 symbols to choose to forward to the other agent, there are very rare cases that they can learn to meet in the same room after communication. Among all 100 groups of agents, there were only 1 or 2 groups which succeed in meeting each other within one step move. The signaling that agents learned to use (while there are only 2 possible signals, we used green and red color to represent the utilization of the signals) and signaling pattern paired with the successful case (the optimal solution) are listed in Fig. 3. The motion policies are colored in the same color of signals received from the other agent. For agent A, the signal it received in one room is as the pattern on the right side of Fig. 3 (i.e., agent B's signaling) and its neighborhood signal is the same whichever room it

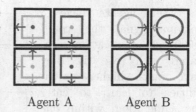

Agent A   Agent B

Fig. 3. Signaling pattern and motion policy pairs agents learned in successful groups when $N = 2$. Agent A and agent B is represented in box and circle, respectively. The signaling policies are showed by the edge color of the agent, and the motion policies are showed by arrow/dot for the received signal.

starts. For agent A, when agent A received the same signal from its neighborhood rooms, it chose actions which allow it to stay in its current position; when agent A received the other signal, it will take other actions to move to an adjacent room. On the other hand, for agent B, the signal it received is as the pattern on the left side of Fig. 3 (i.e., agent A's signaling) and its neighborhood signal is always different. As we can see from Fig. 3, when agent B receives the same signal in one position, it chose actions to move towards the same side of the signals. In this case, agent A's signaling guides the action of agent B and tells it the room it shall goes to. Noticing that agent has three possible next state based on its current position, when it received the same signal based on its current position, it would take the same action.

(ii) $N = 3$

When agents have 3 optional signals they could use for communication, compared with case (i), they have much higher probabilities to learn to enter the same room within one step move, and their signaling patterns also possess more diversity. With meta-parameter tuning, we found an optimal group of parameters $\alpha^p = 0.28$, $\alpha^c = 0.24$, $\tau^p = 0.0012$, and $\tau^c = 0.0021$. The probability of successfully meet in the same room is $63.4 \pm 2.7\%$. There are mainly 3 groups of combined signaling patterns pairs from the overall successful groups, and a visualized signaling pattern is represented in Fig. 4 as follows:

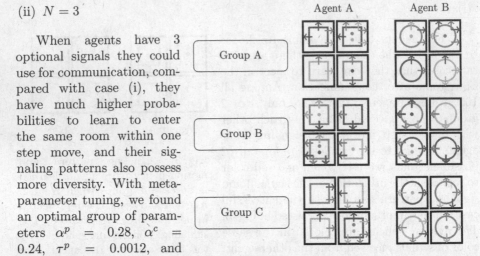

Fig. 4. Signaling patterns of agent A and agent B when $N = 3$, where different colors (green, cyan and red) represent for different signals agent learned after experimentation. Examples of the motion policies are showed by arrow/dot for the received signal. (Color figure online)

- Group A: agents show the same signal on the same side of the game field.
- Group B: agents show the same signal on one side of the game field and have one grid overlap of the same signal.
- Group C: one agents show the same signal in diagonal rooms of the game field.

Table 1 shows the number of each category (group). Group A and B are two most common signaling patterns in this case.

The moving policies that agents learned at the end in the well-learned groups also comply with certain rules. If one agent receives one specific signal, it will move accordingly to this signal, and vice versa for the other agent. In this situation, the signal received from the other agent guides the action of the present agent. As the agents are not in the same grid at the beginning, there exists an optimal solution in this environment when the number of signals is 3. Figure 5 is an example of successful communication policy learned by agent A and agent B in this premise, in which signaling patterns of Group B pairs are listed. As shown in Fig. 5, all 12 possible starting positions conditions are listed with their learned moving policies. For example, column 5–6 and line 2–3 shows the case that agent A sent the same message (colored in green) in the upper and bottom left rooms, and the message sending to agent B directs the direction in which it shall move (moving to the left). While agent A's moving action alters according

Table 1. Numbers of different groups when $N = 3$.

	Groups		
	Group A	Group B	Group C
Numbers	26	34	5

to the message it apprehends from the other agent in this 2 rooms, eventually they could meet in the same room under this signaling pattern within one-step move.

(iii) $N = 4$

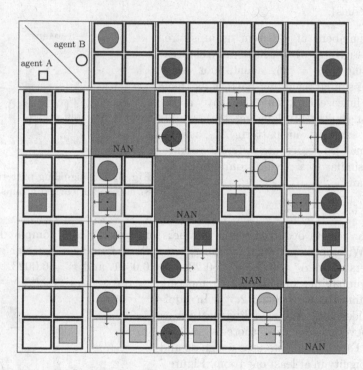

Fig. 5. One example of moving policy between agents when $N = 3$ (Group B). Three signals are colored in green, red and cyan, respectively. Orange box is the room agents meet after one step move. Arrows represent the directions agents move to, and dot is stand action. (Color figure online)

In this case, agents have 4 potential signals they could choose for communication, and the probability for agents to enter the same room within one step move keeps increasing compared with case (ii). Likewise, there are more patterns of signaling. With meta-parameter tuning, we found a group of optimal parameters where $\alpha^p = 0.3$, $\alpha^c = 0.25$, $\tau^p = 0.001$, and $\tau^c = 0.002$. The probability of successfully meet in the same room is $86 \pm 2.2\%$. Here we list one experimental result where the number of successful groups is 87 (out of 100 groups), and patterns of the signaling are in 6 categories as follows:

- A1: Using pure 4 signals (e.g., 2, 3, 1, 4 in four rooms).
- B1: Using all 4 signals but have ambiguity in one position (e.g., 3, [1,4], 2, 1 in four rooms).
- B2: Using all 4 signals, have ambiguity, and 2 signals from the rest 3 positions (e.g., 4, [1,2], 4, 3 in four rooms).
- C1: Using all 4 signals and have ambiguity in two positions (e.g., [1,3], [1,3], 2, 4 in four rooms).
- D1: Using pure 3 signals (e.g., 2, 1, 3, 3 in four rooms).
- E1: Using 3 signals and have ambiguity in one positions (e.g., [1,4], 3, 3, 4 in four rooms).

The numbers of different groups are shown in Fig. 6. As agents have more choices of signaling ($N = 4$), agents not only shows the similar signaling pattern as they emerged in case (iii), but also have more variety of choices of signaling they could use. For example, in pattern A1, agents use 4 signals to represents different rooms, which is similar to a pattern found in [2] as human pairs.

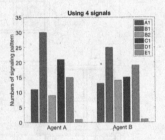

Fig. 6. The signaling pattern overall 87 successful learned groups.

(iv) $N = 5$

Similar results occurred when numbers of signaling is 5 compared with 4 signals. With meta-parameter tuning, we further found an optimal group of parameters where $\alpha^p = 0.25$, $\alpha^c = 0.28$, $\tau^p = 0.0011$, and $\tau^c = 0.0023$.

The probability of successfully meeting in the same room is $86.2 \pm 2.3\%$. In addition, besides the same signaling pattern as listed above in case (iii), there is another category F1 where agents uses 5 signals and have ambiguity in at least one room. Figure 7 shows the number of different patterns.

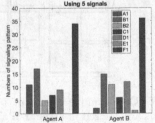

Fig. 7. The signaling pattern overall 83 successful learned groups.

3.2   Meta-Parameter Tuning

During implementation, we further noticed that the learning rate α and temperature τ are the two most contributing factors among other parameters which significantly influence the performance of the adaptive learners. We carried out grid search with learning rate (from 0.10 to 0.30 with step length of 0.01) and temperature (from 0.0010 to 0.0030 with step length of 0.0001) for optimal parameters in this experiment, and we further noticed that both temperatures for moving and communication are not supposed annealing to 0 at the end of each runs, otherwise the success rate will decline significantly.

4 Conclusion

This paper presented an experimental study of the emergence of communication in decentralized reinforcement learning agents with a split-Q learning framework. By the learning framework, RL agents could learn to use signals to enter the same spot in one-step move under message exchange without knowing the position of the other agent, as human participants did in [2,6]. We found that meta-parameter tuning was crucial for descrying the optimal parameters for learning, in which learning rate α and temperature τ are the two contributing factors in determining agents' optimal behavior.

The minimal solution with $N = 2$ was rare found, possibly because the actions are highly depended on the positions of the agent. In [2], a common pattern for signaling found with $N = 4$ in experimental subjects were to use different symbols to represent different positions. In our experiment with $N \geq 4$, besides the clean coding A1, other patterns also emerged for agents to achieve an optimal behavior.

Future work will extend the framework to scenarios where emergence of compositional coding of multiple states, goals, actions, and objects can be investigated, as in [7]. Exploration of the roles of internal models [5] and the theory of mind is also an important future direction.

Acknowledgements. This work was supported by Ministry of Education, Culture, Sports, Science, and Technology KAKENHI Grants 23120007 and 16H06563, and research support of Okinawa Institute of Science and Technology Graduate University to KD.

References

1. Doya, K., Taniguchi, T.: Toward evolutionary and developmental intelligence. Curr. Opin. Behav. Sci. **29**, 91–96 (2019)
2. Galantucci, B.: An experimental study of the emergence of human communication systems. Cogn. Sci. **29**(5), 737–67 (2005)
3. Galantucci, B., Steels, L.: The emergence of embodied communication in artificial agents and humans. In: Wachsmuth, I., Lenzen, M., Knoblich, G. (eds.) Embodied Communication in Humans and Machines, chap. 11, pp. 229–256. Oxford University Press, Oxford (2008)
4. Huang, Q., Uchibe, E., Doya, K.: Emergence of communication among reinforcement learning agents under coordination environment. In: The Sixth Joint IEEE International Conference Developmental Learning and Epigenetic Robotics, pp. 57–58 (2016)

5. Klein, M., Kamp, H., Palm, G., Doya, K.: A computational neural model of goal-directed utterance selection. Neural Netw. **23**(5), 592–606 (2010)

6. Konno, T., Morita, J., Hashimoto, T.: Symbol communication systems integrate implicit information in coordination tasks. In: Dietterich, T., Becker, S., Ghahramani, Z. (eds.) Advances in Cognitive Neurodynamics (III), pp. 453–459. Springer, Dordrecht (2013). https://doi.org/10.1007/978-94-007-4792-0_61

7. Mordatch, I., Abbeel, P.: Emergence of grounded compositional language in multi-agent populations. In: Thirty-Second AAAI Conference on Artificial Intelligence (2018)

8. Sato, T., Uchibe, E., Doya, K.: Learning how, what, and whether to communicate: emergence of protocommunication in reinforcement learning agents. Artif. Life Robot. **12**, 70–74 (2008)

9. Sutton, R.S., Barto, A.G.: Reinforcement Learning: An Introduction. MIT Press, Cambridge (2018)

Arbitrarily Applicable Relational Responding

Robert Johansson[1,2(✉)]

[1] Department of Computer and Information Science, Linköping University,
Linköping, Sweden
robert.johansson@liu.se
[2] Department of Psychology, Stockholm University, Stockholm, Sweden

Abstract. The purpose of this paper is to introduce how contemporary behavioral psychology approaches intelligence and higher-order cognitive tasks, as instances of so-called *arbitrarily applicable relational responding (AARR)*. We introduce the contemporary theory Relational Frame Theory (RFT), that suggests that key properties of AARR are *mutual entailment, combinatorial entailment,* and *transformation of stimulus function.* Furthermore, AARR are *contextually controlled* and developed through *multiple-exemplar training.* We explain these concepts and provide examples of how RFT uses this framework to explain complex cognitive tasks such as language, analogies, a sense of Self, and implicit cognition. Applications of RFT are surveyed. Finally, the relevance of RFT for the AGI audience is discussed.

Keywords: Relational Frame Theory · Behavioral psychology ·
Cognition · Intelligence · Language · Higher-order cognition · Self

1 Introduction

In 1971, Murray Sidman was working with language comprehension with severely developmentally disabled individuals. Unexpectedly, he discovered that if subjects were successfully taught to match pictures and printed words to dictated words (AB and AC relations, respectively; Fig. 1), and to name pictures (BD), they would without explicit training learn how to match printed words to pictures (BC), match pictures to printed words (CB) and to "read" (i.e., name words; CD). From a behavioral psychology point of view, this was very interesting, as it demonstrated a clear example of emitted behavior without a history of reinforcement.

2 Stimulus Equivalence and Derived Stimulus Relations

The above discovery has resulted in over 40 years of research in stimulus equivalence [10]. Stimulus equivalence is a behavioral phenomenon that (with one

© Springer Nature Switzerland AG 2019
P. Hammer et al. (Eds.): AGI 2019, LNAI 11654, pp. 101–110, 2019.
https://doi.org/10.1007/978-3-030-27005-6_10

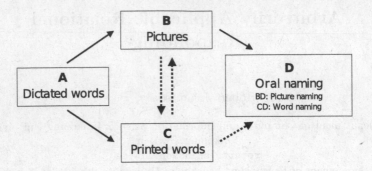

Fig. 1. The relations taught and tested by Sidman in 1971. Trained relations are depicted by solid arrows and derived relations with dashed arrows. Subjects were taught to match pictures and printed words to dictated words (AB and AC, respectively), and to name pictures (BD). Without explicit training they then could match printed words to pictures (BC), match pictures to printed words (CB) and to name words (CD).

possible exception) seems to be limited to humans with verbal abilities. The possible exception is a california sea lion "Rio", that seems to have demonstrated stimulus equivalence [9]. One way to study stimulus equivalence is with the help of matching-to-sample experiments. In such experiments, participants are exposed to series of arbitrary stimuli (e.g., nonsense symbols) where the task is to match a certain symbol to a given sample stimuli. Such experiment is an example of *relational responding*. That is, the task for a participant is not to emit a response in relation to a certain stimulus. It is rather to respond to the relation between symbols.

A formal definition of stimulus equivalence follows. Assume three nonsense symbols, which we for simplicity will refer to as A, B and C (they might be nonsense words, pictures, or something else). Within a given experiment (like the matching- to-sample), participants are taught to select B rather than some other option in the presence of a sample A (i.e., the relation $A \rightarrow B$ will be established through training). In the same way C is trained as the correct response in the presence of B ($B \rightarrow C$). After these relations have been trained, without training in other relations, participants demonstrate an increased probability of selecting A from a set of options when B is presented as a sample ($B \rightarrow A$; symmetry), selecting C when A is displayed ($A \rightarrow C$; transitivity), selecting A when C is displayed ($C \rightarrow A$; equivalence), and also the trivial case of selecting A when A is displayed ($A \rightarrow A$; reflexivity).

Demonstrating symmetry and equivalence are examples of *derived relational responding*, as these stimulus relations are not directly taught but instead derived. Prior to the research by Sidman and colleagues [11] the emergence of these derived stimulus relations was not expected in similar experimental setups. As mentioned above, stimulus equivalence has been very difficult to demonstrate in nonhuman animals (except for the single sea lion). However, there exist research that has demonstrated symmetry in pigeons, monkeys and rats, but the results are somewhat inconclusive [7].

The stimulus equivalence phenomenon opened up for a new way of studying symbolic relations (i.e., how a word "represents" an object in language), and supported the idea that derived stimulus relations were an important component in language and cognition. Importantly though, the idea is not new. William James did already in 1890 regard the abstract concepts of sameness or equivalence as *"the very keel and backbone of our thinking"* [6, p. 459].

3 Arbitrarily Applicable Relational Responding

In the late 1980's, the developers of Relational Frame Theory (RFT) [5] started to ask questions on what was beyond equivalence, for example: What kind of derived relational responding based on other relations than equivalence are human beings capable of? And if so, would such responding also be reflexive, symmetrical, and transitive? For example, consider a situation where someone is showed three identically sized coins, and being told that *"A is worth more than B, and B is worth more than C"*. Not only are the AB and BC relations specified, the BA, CB, AC, and CA relations will immediately be derived. Hence, a question such as *"Is C worth more than A?"* will be possible to answer (The answer would be *"No"*). Not only is this an example of responding to another relation than equivalence (a comparative relation), this is, according to RFT, an example of *arbitrarily applicable relational responding (AARR)*, as A, B and C are related along an arbitrary dimension of worth. In RFT terms, stimulus equivalence (as defined above) could be said to be a special case of AARR [15]. RFT has introduced more generic terms to describe features of derived relational responding, than the ones used to describe stimulus equivalence: *Mutual entailment*, *Combinatorial entailment*, and *Transformation of stimulus function*.

3.1 Mutual Entailment

Like symmetry, *mutual entailment* refers to the fact that arbitrarily applicable relations are always bidirectional. If A is related to B, than a second relation BA is automatically entailed. The type of relation entailed depends on the relation between the two stimuli. For example, as illustrated above, if A is worth more than B, then the novel relation *"B is worth less than A"* is entailed. Another example would be, if A is the opposite to B, then B is also the opposite to A. In the latter case the same relation as the one trained would be entailed.

3.2 Combinatorial Entailment

In line with transitivity, if A is taught to be related to B, and B to C, then a relation between A and C is *combinatorially entailed*. This was illustrated above where the *"A is worth more than C"* statement was derived. Once again, the type of relation entailed doesn't need to be the same as the one trained. For example, if someone is taught that *"A is the opposite to B"* and *"B is the opposite to C"*, then *"A is the same as C"* is combinatorially entailed.

3.3   Transformation of Stimulus Function

If A and B are taught to be related, and a response function (such as appetitive or aversive) is established for A, then the function of B will be *transformed* in accordance with the AB relation. For example, if someone fears dogs and learns that the word *"hund"* means *"dog"*, then the aversive stimulus function of *"dog"* is predicted to transfer through the sameness relation of *"means"*. Another example of non-equivalence follows. If someone learns that two nonsense stimuli are related $A < B$, and A then is paired with a mild electric shock, then the stimulus function of A will be transformed from neutral (as for a nonsense symbol) to aversive. Importantly though, B is predicted to be transformed to even more aversive. Similar effects have been demonstrated experimentally, using skin conductance equipment [3].

3.4   Contextual Control over AARR

Consider the example above, with a person seeing three identically sized coins, learning that *"A is worth more than B, and B is worth more than C"*. Imagine that the person instead learned that *"A is worth the same as B, and B is worth the same as C"*. In the two situations, two different forms of AARR would be triggered, for example as part of a decision-making scenario involving money. More specifically, the *"more than"* and *"same as"* are two different forms of *contextual cues*. This highlights the contextual nature of AARR.

3.5   Multiple-exemplar Training

How is arbitrarily applicable relational responding developed during lifetime? RFT assumes this is due to a history of *multiple exemplar training*. Imagine for example a small child who hasn't learned to apply the concept of comparison. Through interaction with the environment, the child might hear that *"the horse is larger than the duck, and the duck is smaller than the horse"*, and *"the man is longer than the child, and the child is shorter than the man"*, etc. RFT assumes that these multiple examples over time leads to the applicable abstract pattern of comparison that fulfills the properties of relational frames mentioned above.

3.6   AARR and Relational Frames

In summary, *arbitrarily applicable relational responding (AARR)* is defined as *abstract response patterns*, that have the properties of *mutual entailment, combinatorial entailment* and *transformation of stimulus functions*, that are controlled by *contextual cues* and learned through a history of *multiple exemplar training*.

Specific instances of AARR (for example sameness and comparison), are referred to as different types of *relational frames*. The term is based on a metaphor of a picture frame. Just as a picture frame can hold many pictures, a response frame can include many different features while still being a specific instance of an overall pattern.

4   Families of Relational Frames

In this section, we will elaborate further on RFT by describing the most common types of relational frames. Importantly, RFT is not limited to these frames. These are overall patterns that have been found useful to distinguish from one another.

Coordination. A frame of *coordination* is essentially a relation of sameness. If someone is taught that *"A is the same as B"*, and *"B is the same as C"*, then the *BA*, *CB*, *AC*, and *CA* relations of sameness will be entailed. This is essentially the same as stimulus equivalence. Furthermore, if the person is taught *"C tastes disgusting"*, then the aversive stimulus function of *C* will transfer to *A* and *B*, both being about equally aversive. RFT research has suggested that sameness is the earliest relational frame to develop, and arguably the most fundamental. This seems related to the fact that children early in their development tend to learn that words "refers" to things and events, that is, being the "same as".

Opposition. A more complex relational frame is that of *opposition*, that is relating stimuli in the presence of cues such as *"is opposite of"*. For example, a statement such as *"If Aaron (who is very tall) is opposite to Bill, and Bill is opposite to Charlie, then what is Charlie like?"* involves this frame. The statement needs to involve explicit or implicit information on which dimension along with the stimuli may be differentiated. These dimensions could be physical such as size, temperature, and brightness, but also arbitrary dimensions, as for example in the following statements: *"easy is the opposite of hard"*, *"valuable is the opposite of worthless"*, and *"A is opposite to B, and B is opposite to C. A is funny. Is C funny? Is B?"*.

Distinction. The frames of *distinction* are controlled by cues such as *"is different from"* and *"is not the same as"*. For example, if *A* is taught to be of different color from *B*, then it is entailed that *B* is of different color from *A*. However, the frame of distinction doesn't have the same specificity as the previously described frames when the relational networks grow, as shown in the following example: *"A has a different color from B, and C has a different color from B. A is green. Is B green? (No) Is C green? (Don't know)"*.

Comparison. *Comparative frames* involve responding to stimuli or events in terms of a quantitative or qualitative relation along some specified dimension. For example, *"If a dime is worth more than a nickel, and a nickel is worth more than a penny, is a dime worth more or less than a penny?"* is a statement which would require a person to derive the comparative relation between a dime and a penny. More specifically, the cue *"is worth more"* signals that the frame of comparison could be applied. Other examples of cues that control this kind of relating are *"heavier/lighter"*, *"better/worse"*, and *"larger/smaller"*.

Hierarchy. These are frames involving membership, attributes, class containment, etc. For example, *"If an object A is a type of object B and an object B is a type of object C, then is an object A a type of object C?"*. Also consider this example: *"If coffee is a type of drink, and tea is a type of drink, is then coffee a type of tea?"* In that example, the relationship isn't specified.

Temporal Frames. Responding to events in terms of temporal displacement from other events represents an example of responding in accordance with temporal relations, such as *"before/after"*. For example, *"If Tuesday comes before Thursday, and Thursday comes before Friday, does Friday come before or after Tuesday?"*

Spatial Frames. These frames involve relating along a spatial dimension, and may be triggered by cues such as *"above/below"*, *"left/right of"*, *"here/there"*, *"front/back"*, etc. For example, given that *"If A is above B, and B is above C"*, a person will derive that *"C is below A"*, *"A is above C"*, *"B is above A"*, and *"C is above B"*.

Deictic Frames. Finally, *deictic* frames are those that specify a relation between stimuli from the perspective of the speaker. RFT suggests that these deictic frames are a combination of three types of relations: *spatial* (*"here/there"*), *temporal* (*"now/then"*), and *interpersonal* (*"me/you"*). An example of a statement involving deictic framing is *"If I am here and you are there, and if I were you and you were me, where would you be? Where would I be?"*. Another example is *"If I feel sad and you feel happy, and if I were you and you were me, how would you feel? How would I feel?"*. The latter could be said to be an example of how something such as empathy could be analyzed through RFT.

5   Cognition and Intelligence from an RFT Perspective

From an RFT perspective, *cognition* is not a mental event that mediates between environment and behavior. It is rather a behavioral event (AARR), and hence, it can be studied and understood within a behavioral psychology framework, using experiments such as the matching-to-sample task described above. Another way to put it: arbitrarily applicable relational responses are what "minds" are full of, and when we speak of "cognitive" phenomena (such as thinking, planning, remembering, decision making) we are referring to complex instances of relational framing that are more or less evident under different environmental conditions [15].

Regarding *intelligence*, the core idea from RFT is that AARR represents the basic functional "building block" of cognitive and linguistic skills, such as deductive and inductive reasoning, communication, etc., all of which underpin intelligent behavior. In essence, intelligent acts involve the ability to elaborate networks of derived stimulus relations fluently and flexibly, to transform stimulus functions through entire networks, and to bring relational responses under increasingly subtle forms of contextual control, by abstracting relevant contextual features with high precision.

6   Higher-Order Cognitive Tasks and Complex Relational Responding

In this section, we will provide some examples on how RFT approaches various complex cognitive skills given the framework introduced above.

6.1   Language

RFT approaches language as verbal behavior [15]. A person learns "how to language" by learning how to respond relationally to stimuli and events. Hence, verbal behavior and language from an RFT perspective is really about the act of "framing events relationally". Stimuli such as words (spoken or written) or pictures become "verbal stimuli" when they participate in relational networks with contextual cues. It is this process that enables "meaning" to something as the stimuli acquire various stimulus functions. Someone speaks "with meaning" when they frame events relationally and produce sequences of verbal stimuli as a result. Someone else will "listen with understanding" whenever they respond as a result of framing events relationally. In essence, understanding something is not an outcome of an "inner/mediating" mental event, but is rather a type of contextually controlled behavior.

6.2   Analogies

All of the examples above have focused on how stimuli or events can be related. However, sets of relations can also be related. Relating relations is, from an RFT perspective, the basis of how analogies are developed and used [12]. For example, a quite simple analogy might be "*Apples are to oranges as dogs are to sheep*". This can be described as an equivalence relation between equivalence relations. More specifically, apples and oranges participate in a relation of equivalence (fruits), while dogs and sheep also participate in a relation of equivalence (animals). An example of analogical reasoning given this is deriving these two equivalence relations and the derivation of another equivalence relation between the relations. In other words, apples are equivalent to oranges in the same way that dogs are equivalent to sheep, because they are members of the same respective class). A further example could be someone who already knows about the solar system, and is learning physics. The statement "*An electron is to the nucleus as a planet is to the sun*" involves an equivalence relation between spatial relations. Given that the person knows this relation between planets and the sun, he/she could then derive a new spatial relation between electrons and nuclei.

6.3   The Self and Perspective Taking

As described previously, deictic frames involve temporal (*"now/then"*), spatial (*"here/there"*), as well as interpersonal relations (*"Me/You"*). While coordination, distinction and comparative relations (see above) develop based on what people learn about stimuli that are physically similar, dissimilar, or quantitatively different along some dimension, deictic frames are typically not. Instead, they develop based on the invariance of the speaker's perspective throughout time and location. A child might learn this by being asked questions such as *"Who are you?"*, *"What are you doing here?"*, *"What will you do there?"*, and *"What will I do tomorrow?"*, with many variations, in several different contexts. By taking part of a constant relating of *"Me/You"*, *"here/there"*, *"now/then"*, a child learns about itself, as something being different from others, and being *"here and now"* as compared to *"there and then"*. Hence, in line with how RFT provides an understanding of "languaging" as framing events relationally, "selfing" is approached similarly. Understanding how it is possible to take someone else's perspective also follows naturally from this analysis [8].

6.4   Implicit Cognition

To account for both "thinking fast and slow", RFT introduces dimensions to AARR such as *levels of complexity, derivation*, and *coherence* [1]. Complexity refers to the number of stimuli or events involved, with for example a mutually entailed response being "less complex" than a relating of relations. Levels of derivation is a continuum from a relating with very few new derivations on one end, and a response involving a large amount of new derivations on the other end. A response that is low is coherence is very little in agreement with a larger relational network that the response is taking place in. On the contrary, a response with high overlap with previous experience, is said to be high in coherence.

In an experimental task that studies implicit cognition from an RFT perspective, there is an assumption that responses that requires low levels of complexity and derivation, and being high in coherence, will be very quickly emitted. However, responses that require a high level of complexity and derivation, and/or being low in coherence, are assumed to be slower emitted, and therefore lead to longer response times.

7   Applications of RFT

Below, we will provide examples of how RFT can be used in applied settings, outside experimental psychology.

7.1   Education

It follows naturally from the above description, how teaching based on sameness, opposition, comparison, etc, could be conducted. The importance of multiple-exemplar training is highlighted by RFT. Furthermore, RFT provides the tools on how various new relational networks could be established, set in relation to existing networks, affected by transformation of function, etc. RFT provides the details on how analogies could be used as part of education, and provides an account of experiential learning through transformation of stimulus function. Furthermore, skills training involving perspective taking, such as training in empathy, could be understood through the lens of RFT [13].

7.2 Clinical Applications

Human suffering seems to be very much related to our capacity for language [2]. Statements such as *"Deep down I'm a bad person"* or *"I am not worthy of love"* or *"Everybody else is much better than me in most aspects"* are common in depression and related problem presentations. For anxiety disorders, simple statements such as *"Spider"* can trigger a whole host of physiological reactions. Similarly, when other terms are taught to be in equivalence with *"Spider"*, then these terms are predicted to trigger similar reactions. Furthermore, RFT provides an understanding of how other stimuli and events can become closely related to spiders, which could result in that the fear will generalize to other similarly looking things [4]. In summary, RFT provides accounts of a whole range of clinical phenomena, and provides tools on how to resolve these issues.

7.3 Prejudices

Today's society undoubtedly face massive problems related to hate, discrimination and violence due to prejudice. From an RFT perspective, prejudice could be defined as objectification and dehumanization of individuals because of their participation in verbal evaluative categories [14]. A major challenge seems to be due to the fact that prejudice and related processes seem to stem from the same source as our most successful problem-solving processes. RFT might be able to provide the means to deal with this verbal entanglement.

8   How Could RFT Be Relevant for AGI Researchers?

One could argue that RFT is essentially a behavioral psychology approach to general intelligence. While the AGI field has benefited from theories from diverse fields such as computer science and neuroscience, we believe that behavioral psychology also has something to offer. In the complex task of building thinking machines, clear definitions of cognitive phenomena are likely to be very helpful. RFT suggests that AARR is a necessity for intelligence and higher-order cognitive tasks. Possibly, RFT could provide a roadmap based on a science of derived stimulus relations, starting with symmetry and stimulus equivalence, going up to relations between relational networks, with models of language development, higher-order cognitive tasks, and the Self, with potential applications within diverse fields such as education, psychological treatments, and prejudices. We hope by writing this text that the AGI field finds such roadmap potentially helpful.

References

1. Barnes-Holmes, D., Barnes-Holmes, Y., Luciano, C., McEnteggart, C.: From the IRAP and REC model to a multi-dimensional multi-level framework for analyzing the dynamics of arbitrarily applicable relational responding. J. Context. Behav. Sci. **6**(4), 434–445 (2017)
2. Barnes-Holmes, Y., Barnes-Holmes, D., McHugh, L., Hayes, S.C.: Relational frame theory: some implications for understanding and treating human psychopathology. Int. J. Psychol. Psychol. Ther. **4**, 355–375 (2004)
3. Dougher, M.J., Hamilton, D.A., Fink, B.C., Harrington, J.: Transformation of the discriminative and eliciting functions of generalized relational stimuli. J. Exp. Anal. Behav. **88**(2), 179–197 (2007)
4. Dymond, S., Schlund, M.W., Roche, B., Whelan, R.: The spread of fear: symbolic generalization mediates graded threat-avoidance in specific phobia. Q. J. Exp. Psychol. **67**(2), 247–259 (2014)
5. Hayes, S.C., Barnes-Holmes, D., Roche, B.: Relational Frame Theory: A Post-skinnerian Account of Human Language and Cognition. Kluwer Academic/Plenum Publishers, New York (2001)
6. James, W.: The Principles of Psychology, vol. I. Henry Holt and Co Inc., New York (1890)
7. Lionello-DeNolf, K.M.: The search for symmetry: 25 years in review. Learn. Behav. **37**(2), 188–203 (2009)
8. McHugh, L., Stewart, I.: The Self and Perspective Taking: Contributions and Applications from Modern Behavioral Science. New Harbinger Publications, Oakland (2012)
9. Schusterman, R.J., Kastak, D.: A california sea lion (Zalophus californianus) is capable of forming equivalence relations. Psychol. Rec. **43**(4), 823–839 (1993)
10. Sidman, M.: Equivalence relations and behavior: an introductory tutorial. Anal. Verbal Behav. **25**(1), 5–17 (2009)
11. Sidman, M., Tailby, W.: Conditional discrimination vs. Matching to sample: an expansion of the testing paradigm. J. Exp. Anal. Behav. **37**(1), 5–22 (1982)
12. Stewart, I., Barnes-Holmes, D.: Relational frame theory and analogical reasoning: empirical investigations. Int. J. Psychol. Psychol. Ther. **4**(2), 241–262 (2004)
13. Vilardaga, R.: A relational frame theory account of empathy. Int. J. Behav. Consult. Ther. **5**(2), 178 (2009)
14. Weinstein, J.H., Wilson, K.G., Drake, C.E., Kellum, K.K.: A relational frame theory contribution to social categorization. Behav. Soc. Issues **17**(1), 40–65 (2008)
15. Zettle, R.D., Hayes, S.C., Barnes-Holmes, D., Biglan, A.: The Wiley handbook of contextual behavioral science. Wiley Online Library (2016)

Programmatic Link Grammar Induction for Unsupervised Language Learning

Alex Glushchenko[1], Andres Suarez[1,2], Anton Kolonin[1(✉)], Ben Goertzel[1,2], and Oleg Baskov[1]

[1] SingularityNET Foundation, Amsterdam, The Netherlands
{anton, ben}@singularitynet.io
[2] Hanson Robotics, Hong Kong, China

Abstract. Although natural (i.e. human) languages do not seem to follow a strictly formal grammar, their structure analysis and generation can be approximated by one. Having such a grammar is an important tool for programmatic language understanding. Due to the huge number of natural languages and their variations, processing tools that rely on human intervention are available only for the most popular ones. We explore the problem of unsupervisedly inducing a formal grammar for any language, using the Link Grammar paradigm, from unannotated parses also obtained without supervision from an input corpus. The details of our state-of-the-art grammar induction technology and its evaluation techniques are described, as well as preliminary results of its application on both synthetic and real world text-corpora.

Keywords: Categorization · Clustering · Computational linguistics · Dimensionality reduction · Formal grammar · Grammar induction · Natural language processing · Unsupervised learning · Vector space

1 Introduction

This work is grounded on the premise that the grammar of any language may be derived (at least to some extent) in an unsupervised way from statistical evidence of word co-occurrences observed in large unannotated corpora [1]. Following this idea, Vepstas and Goertzel [2] proposed to use such learned grammar for programmatic unlabeled dependency text parsing and part-of-speech tagging of raw text, for further extraction of semantics. The Link Grammar (LG) formalism [3] is proposed to represent the learned grammars, while parses are built by a maximum spanning tree (MST) algorithm [2].

In earlier work [4] we have described the implementation of the software framework capable to solve the described unsupervised language learning problem (to some extent) for synthetic English corpora, and approach the solution for real-world English corpora. The major components of our research pipeline (see Fig. 1) are: text tokenization, word-sense disambiguation (WSD), parsing, and grammar learning, with subsequent indirect evaluation of the produced grammar (by producing LG parses for a test corpus using the synthetic grammar and comparing them against expected parses).

P. Hammer et al. (Eds.): AGI 2019, LNAI 11654, pp. 111–120, 2019.
https://doi.org/10.1007/978-3-030-27005-6_11

Although text tokenization is a problem that can be attacked in an unsupervised manner [5], our current work has not attempted this seriously; for now, we rely on a rule-based English tokenizer. The WSD part of pipeline has shown promising results in earlier works [4, 6], providing noticeable improvement in the quality of the learned grammars and it is not discussed herein.

The MST-parser has proved to be a critical component of our pipeline, as it provides input to the grammar induction process. Ongoing development in this area is worth separate discussion, but its importance is confirmed by the findings presented below.

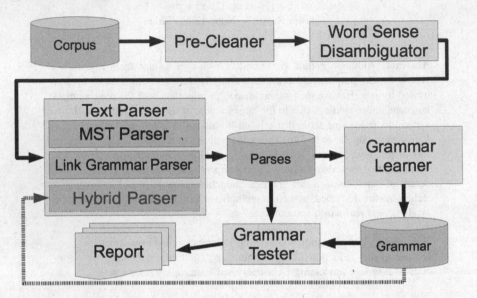

Fig. 1. Overall architecture of the unsupervised language learning pipeline, composed of a Pre-Cleaner responsible for tokenization, Text Parser (using either MST-Parser, or Link Grammar Parser or Hybrid Parser combining results of the previous two), Grammar Learner which induces a grammar from parses, and Grammar Tester that evaluates the learned grammar.

This paper focuses on the part of the pipeline responsible for induction of a Link Grammar dictionary from input parses, on the process for evaluation of such grammars, as well as on the results obtained from our research efforts.

The fundamental importance of this research is based on the assumption that understanding natural human language acquisition is one of the keys to decipher the nature of human intelligence [7] and unlock the path to artificial general intelligence (AGI) [8]. Unlike other approaches to unsupervised language acquisition [9], our framework creates a language model that, in contrast to a neural network "black box", consists of a human-comprehensible formal grammar contained in a LG dictionary file. Such file lists grammar rules that can be further reviewed, edited and extended by human computational linguists, or used by the Link Parser software (https://github.com/opencog/link-grammar) to parse previously unseen text in the target language. The latter possibility is compliant with latest trend in artificial intelligence domain called "explainable artificial intelligence" (XAI) [10].

From a practical standpoint, the goal of the unsupervised language learning (ULL) project is to automate the process of building, or extending, formal grammars of human languages. These grammars could then be applied on the comprehension and production of text and speech in computer software, and artificial intelligence applications involving natural language processing.

2 Grammar Induction Architecture and Implementation

Our proposed method for grammar induction, part of the open-source OpenCog Unsupervised Language Learning (ULL) project, is implemented as its Grammar Learner (GL) component and is represented on Fig. 2 (code can be found at https://github.com/singnet/language-learning). This section dissects the steps necessary for this process.

The Grammar Learner component takes as input a set of dependency parses with undirected unlabeled links, which are used to create a word-vector space. Inspired by representations using a Shifted Positive Pointwise Mutual Information word-context matrix [11], the created word space is described by a sparse matrix M in which each row i corresponds to a word, each column j to a context in which the word appeared, and each matrix entry Mij corresponds to some association measure between the word and the context. From a given input parse, we extract each word's connectors as those context-words linked to it, as well as a label "-" if the context-word appears to the left of the reference word in the sentence, or a label "+" otherwise. A connector-set for a word (also called a "disjunct" [4]) is composed of all the connectors it has in a given parse tree. We then build the word-vector space matrix using either connectors-sets (for smaller corpora) or plain connectors (for the larger "Gutenberg Children Books" dataset) as the words contexts.

A variety of interaction metrics can be used as association measures: mutual information [12] and co-occurrence frequency were implemented, resulting in dense and sparse matrix representations, respectively.

The Space Formation sub-component implements cleanup options for the sparse word space, filtering low frequency words and links. Further development suggests pruning words, connector sets, and word-context links based on mutual information or other interaction information criteria.

Singular Value Decomposition (SVD) [13] can be applied to the sparse vector space to produce dimensionally-reduced dense vector representations (word embeddings). However, this approach provided unstable results when applying K-means clustering, so totally different distributions of words across clusters were formed with different random seeds. Using other clustering algorithms, no clusters were obtained at all.

An alternative approach was to project the filtered word space onto a vector space similar to multivariate Bernoulli distribution [14], with each word represented as a sparse j-dimensional vector of binary variables. In this space, each variable describes the interaction between a word and a context (connector or connector-set), taking the values 1 if a word appears in a given context, or 0 otherwise. Exploring the properties of the resulting word space and whether these variables are correlated or dependent is an objective of further exploration. This approach smooths the influence of word frequencies and the distribution of interaction metrics on word vector similarities. However, preliminary studies have shown that rarely occurring words may have negative impact on the quality of space and consistency of the following results obtained from it. That means, more research is required to suppress such "noise" based on frequency filters.

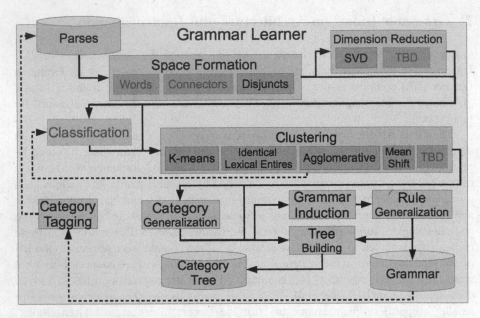

Fig. 2. Detailed architecture of the Grammar Learner component of the ULL pipeline. Grayed (dimmed) components of the architecture are designed but not currently implemented, and "TBD" blocks specify that new algorithms for a given stage of the process may be added in the future. Dashed lines indicate reverse flow direction, introducing loops in the pipeline.

The Clustering component may use various algorithms: beyond common K-means, the present research effort implemented and studied mean shift and agglomerative (ALE) clusterings, as well as grouping Identical Lexical Entries (ILE).

K-means clustering [15] of word embeddings used in our previous studies [4] turned out to introduce instability during the optimization of the entire pipeline parameters, so it was used only during earlier phases of the research. Also, our first results for mean shift clustering [16] were not significantly better than ALE. Hence, results for K-means and mean-shift clustering are not presented in the next section.

Agglomerative clustering in sparse vector space (implementation from https://scikit-learn.org/stable/modules/generated/sklearn.cluster.AgglomerativeClustering.html), further referred to as "ALE" (Agglomerating Lexical Entries), proved to be the best fit for larger datasets.

While testing similarity metrics for ALE, Euclidean distance provided better results for larger datasets than cosine and Manhattan distances. The clustering quality was evaluated with the Silhouette index for cosine, Jaccard, Euclidean, and Chebyshev similarities; cosine distance was preferred for smaller datasets. For larger corpora, all tested variations of the Silhouette index were close to zero, so no programmatic determination of the optimal number of clusters to create was possible (as opposed to our earlier work with K-means [4]). Therefore, we explored the target-clusters parameter space using 20, 50, 500, 1000, and 2000 clusters.

The ILE algorithm introduced in our previous work [2, 4] actually implements lossless compression of a vector space by grouping words with the same sets of associated connectors or connector-sets into grammatical categories. The resulting space can be considered a straight projection of a fine-grained LG dictionary with the maximum number of word categories onto the space of connectors or connector-sets. However, ILE clustering creates very sparse LG dictionaries that could not be processed by the LG parser in its current version, due to combinatorial explosions and stack overflow issues in run-time.

Further development suggests iterative clustering process, involving incrementally increasing volume of input data from smaller amount of high-frequency words to larger amounts of less frequency words. In such case, the dimmed Classification component in Fig. 2 could be used to attempt to classify newly experienced words to some of the categories learned from the previous iterations. Then, if some of words are not classified, they can be used to learn new clusters to be added to set of the categories. Still, exploration of the described flow has been not included in this study.

Category Generalization can be applied after Clustering for further aggregation of the learned word categories, based on Jaccard similarities of sets of connectors or connector-sets associated with them. Similarity thresholds can be set as generalization parameters; by gradually decreasing the threshold from the maximum found in the category distribution to a desired value, an iterative generalization process can be set up to provide hierarchical category trees showing the inner structure of categories agglomeration. Category Generalization results are not presented below, as Grammar Rules Generalization with the same algorithm demonstrated more efficiency.

The Grammar Induction component infers a grammar in the LG formalism [3] by processing links from input parses and replacing words with their corresponding learned word categories. Sets of links corresponding to each word, expressed in terms of word categories, form Link Grammar disjuncts for the category of the word. Link Grammar rules are sets of disjuncts associated with word categories.

Finally, the Grammar Rule Generalization component may be used to further cluster the learned word categories based on Jaccard similarities of sets of Link Grammar disjuncts associated with the categories in the Link Grammar rules. This component also adds an "upper layer" to the grammatical category tree on top of the "middle" layer representing word categories, which is anticipated to correspond to higher-level grammatical and semantic categories.

Optionally, the grammar learning process may be run in an iterative loop, using word categories from grammar rules found in a previous iteration as input to categorize words in subsequent iterations. The Category Tagging component replaces the words in input parses with learned categories (when available) so that more and more dense vector spaces may be created on subsequent iterations. The same iterative approach may be employed for incremental grammar learning, where the scope of the input parses gradually increases by adding previously unseen data to the training corpus.

3 Grammar Testing and Evaluation Metrics

The Grammar Tester (GT) component of the ULL pipeline implements a quality assurance procedure on the induced grammar obtained by the Grammar Learner. Two metrics are employed for this purpose: parse-ability and F1-score, as shown in Fig. 4.

The first quality criterion determines the extent to which the reference corpus is parsed at all – it is called "parse-ability" (PA) and computes the average percentage of words in a sentence recognized by the GT: $PA = (\Sigma(k_i/n_i))/N$, where N is the number of evaluated sentences, k_i is the number of words in the i-th sentence recognized by the GT, and n_i is the total number of words in i-th sentence.

As a second metric, we use the conventionally defined F-measure or F-score ($F1$), a function of recall (R) and precision (P): $F1 = 2 *R * P/(R + P)$. Recall is defined as $R = (\Sigma(c_i/e_i))/N$, and precision as $P = (\Sigma(c_i/l_i))/N$, where c_i is the number of correctly identified links in i-th sentence, e_i is the number of expected links and l_i is the number of identified links, including false positives. That is, for recall we take the average per-sentence number of overlapping links in test and reference parses divided by the total number of links in the reference parses. Respectively, for precision we take the same overlapping number, divided by the total number of links in the test parses.

4 Methodology of Studies and Intermediate Results

Our experiments for the ULL pipeline were performed with the three English text corpora referenced in earlier work [4] and presented on Fig. 3: (1) an artificial corpus created for basic testing purposes, the Proof-of-Concept English (POCE) corpus; (2) the Child Directed Speech (CDS) corpus obtained from subsets of the CHILDES corpus – a collection of English communications directed to children with limited lexicon and grammar complexity (https://childes.talkbank.org/derived/) [17–19]; (3) the Gutenberg Children (GC) corpus – a compendium of books for children contained within Project Gutenberg (https://www.gutenberg.org), following the selection used for the Children's Book Test of the Babi CBT corpus [14] (https://research.fb.com/downloads/babi/).

For each of these corpora, we ran our Grammar Learner using two different kinds of parses as input: first, our "standard" parses created either manually (for the POCE corpus), or parsed by the LG parser using the standard human-crafted Link Grammar

Corpus	Total words	Unique words	Occurrences per word	Total sentences	Average sentence length
POC-English	388	55	7	88	4
Child-Directed Speech	124185	3399	37	38181	4
Gutenberg Children	2695151	54054	50	207130	13

Fig. 3. Some features of the English text corpora used for studies. See [4] for more details.

Dictionary for the English language – further called LG-Parses. The second type of parses used are MST-Parses created by the previous segment of the ULL pipeline, including parses with WSD applied [4]. The human-knowledge-based LG-parses were used as a reference to asses the quality of MST-parses, as well as to create a baseline input for the GL to gauge its ability to induce grammar from "ideal" parses.

Based on the study of the various configurations of the Grammar Learner with different parses for each given corpora, and having generated approximately 100 induced grammars and evaluated them as specified before, we present the best results obtained in Fig. 4. From this experience, the following observations can be made:

Corpus	Parses	Parses F1	Clustering	Grammar PA	Grammar F1
POC-English	Manual	1.0	ILE	100%	1.0
POC-English	Manual	1.0	ALE-400	100%	1.0
POC-English	MST	0.71	ILE/G	100%	0.72
POC-English	MST	0.71	ALE-400	100%	0.73
Child-Directed Speech	LG	1.0	ILE	99%	0.98
Child-Directed Speech	LG	1.0	ALE-400	99%	0.97
Child-Directed Speech	MST	0.68	ILE/G	71%	0.45
Child-Directed Speech	MST	0.68	ALE-400/G	82%	0.50
Gutenberg Children	LG	1.0	ALE-50	90%	0.61
Gutenberg Children	LG	1.0	ALE-500	56%	0.55
Gutenberg Children	MST	0.52	ALE-50	N/A	N/A
Gutenberg Children	MST	0.52	ALE-500	81%	0.48

Fig. 4. Best scores for F-measure (F1) and parse-ability (PA) for different corpora and parse types using different clustering algorithms: ILE – Identical Lexical Entries, ILE/G – ILE with Grammar Rule Generalization, ALE-400 – Agglomerative clustering for 400 target categories, ALE-400/G – same with Grammar Rule Generalization, ALE-50 and ALE-500 – Agglomerative clustering for 50 and 500 target categories, respectively.

1. It is possible to perform grammar learning using a non-dimensionally-reduced discrete vector space of lexical entries (Link Grammar "disjuncts") without dimension reduction, based on identical lexical entries (ILE clustering) and using agglomerative clustering for English corpora of different scales, achieving reasonable scores for parse-ability and F-measure (PA/F1), using either parses obtained with English Link-Grammar dictionary (LG-parses) or MST-parses, as shown on Fig. 4.
2. It has been found that for real-world corpora such as CDS and GC, better PA/F1 scores are obtained if the evaluation of the grammar is performed only for sentences

for which the LG-parses are complete (the LG parser is allowed to ignore some words from a parse if a "cheaper" parse tree is found with an incomplete sentence). This way, the comparison is less likely to be done against originally incorrect parses.

3. We found a large Pearson correlation (93–100%) between the distributions of F-scores of MST-parses against LG-parses, and that of the parses obtained based on the grammar induced from these MST-parses against the same LG-parses. This effectively means that the quality of a learned grammar is linearly related to the quality of its input parses.

4. No reliable correlation between PA and F1 was found across corpora: in some cases (POCE, cleaned version of CDS and raw GC) it is positive, for another one it is close to zero (raw CDS), and for a third one it is negative (cleaned version of GC). That means PA can not be used as a metric for hyper-parameters optimization when we lack a standard (like LG-parses) to measure F1.

5. It has been shown that applying word-sense disambiguation before MST-parsing can improve the parses, providing higher F1 against their LG-parses standard. For the POCE corpus, F1 (on MST-parses only, not from grammar induction) improves from 0.70 to 0.75; in the case of the GC corpus, it grows from 0.50 to 0.52. As predicted by the point 3 above, the quality of the learned grammar increases as well.

6. The results shown in Fig. 5 were achieved by either grouping identical lexical entries (ILE) or agglomerative clustering (ALE), both starting from a discrete vector space of lexical entries (Link Grammar disjuncts) without dimension reduction. These results replace the ones from previously-used dimension reduction with singular value decomposition (SVD) and K-means clustering. Such changes provide higher F-scores and reproducibility, allowing optimization of the pipeline's hyper-parameters.

7. It has been found that the number of clusters, representing grammatical categories, that provides the best F1 for produced parses is about 500 for the real-world English corpora (CDS and GC). A decrease in the number of clusters/categories tends to increase PA and decrease F1 rapidly; using more clusters tends to reduce both PA and F1 slowly. Also, inducing grammars with less than 50 categories on the GC corpus causes exponential run-time growth for the LG parser using them, as well as segmentation faults on particular sentences.

8. We noticed that removing parses with low-frequency words from the GL input may decrease the grammar induction run-time, but never increase quality (either PA or F1) given our corpora; literally "the more words, the better".

9. Figure 5 shows that it is possible to use generalization of the learned grammatical categories into hierarchical trees to unravel the grammatical and semantic nature of their vocabulary in a reasonable way, corresponding to the context of the training corpora. These categorical trees can be useful for feature engineering in NLP applications, as well as for studies of new languages or domains by computational linguists.

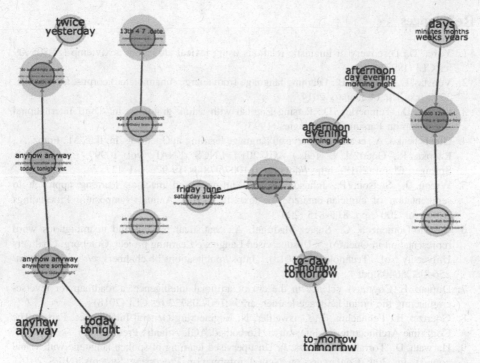

Fig. 5. Fragment of a category tree learned from the Gutenberg Children corpus in an unsupervised way, showing subgraphs matching the word "day". Visualized with the Aigents Graphs framework (https://github.com/aigents/aigents-java/blob/master/html/graphs.html).

5 Conclusion

We can conclude that it is generally possible to perform programmatic unsupervised induction of formal grammars from unannotated sentence parses for tiny, small and large text corpora, using the Link Grammar formalism and parser. We have found that quality of the grammar is linearly correlated with quality of the input parses used to induce the grammar. That is, the quality of the input parses seems to be the major obstacle for obtaining high quality grammars.

Future plans for our work include searching for ways to improve the quality of the input parses obtained in an unsupervised way from unannotated text corpora, as well as enhancing the grammar-induction technology itself. For the latter, we intend to improve the GL component to learn generalized parts of speech and grammatical relationships through better clustering.

Acknowledgements. We appreciate contributions by Linas Vepstas, including insightful discussions and critique on our research. We thank Amir Plivatsky for valuable feedback and maintenance and incremental improvements of the LG parser technology used in our work.

References

1. Yuret, D.: Discovery of linguistic relations using lexical attraction. arXiv:cmp-lg/9805009 [cs.CL] (1998)
2. Vepstas, L., Goertzel, B.: Learning language from a large (unannotated) corpus. arXiv:1401.3372 [cs.CL], 14 January 2014
3. Sleator, D., Temperley, D.: Parsing English with a link grammar. In: Third International Workshop on Parsing Technologies (1993)
4. Glushchenko, A., et al.: Unsupervised language learning in OpenCog. In: Iklé, M., Franz, A., Rzepka, R., Goertzel, B. (eds.) AGI 2018. LNCS (LNAI), vol. 10999, pp. 109–118. Springer, Cham (2018). https://doi.org/10.1007/978-3-319-97676-1_11
5. Wrenn, J., Stetson, P., Johnson, S.: An unsupervised machine learning approach to segmentation of clinician-entered free text. In: AMIA Annual Symposium Proceedings 2007, vol. 2007, pp. 811–815 (2007)
6. Castillo-Domenech, C., Suarez-Madrigal, A.: Statistical parsing and unambiguous word representation in OpenCog's Unsupervised Language Learning project. Göteborg: Chalmers University of Technology (2018). https://publications.lib.chalmers.se/records/fulltext/256408/256408.pdf
7. Dupoux E: Cognitive science in the era of artificial intelligence: a roadmap for reverse-engineering the infant language-learner. arXiv:1607.08723 [cs.CL] (2018)
8. Goertzel, B., Pennachin, C., Geisweiller, N: Engineering General Intelligence, Part 2: The CogPrime Architecture for Integrative, Embodied AGI. Atlantis Press (2014)
9. Harwath, D., Torralba, A., Glass, J.: Unsupervised learning of spoken language with visual context. In: 30th Conference on Neural Information Processing Systems (NIPS 2016), Barcelona, Spain (2016)
10. Došilović, F., Brčić, M., Hlupić, N.: Explainable artificial intelligence: a survey. In: 2018 41st International Convention on Information and Communication Technology, Electronics and Microelectronics (MIPRO) (2018)
11. Levy, O., Goldberg, Y.: Neural word embedding as implicit matrix factorization. In: NIPS 20114 Proceedings of the 27th International Conference on Neural Information Processing Systems, vol. 2, pp. 2177–2185 (2014)
12. Church, K., Hank, P.: Word association norms, mutual information, and lexicography. Comput. Linguist. Arch. 16(1), 22–29 (1990)
13. Wall, M., Rechtsteiner, A., Rocha, L.: Singular value decomposition and principal component analysis. arXiv:physics/0208101 (2002)
14. Dai, B., Ding, S., Wahba, G.: Multivariate Bernoulli distribution. Bernoulli 19(4), 1465–1483 (2013)
15. Sculley, D.: Web-scale k-means clustering. In: WWW 2010 Proceedings of the 19th International Conference on World-Wide-Web, Raleigh, NC, USA, pp. 1177–1178 (2010)
16. Comaniciu, D., Meer, P.: Mean shift: a robust approach toward feature space analysis. IEEE Trans. Pattern Anal. Mach. Intell. 24(5), 603–619 (2002)
17. Bernstein-Ratner, N.: The phonology of parent child speech. Children's Lang. 6(3), 159–174 (1987)
18. Brent, M., Cartwright, T.: Distributional regularity and phonotactic constraints are useful for segmentation. Cognition 61, 93–125 (1996)
19. Brent, M., Siskind, J.: The role of exposure to isolated words in early vocabulary development. Cognition 81(2), B33–B44 (2001)

Mental Actions and Modelling of Reasoning in Semiotic Approach to AGI

Alexey K. Kovalev[1,2] and Aleksandr I. Panov[2,3(✉)]

[1] National Research University Higher School of Economics, Moscow, Russia
[2] Artificial Intelligence Research Institute, Federal Research Center "Computer Science and Control" of the Russian Academy of Sciences, Moscow, Russia
panov.ai@mipt.ru
[3] Moscow Institute of Physics and Technology, Moscow, Russia

Abstract. The article expounds the functional of a cognitive architecture Sign-Based World Model (SBWM) through the algorithm for the implementation of a particular case of reasoning. The SBWM architecture is a multigraph, called a semiotic network with special rules of activation spreading. In a semiotic network, there are four subgraphs that have specific properties and are composed of constituents of the main SBWM element – the sign. Such subgraphs are called causal networks on images, significances, personal meanings, and names. The semiotic network can be viewed as the memory of an intelligent agent. It is proposed to divide the agent's memory in the SBWM architecture into a long-term memory consisting of signs-prototype, and a working memory consisting of signs-instance. The concept of elementary mental actions is introduced as an integral part of the reasoning process. Examples of such actions are provided. The performance of the proposed reasoning algorithm is considered by a model example.

Keywords: Cognitive agent · Sign-based world model · Semiotic network · Modeling of reasoning

1 Introduction

Cognitive architectures as a way to model the higher mental functions of a person to this day remain the main tool for creating global models of thinking, activity and decision making. On the one hand, this approach uses research materials in neuroscience and psychology. On the other hand, it allows combining a variety of methods and techniques to achieve the goal. For example, in [1–3] the cognitive architecture of the DSO based on the Paul McLean model of the triune brain [4] and extended by using Bernard Baars' global workspace theory [5, 6] is presented. In [7] several formal models are proposed, each of which can be considered as a cognitive architecture. The proposed models are organized in a hierarchy, starting with a basic RL agent capable of observing, exploring the environment, as well as performing actions affecting this environment, and ending with PrimeAGI agent [8, 9], implemented on top of OpenCog platform, which is capable of selecting cognitive actions through the process PGMC [10]. Recently, there has been a process of "equipping" cognitive architectures with the

© Springer Nature Switzerland AG 2019
P. Hammer et al. (Eds.): AGI 2019, LNAI 11654, pp. 121–131, 2019.
https://doi.org/10.1007/978-3-030-27005-6_12

latest advances in machine learning, which often do not simulate any mental process at all. For example, in [11], an approach to generate a description of an image (semantic image retrieval) is proposed, using deep convolutional networks for detecting objects and the cognitive architecture OpenCog for semantic analysis and query processing. Another approach to developing cognitive architectures is to use data derived from neurobiological research. Obvious examples are the HTM [12, 13] and eBICA [14] architectures.

Of particular interest is the above paper [7], which uses the graph approach. The agent's memory is represented by a large hypergraph, called Atomspace. Atoms in such a model are called both vertices and edges of the graph. Moreover, Atoms are accompanied by labels which can mean "variable", "or", "implication", etc. Then an atomic cognition, called "cognit", is an Atom or a set of Atoms. Activation of the cognit, depending on the label, can lead to such results as the creation of a new cognit, activation of one or more cognits, etc. This allows us to consider "graph programs" embedded in a common hypergraph. Additionally, the following hypothesis is applied: most of the operations performed by cognitive processes are a composition of elementary homomorphisms. This approach is close to the SBWM architecture, since the world model, as it will be described in detail below, in SBWM is a complex semiotic network formed by several semantic networks and transition functions between them. However, an important distinction of the model described below presents a process of activity propagation on the network, which allows to model unconscious processes.

2   Cognitive Architecture SBWM

In a broad sense, cognitive architecture is said to specify a computational infrastructure that defines various regions/functions working as a whole to produce human-like intelligence [15]. Such a definition in practice is expressed in the fact that cognitive architectures are built on the block principle, where each block performs a specific function, and partial modeling of human intelligence is achieved by the interaction of these blocks.

However, this approach has its drawbacks. For instance, modern works on neurophysiology speak of a uniform structure of the brain and the absence of an exact localization of the processes occurring in it. Also, most architectures are limited to modeling the memory of the agent and the set of some actions on this memory and do not use developments in the field of activity theory of behavior. As another drawback, one can point out a situation where a group of agents operates acting as carriers of cognitive architecture. In this case, the agents will be identical, copies of one system, up to the data loaded in them, which does not allow to model the individual characteristics of the agents obtained in the process of functioning. There are approaches to the development of so-called lifelong learning systems, in which it supports an iterative process of additional training due to which individual characteristics can arise, however, this has not yet become widespread in the construction of cognitive architectures.

The sign-based world model (SBWM) architecture is based on principles of the cultural-historical approach of L.S. Vygotsky and activity theory of A.N. Leontiev, which allow to eliminate these shortcomings. The main element of architecture is a sign, a distinctive feature of which is the presence of a personal meaning component. This component allows to store and use the individual characteristics of the agent, obtained in the course of activities in the environment and, as a result of processing the experience is gained. The main idea of the approach is that the agent acting in the environment keeps its own view on this environment. Moreover, on the one hand, this view represents the assimilation of well-known rules and patterns of behavior (the cultural and historical heritage of the collective), and on the other hand, is the result of accumulated experience gained in the process of performing any actions in this environment. Thus, the agent's view on the environment is subjective, depends on experience, and may be different for different agents. In contrast to the classical approach to cognitive architectures, in which the resulting system is a collection of individual blocks, the SBWM uses a uniform representation of knowledge and processes: on the semantic level, in the form of signs, and on the structural, in the form of distinct networks on a set of causal matrices. Such an approach shows its expediency in the tasks of cognitive hierarchical planning [16, 17] and anomaly detection [18], etc. In this paper, SBWM architecture is used to model a particular case of reasoning with a cognitive agent. The ability to reason is one of the most important tools necessary for functioning in a partially observable and/or non-deterministic environment. With the help of reasoning, the agent is able to generate new knowledge that is not in their world model, using available knowledge, known patterns, and connections between them. Although the processes of reasoning and planning are often considered separately, in essence, they complement each other. In [17], an alternating approach is considered for planning and reasoning. The updated agent's world model, obtained at the stage of reasoning, is used at the subsequent planning stage.

Further, we will describe the principles of SBWM in more detail, following [18, 19], originally described in [20, 21]. The main element of the system is the sign, which corresponds with the agent's view on an object, action or situation. Further, for simplicity, an object, action or situation will be called an entity. The sign consists of four components: *image p*, *significance m*, *personal meaning a*, and *name n*. The *image component* corresponds to the characteristic feature of the described entity. In the simplest case, the image refers to signals from the agent's sensors that is consistent with an entity. In general, one can say that the image of the sign is relative to the set of characteristic features of the entity which the sign corresponds with. The *significance of the sign* describes the standard application of the entity, taken from cultural and historical experience. In practice, this is expressed in a priori knowledge obtained by an agent from outside, for example, when processing a corpus of texts, and not depending on experience. The *meaning of a sign* is understood as a relation of the agent to the entity or experience of the agent's interaction with this entity. Thus meanings are formed in the interaction process of the agent with the environment.

To describe the components of the sign, we introduce a special structure – the causal matrix. A *causal matrix* is a tuple $z = \langle e_1, e_2, \ldots, e_t \rangle$ of length t where events e_i are represented by a binary vector (column) of length h. For each index j of the event vector e_i (row of the matrix z), we will associate a tuple, possibly empty, of causal matrices Z_j, such that $z \notin Z_j$. We divide the set of columns indices of the causal matrix z into two disjoint subsets I^c and I^e. The set I^c for the matrix z will be called the indexes of the condition columns, and the set I^e – the indexes of the effect columns of the matrix z. If there are no effect columns in the matrix, then we will say that such a matrix corresponds with the object. The presence of effect columns in the matrix means that such a matrix corresponds with an action or process. It is also worth noting that the matrix cannot consist only of effect columns. Thus, the structure of the causal matrix makes it possible to encode uniformly both static information and features of an object, as well as dynamic processes. The ability to specify causes and effects allows to represent a causal relationship.

A sign means a quadruple $s = \langle n, p, m, a \rangle$, where the name of a sign n expressed by a word in some finite alphabet, $p = Z^p$, $m = Z^m$, $a = Z^a$ are tuples of causal matrices, which are respectively called the *image*, *significance*, and *meaning* of the sign s. Based on this, the whole set of causal matrices Z can be divided into three disjoint subsets: images Z^p, significances Z^m, and meanings Z^a which are organized into semantic networks, which we will call causal.

A *causal network on images* will be a labeled directed graph $W_p = \langle V, E \rangle$, in which each node $v \in V$ is assigned a causal matrices tuple $Z^p(s)$ of the image of a certain sign s, an edge $e = (v_1, v_2) \in E$, if the sign s_1 is an element of the image s_2.

Causal networks on significances and meanings are defined in a similar way. The network on names is a semantic network whose vertices are the names of signs, and the edges correspond to special relationships. Thus, each component of the sign forms a causal network with a specific set of relationships. These four causal networks are connected by using transition functions Ψ_i^j, $i, j \in \{p, m, a, n\}$ to the semiotic network. The transition function Ψ allows to switch from one component of the sign to another, for instance. A semiotic network can be considered an agent's knowledge base of the environment, taking into account the experience. In other words, the semiotic network is a sign-based world model of an agent.

Formally, we will call the semiotic network $\Omega = \langle W_m, W_a, W_p, W_n, R, \Theta \rangle$ a sign-based world model, where W_m, W_a, W_p, W_n are causal networks of significances, meanings, images, and names, respectively, $R = \langle R^m, R^a, R^p, R^n \rangle$ is a family of relations on sign components, Θ is a family of operations on a set of signs. Operations Θ include such actions on signs as unification, image comparison, updating while learning, etc.

An important element of the SBWM is the concept of the *spread of activity* on the semantic network. By the *activation level of the sign component* λ_i, $i \in \{p, m, a\}$ will be called a real number $0 \leq \lambda \leq 1$ where 0 corresponds to the absence of activation, and 1 is the maximum possible activation. The *activation threshold* $\theta_i^S, i \in \{p, m, a\}$ sets the activation level so that when $\lambda \geq \theta^S$, i.e. activation of a component is equal to or exceeds the threshold, the sign component becomes *active* and is assigned an *activity label* α. The component of the sign, the activation level of which is not zero, but less than the threshold, i.e. $0 < \lambda < \theta^S$, considered *pre-activated*. A sign becomes active and an activity label is assigned to it if its components are active. Thus, the activation of the sign components corresponds to replenishment of the sets of active causal matrices Z_i^*, $i \in \{p, m, a\}$, and the activation of the sign corresponds to replenishment of the set of active signs S^*. Activation of components and signs occurs in the process of spreading activity on a semiotic network. It is worth noting that in the simplest case, the activity of the components can only increase with time, however, situations are possible when signs and their components are no longer active, excluded from the sets Z^* and S^*, then the *attenuation coefficient of the activity* γ_i, $i \in \{p, m, a\}$ can be entered at which the activity will decrease at each step: $\lambda^l = \lambda^{l-1} - \gamma$. The need for the attenuation coefficient of the activity may arise, for example, when the power of the sets Z^* and S^* greatly increases in the course of the agent activity in the environment.

Spreading activity on a semiotic network is subject to *global* and *local* rules (*ascending, predicting, descending, causal*) for spreading activity listed in Table 1.

Table 1. Local and global rules

Rule name	Description
Ascending	If at some point in time the component of the sign becomes active, then all occurrences of this component in the causal matrix of other signs become active
Predicting	If at the time moment t an event e_t is active in any component of the sign s, then the events e_{t+1} of the same component are pre-activated
Descending	If at some point in time each event in the tuple of causal matrices of some component of the sign is active, then these components of all signs included in the event are pre-activated
Causal	If an event is active at some point in time, then predictive and descending rules are consistently applied to all event-effects, with the amendment that the maximum activity applies
Global	If one of the components of the sign becomes active at some point in time, the other components become pre-activated, i.e. their activity level is changed by a certain value determined for each component

The process of spreading activity is iterative, i.e. at each i step, new active matrices and signs are added to the sets of active matrices and signs for the step $i - 1$.

3 Reasoning in SBWM

We introduce some concepts that we need in the future.

A semiotic network expressing the agent's knowledge of the environment can be divided into *long-term* and *working memory*. The conditionality of such a division arises because of impossibility to localize a region in a semiotic network that would be responsible only for one of them. They differ only in the types of signs they may contain. Abstract knowledge of an agent of a certain entity, its characteristics and possible interactions with this entity, obtained as a result of the assimilation in which cultural and historical experience are integrated or the experience of the agent, will be called a *sign-prototype* $\dot{S}$.

By a *sign-instance* $\hat{S}$, we mean the specific implementation of the sign-prototype. The sign-instance does not reflect all the properties available to the sign-prototype, but only those that are important at the moment. At the same time, the connection with the prototype through the name component is retained, which allows updating the description of the sign-instance as necessary. Updating occurs due to the removal (forgetting) of the current sign-instance and the creation (recall) of the sign-instance with an extended set of properties. The fact that the sign $\hat{S}$ is an instance of the sign-prototype $\dot{S}$ will be denoted as $\hat{S} \simeq \dot{S}$.

Long-term memory M_L, or simply *memory*, will be called a part of the agent's sign-based world model, expressed with the help of signs-prototype. Although structurally long-term memory is a network, it can be described as the set of all signs-prototype.

Working memory M_W is part of the agent's sign-based world model in which information that is actively processed is stored. Such information is expressed by means of signs-instance. As well as long-term memory, working memory can be represented as a set of all signs-instances.

By *active edges*, we will mean edges, which are currently spreading activity. The *activation of the edge* corresponds to the beginning of the spread of activity along this edge.

We proceed directly to the formalization of reasoning. To begin with, we define that a binary predicate $P(x, y)$ can be regarded as a binary relation, then the predicate $P(x, y)$ is true if and only if the pair (x, y) belongs to the relation P. We will use the terms binary predicate or, simply, the predicate and relations interchangeably.

We define a *situation* as any fixed state of the environment. Then, the configuration of the environment in which the agent operates is generally specified by listing the objects in the situation and the relations between them. We denote D_f the set of all possible relationships between all objects presented in the situation. Such a set will call a *complete description of the situation*. Obviously, such a complete description of the situation is redundant, for example, if it is known that "object A to the left of object B", using the interrelation between relationships, can be inferred that "object B to the right of object A". We will say that D is *a description of a situation* if $D \subseteq D_f$.

We formulate the problem solved by the agent as follows: the agent is given a description of the situation D and asked a question Q in the form of predicate conjunction $P_1(x_1, y_1) \cdot P_2(x_2, y_2) \cdot \ldots \cdot P_n(x_n, y_n)$. The agent must determine whether the question is fulfilled (the predicate conjunction takes the value true) in the given description. The task of the agent is to replenish the description D to some description D', in which the question is solved or to establish the impossibility of its implementation.

At the initial moment of time, the agent has access to a set of active signs S_0^*, from which they can choose one of the signs to start the reasoning. We will assume that the signs are chosen randomly and equally likely. Having chosen a sign, the agent gets access to the incoming and outgoing edges of this sign. With the selected sign, the agent can perform one of the available elementary mental actions. An *elementary mental action* corresponds to a transition along one of the edges of a chosen sign, as a result of which a sign is activated at the other end of the edge. Depending on the types of signs connecting the edge, different elementary actions arise listed in Table 2.

For signs corresponding to some objects or other agents, an elementary action *"transition to action/relation"* occurs, in which the entity described by the sign plays the role of an object $obj2act(S)$ or a subject $subj2act(S)$. Formally, actions $obj2act(S)$ and $subj2act(S)$ are written in the same way as actions $act2subj(S)$ and $act2obj(S)$.

Table 2. Types of elementary mental actions

Name	Label	Description
Abstraction	$inst2prot(\hat{S})$	A transition along an edge from the sign-instance to the corresponding sign-prototype
Concretization to the instance	$prot2inst(\dot{S})$	A transition along the edge from the sign-prototype to the corresponding sign-instance
Generalization	$cl2supcl(\dot{S})$	A transition along the edge from the sign-prototype of the class to the sign-prototype of the superclass
Concretization to a subclass	$cl2subcl(\dot{S})$	A transition along the edge from a sign-prototype of a class to a sign-prototype of a subclass
Transition to the action subject	$act2subj(S)$	Records that the sign S_j is a subject for the action corresponding to the sign S_i
Transition to the action object	$act2obj(S)$	Records that the sign S_j is an object for the action corresponding to the sign S_i

Despite the fact that edges can connect different components of signs, information about available mental actions is recorded on a network of names. This allows to shorten the chain of actions with a sign.

Elementary mental actions can be organized in chains, such a chain will be called a *compound mental action*, or simply, a *mental action*. For example, the transition from one sign-instance to another sign-instance of the same sign-prototype is carried out as follows: abstraction followed by concretization to an instance. Thus, mental action can be understood as any stable sequence of elementary mental actions. A stable sequence means a sequence of elementary actions, which is often repeated when the agent solves problems.

If we denote s_i the active sign chosen by the agent in the i-th step, a_i is the mental action is chosen at the same step, and the application of this action a_i to the sign s_i is denoted as $v(s_i, a_i)$, then $v(s_i, a_i) = s^i$ where s^i is the sign activated in the i-th step. Then the set of active signs on the $i + 1$-th step will be equal to $S_{i+1}^* = S_i^* \cup s^i$. To simplify writing, we will denote $v(s_i, a_i)$ as $s_i a_i$, and the set S_{i+1}^* as r_i, i.e. as a result of applying a mental action at the i-th step. Then the sequence $s_1 a_1 r_1 s_2 a_2 r_2 \ldots s_n a_n r_n$ will be called *reasoning*.

The process described above corresponds to the perceived or verbalized part of the reasoning. However, this is not the only way to replenish the set r_i. The set r_i can also be replenished by spreading the activity using the rules for spreading activities.

Let us replenish rules for spreading activity by the following list:

- on the significance network, the activity spreads both in the direction of the edge and against the direction;
- on networks of images, personal meanings and names, the activity spreads only in direction of the edge.

Let us add the rules for activating the sign components and the sign itself with the following rules:

- on the significance network, the sign component becomes active if at least one outgoing or incoming edge is active;

- on the network of images and personal meanings the sign component becomes active if all incoming arcs are active;
- if the name of the sign s is activated at the step t, then, regardless of the activation level of the components of the sign s at the step $t-1$, the sign s is activated, and all its components are activated accordingly.

We denote the set of signs that were activated at the i-th step by spreading the activity as r_i^{sa}, then the set of all active signs after the i-th step r_i' can be written as $r_i' = r_i \cup r_i^{sa}$.

It is worth noting that in order to proceed and lead to any results in the reasoning process, it is necessary that the agent's long-term memory stores information about the interrelation of the relationships presented in the situation (such as "left", "right", etc.). Such information can be obtained in several ways: (1) from a priori knowledge of an agent, for example, as a result of processing a corpus of texts, where these connections are clearly indicated; (2) obtained during the processing of the agent's experience; (3) be part of the input information along with the relationship itself, information about the situation and the question. These interrelations are also represented as causal matrices.

Also, in the working memory, a sign is created corresponding the reflection of the agent over their own reasoning, and a sign corresponding to the stage of reasoning. The agent begins the reasoning "by focusing attention" on the active sign-instance in the working memory.

The algorithm for implementing the mechanism of reasoning in the sign-based world model listed in Table 3. Currently, this algorithm is being implemented on the basis of the library "map-core" developed at FRC CSC RAS [22].

Table 3. Algorithm for implementing the mechanism of reasoning in SBWM

Algorithm	
0	**INPUT:** Description of the situation D, question Q
1	Creation of signs-instance of the objects and relations specified by D
2	Creation of signs-instance of question and answers "Yes", "No"
3	Activation of signs in working memory
4	**WHILE** question sign is not active **AND** (there are not considered active signs **OR** not applied actions)
5	Choose one of the sign from set of active signs
6	Choose one of the possible mental actions for the sign and apply to it
7	Update set of active signs due to the spread of activity
8	**END**
9	**IF** question sign is active **THEN**
10	Activate the "Yes" sign
11	**ELSE**
12	Activate the "No" sign

4   Model Example

We briefly illustrate the above algorithm without following formalities and omitting the technical details. We will consider the problem of modeling reasoning in a modified world "World of cubes". The objects will be cubes and tables with specified identifiers. An example of the environment configuration is shown in Fig. 1.

Fig. 1. Possible configuration of the "World of cubes" environment.

The environment has the following relationships: On (x, y), Left (x, y), Right (x, y), Above (x, y), Below (x, y), Near (x, y), Far (x, y). A complete description of the situation depicted in Fig. 1, as mentioned above, will be redundant.

Two obvious extreme cases where the question is contained in the description or when the description does not contain the object of the question are not considered.

The following example is of greater interest: a description $D = \{On(A, T),$ $On(B, T), Left(A, B), On(C, B)\}$ is given and a question $Q = Right(B, A) \cdot Above(C, T)$ is asked – the answer is not presented clearly in the description, but all objects appearing in the question are contained in it.

In this case, at some stage of the reasoning, the agent will select a sign-instance of block "A", denote it $\hat{S}_A$, apply a mental action $obj2act(S)$ to it: $obj2act(\hat{S}_A) = \hat{S}_{Left1}$ and proceed to the sign-instance of the corresponding relation "Left", we denote it as $\hat{S}_{Left1}$. Next, applying to the $\hat{S}_{Left1}$ action $inst2prot(\hat{S})$ will go to the sign-prototype of the relationship "Left": $inst2prot(\hat{S}_{Left1}) = \dot{S}_{Left}$. On the significance network at the sign $\dot{S}_{Left}$ there is a causal matrix $Z_{Left \leftrightarrow Right}$, encoding that if the object X is to the left of the object Y, then the object Y to the right of the object X, i.e. if $Left(X, Y)$, then $Right(Y, X)$. Using this interrelation of relations, the agent will replenish the description of the situation with a new fact: $D := D \cup Right(B, A)$. The relation $Above(C, T)$ is derived in a similar way using the rule: if $On(X, Y)$ and $On(Y, Z)$, then $Above(X, Z)$. Thus, the final description of the situation will be $D = \{On(A, T), On(B, T), Left(A, B), On(C, B), Right(B, A), Above(X, Z), \ldots\}$ where the dots correspond to other facts obtained in the course of the reasoning. This description contains a question and, therefore, the agent will give a "Yes" answer.

5 Conclusion

The article considers the cognitive architecture SBWM and proposes an algorithm that simulates a particular case of reasoning in it. The concept of long-term and working memory, as well as signs-prototype and signs-instance are introduced. A model example of the use of reasoning in a modified world "World of cubes" is given. However, all the capabilities of this algorithm will be fully revealed in more complex examples, which will be considered in subsequent works. The results will form the basis for the further development of reasoning algorithms in the SBWM.

Acknowledgements. The reported study was supported by RFBR, research Projects No. 18-07-01011 and No. 18-29-22027.

References

1. Ng, G.W., Tan, Y.S., Teow, L.N., Ng, K.H., Tan, K.H., Chan, R.Z.: A cognitive architecture for knowledge exploitation. In: 3rd Conference on Artificial General Intelligence AGI-2010, pp. 1–6. Atlantis Press, Lugano (2010)
2. Ng, K.H., Du, Z., Ng, G.W.: DSO cognitive architecture: unified reasoning with integrative memory using global workspace theory. In: Everitt, T., Goertzel, B., Potapov, A. (eds.) AGI 2017. LNCS (LNAI), vol. 10414, pp. 44–53. Springer, Cham (2017). https://doi.org/10.1007/978-3-319-63703-7_5
3. Ng, K.H., Du, Z., Ng, G.W.: DSO cognitive architecture: implementation and validation of the global workspace enhancement. In: Iklé, M., Franz, A., Rzepka, R., Goertzel, B. (eds.) AGI 2018. LNCS (LNAI), vol. 10999, pp. 151–161. Springer, Cham (2018). https://doi.org/10.1007/978-3-319-97676-1_15
4. MacLean, P.D.: The Triune Brain in Evolution: Role in Paleocerebral Functions. Plenum Press, New York (1990)
5. Baars, B.J.: A Cognitive Theory of Consciousness. Cambridge University Press, Cambridge (1993)
6. Baars, B., Franklin, S., Ramsoy, T.: Global workspace dynamics: cortical "binding and propagation" enables conscious contents. Front. Psychol. **4**, 200 (2013)
7. Goertzel, B.: From abstract agents models to real-world AGI architectures: bridging the gap. In: Everitt, T., Goertzel, B., Potapov, A. (eds.) AGI 2017. LNCS (LNAI), vol. 10414, pp. 3–12. Springer, Cham (2017). https://doi.org/10.1007/978-3-319-63703-7_1
8. Goertzel, B., Pennachin, C., Geisweiller, N.: Engineering General Intelligence, Part 1: A Path to Advanced AGI via Embodied Learning and Cognitive Synergy. Atlantis Thinking Machines. Springer, New York (2014). https://doi.org/10.2991/978-94-6239-027-0
9. Goertzel, B., Pennachin, C., Geisweiller, N.: Engineering General Intelligence, Part 2: The CogPrime Architecture for Integrative, Embodied AGI. Atlantis Thinking Machines. Springer, New York (2014). https://doi.org/10.2991/978-94-6239-030-0
10. Goertzel, B.: Probabilistic growth and mining of combinations: a unifying meta-algorithm for practical general intelligence. In: Steunebrink, B., Wang, P., Goertzel, B. (eds.) AGI - 2016. LNCS (LNAI), vol. 9782, pp. 344–353. Springer, Cham (2016). https://doi.org/10.1007/978-3-319-41649-6_35

11. Potapov, A., Zhdanov, I., Scherbakov, O., Skorobogatko, N., Latapie, H., Fenoglio, E.: Semantic image retrieval by uniting deep neural networks and cognitive architectures. In: Iklé, M., Franz, A., Rzepka, R., Goertzel, B. (eds.) AGI 2018. LNCS (LNAI), vol. 10999, pp. 196–206. Springer, Cham (2018). https://doi.org/10.1007/978-3-319-97676-1_19
12. George, D., Hawkins, J.: Towards a mathematical theory of cortical micro-circuits. PLoS Comput. Biol. **5**(10) (2009). https://doi.org/10.1371/journal.pcbi.1000532
13. George, D.: How the brain might work: a hierarchical and temporal model for learning and recognition. Stanford University (2008)
14. Samsonovich, A.V.: Emotional biologically inspired cognitive architecture. Biol. Inspired Cogn. Arch. **6**, 109–125 (2013). https://doi.org/10.1016/j.bica.2013.07.009
15. Newell, A.: Unified Theories of Cognition. Harvard University Press, Cambridge (1990)
16. Aitygulov, E., Kiselev, G., Panov, A.I.: Task and spatial planning by the cognitive agent with human-like knowledge representation. In: Ronzhin, A., Rigoll, G., Meshcheryakov, R. (eds.) ICR 2018. LNCS (LNAI), vol. 11097, pp. 1–12. Springer, Cham (2018). https://doi.org/10.1007/978-3-319-99582-3_1
17. Kiselev, G., Kovalev, A., Panov, A.I.: Spatial reasoning and planning in sign-based world model. In: Kuznetsov, S.O., Osipov, G.S., Stefanuk, V.L. (eds.) RCAI 2018. CCIS, vol. 934, pp. 1–10. Springer, Cham (2018). https://doi.org/10.1007/978-3-030-00617-4_1
18. Osipov, G.S., Panov, A.I.: Relationships and operations in a sign-based world model of the actor. Sci. Tech. Inf. Process. **45**(5), 317–330 (2018)
19. Panov, A.I.: Behavior planning of intelligent agent with sign world model. Biol. Inspired Cogn. Arch. **19**, 21–31 (2017)
20. Osipov, G.S., Panov, A.I., Chudova, N.V.: Behavior control as a function of consciousness. II. Synthesis of a behavior plan. J. Comput. Syst. Sci. Int. **54**, 882–896 (2015)
21. Kiselev, G.A., Panov, A.I.: Synthesis of the behavior plan for group of robots with sign based world model. In: Ronzhin, A., Rigoll, G., Meshcheryakov, R. (eds.) ICR 2017. LNCS (LNAI), vol. 10459, pp. 83–94. Springer, Cham (2017). https://doi.org/10.1007/978-3-319-66471-2_10
22. Map-core library. https://github.com/cog-isa/map-planner/tree/map-core

Embodiment as a Necessary a Priori of General Intelligence

David Kremelberg[(✉)]

Icelandic Institute for Intelligent Machines, Reykjavik, Iceland
`david.kremelberg@uconn.edu`

Abstract. This paper presents the most important neuroscientific findings relevant to embodiment, including findings relating to the importance of embodiment in the development of higher-order cognitive functioning, including language, and discusses these findings in relation to
Artificial General Intelligence (AGI). Research strongly suggests the
necessity of embodiment in the individual development of advanced cognition. Generalizing from this body of literature, conclusions focus on
the importance of incorporating a physical body in the development of
AGI in a meaningful and profound way in order for AGI to be achieved.

1 Introduction

Work conducted in the field of neuroscience suggests the presence of a physical
body may be necessary for the development of advanced cognitive functions,
including language, and it has been argued that embodiment may be necessary for abstract and symbolic thought. Despite this, a focus on robotics, or
more specifically, embodiment within AGI remains rare, with theoretical and
philosophical discussion pertinent to embodiment and its importance also being
uncommon. This paper presents a summary of evidence drawn from neuroscience
suggesting the necessity of embodiment in achieving advanced cognitive functioning, along with the importance of real experience, and how embodiment
may solve the symbol grounding problem. All of the above produces a number of important implications in relation to AGI, and by extension, general
intelligence.

2 The Neuroscientific Basis Behind Embodiment

There exists a substantial body of evidence from the field of neuroscience suggesting the importance, or more strongly, necessity of embodiment in the achievement of advanced cognitive functions in humans. Within this and related fields,
theories of embodied cognition suggest no separation between cognitive processing considered more rudimentary, such as perception and action, and what are
considered higher-level processes, including language and thought [7]. According
to this view, cognition associated with these "high" and "low" level processes is

© Springer Nature Switzerland AG 2019
P. Hammer et al. (Eds.): AGI 2019, LNAI 11654, pp. 132–136, 2019.
https://doi.org/10.1007/978-3-030-27005-6_13

not processed in different domains. Similarly, language comprehension is thought to recruit the same sensorimotor areas as are recruited when interacting with the environment [3,4,7,11] and the state of the world described using language is thought to be simulated when this language is comprehended [5,16]. The key issue here is grounding; theories of embodied cognition suggest not only that the same neural units ground both actions as well as the language which refers to actions, but within this sensorimotor basis for cognition [12,14], the sensorimotor system also provides the grounding for abstract concepts [7]. Various proposals have been put forth within this school of thought with regard to how these abstractions might work [6]. Additionally, the embodied view of cognition is further supported by thoughts being composed of modality-specific representations, and with perception, thought, and action being co-constituted, or constitutively interdependent [12].

In particular, visio-motor processing, and specifically, manipulation, have been cited as necessary for higher cognitive development - which includes abilities such as social behavior and language [10]. Within the context of language comprehension, sensorimotor areas in the brain have been found to be closely linked to language processing, and with the motor system having an important role in language comprehension [7]. All of this suggests sensorimotor capabilities and relevant components of the brain are necessary for the achievement of our language abilities, and that mechanical or electronic counterparts of these may be necessary for language acquisition in machines, along with other advanced cognitive functions.

3   The Necessity of Embodiment and Sense Experience

An issue rarely discussed is the potential necessity of a body for the purposes of achieving general intelligence. One question that has been raised is the extent to which the body influences the brain, whether it impacts the way in which we think, and if the world must be experienced in order to be understood [15]. Work in the field of embodied cognition suggests that cognition is much more dependent on a physical body as has been assumed [12,15], with some stating that interactions are imperative for shaping the rapidly growing brain [10], and others arguing that the body is intimately connected with learning, even the learning of abstract concepts, such as mathematics [1], and that even symbol manipulation is embodied, activating "naturalistic perceptuomotor schemes that come from being corporeal agents operating in spatial-dynamical realities" [1, p. 2].

Evolutionarily, brains have always developed within the context of a body that interacts with the world to survive [15], while the vast majority of the work done in AGI has ignored this fact. Some have cited the necessity of machines acquiring their own experiences if human-level intelligence is a goal - and the fact that memories relate to something done with the body, or some real experience [15]. Without embodiment, agents cannot learn through experience, while approaches not incorporating embodiment assume that representations of physical objects can be sufficiently constructed through only theoretical measures [15].

However, simulations are inherently limited, while goal-oriented behavior derives its success from experience: even the simple task of picking up an object is easily accomplished only due to our past physical experiences with such objects.

All of this suggests that intelligence requires a physical body that interacts with the world, and that intelligence needs to grow and develop over time concomitant with experience, as opposed to being pre-programmed, with embodiment and sense experience being intimately connected with cognition. It has been argued that even abstract thought is rooted in our physical experiences with the world - that we have a large set of basic concepts which relate to our body and how we move in space, and that more advanced and abstract concepts build upon these [8,9]. It has even been suggested that conceptions like happiness would differ in different bodies [8,9] - which implies that all emotions, and maybe all concepts, as well as the nature and form of consciousness, may vary on the basis of the physical form of the agent.

Additionally, embodiment also assists with the symbol grounding problem [12]. In humans, meaning is imbued in objects and the words that represent them through our experiences with these objects, our history with them, our memories, and so forth. Grounding even a single concept is thought to require a set of physical skills and experiences which are very specific; for example, grounding the word "chair" involves reliable detection of these objects, as well as responding appropriately to them [2]. Incorporating physicality in agents should allow them to gain similar experiences to ours, which should allow for grounding by attaching meaning to physical objects as well as their representation of these objects. This grounding would allow for a connection to the real world which, so far, has not been attained by any artificial agent, while also allowing for cooperation and communication, which have been said require symbolic thought [10]. This is also highlights the importance of the extent to which this physicality may need to be similar to ours, and with all forms of sensory perception being active processes, with sensory experiences being tied to movement, this would suggest the insufficiency of simply adding sensors to a robot [15].

4   Conclusions

Searle argues that machines cannot understand, as they simply operate on the level of symbol manipulation [13]. Agreeing that an agent that only manipulates meaningless symbols is qualitatively different from one whose symbols are grounded and are linked to other grounded symbols, the question then becomes how to imbue meaning in the symbols used by machines. With the literature suggesting that meaning is imbued through embodied experience, if this is not the only way in which machines can be created whose symbols are meaningful to themselves, it may at least be an efficient approach to creating such an entity.

While those in AGI have realized the probable errors of the approaches used in AI in the attempt to create general intelligence, the work done in the field still largely encapsulates the view that cognition can be reduced to a series of algorithms; input, processing, and output. Furthermore, the idea that knowledge of how intelligence develops may be necessary in order to replicate it has largely been ignored. All of this would suggest an embodiment-focused approach to AGI, which, as stated, would not simply involve the addition of sensors to a robotic body, but would allow for a richer and fuller qualitative experience, akin to the qualitative deepness of the sensory experience and the nature of embodiment experienced by humans. In addition, this would further suggest a strong focus on the use of learning algorithms similar to those manifested in the human brain, and that through extensive and continuous interaction with the environment, AGI would be achieved. AGI may not be expected to bootstrap from nothing; in the case of many artificial agents, some innate abilities as those manifested in babies are pre-programmed [10]; this may at least be conducive to the bootstrapping process without impeding the path to AGI. Similar arguments could be made for our other innate abilities such as language.

In sum, strong evidence exists for the necessity of embodiment in grounding and the development of advanced cognitive functions, including language, and this evidence likely applies to all agents, which suggests that embodiment and experience is a necessary a priori for AGI. An embodiment approach should allow machines to think about and understand concepts in a manner which is no less in quality than that of a human. This suggests the great importance of those in AGI to not simply put their system in a robotic body or to add sensors, but for the entire process of development to be intimately connected with embodiment; great detail should be afforded to the body from the earliest planning stages, and with no detail planned or made without consideration of the body, and for the artificial body to be as similar as possible to a human body. This then suggests the importance of those in AGI to be working closely with those in the field of robotics; associations should be made, and these two groups of researchers should be closely collaborating on AGI projects as partners.

Acknowledgments. I would like to thank Kristinn R. Thórisson for his generous assistance as a mentor and in reviewing this paper.

References

1. Abrahamson, D., Lindgren, R.: Embodiment and embodied design. In: Sawyer, R.K. (ed.) The Cambridge Handbook of the Learning Sciences, 2nd edn, pp. 358–376. Cambridge University Press, Cambridge, UK (2014)
2. Anderson, M.L.: Embodied cognition: a field guide. Artif. Intell. **149**, 91–130 (2003)
3. Barsalou, L.W.: Grounded cognition. Annu. Rev. Psychol. **59**, 617–645 (2008)
4. Fischer, M., Zwaan, R.: Embodied language: a review of the role of the motor system in language comprehension. Q. J. Exp. Psychol. **61**, 825–850 (2008)
5. Gallese, V.: Mirror neurons and the social nature of language: the neural exploitation hypothesis. Soc. Neurosci. **3**, 317–333 (2008)
6. Glenberg, A.M., Sato, M., Cattaneo, L., Riggio, L., Palumbo, D., Buccino, G.: Processing abstract language modulates motor system activity. Q. J. Exp. Psychol. **61**, 905–919 (2008)
7. Jirak, D., Menz, M.M., Buccino, G., Borghi, A.M., Binkofski, F.: Grasping language - a short story on embodiment. Conscious. Cogn. **19**, 711–720 (2010)

8. Lakoff, G., Johnson, M.: Metaphors We Live By. University of Chicago Press, Chicago (1980)
9. Lakoff, G., Johnson, M.: Philosophy in the Flesh: The Embodied Mind and Its Challenge to Western Thought. Basic Books, New York (1999)
10. Nosengo, N.: The bot that plays ball. Nature **460**, 1076–1078 (2009)
11. Pulvermuller, F.: Brain mechanisms linking language and action. Nat. Rev. Neurosci. **6**(7), 576–582 (2005)
12. Robbins, P., Aydede, M.: A short primer on situated cognition. In: Robbins, P., Aydede, M. (eds.) The Cambridge Handbook of Situated Cognition, pp. 3–10. Cambridge University Press, New York (2012)
13. Searle, J.: Minds, brains and programs. Behav. Brain Sci. **3**(3), 417–457 (1980)
14. Wang, P.: Embodiment: does a laptop have a body? In: Proceedings of the Second Conference on Artificial General Intelligence, pp. 174–179 (2009)
15. Weigmann, K.: Does intelligence require a body? EMBO Rep. **13**(12), 1066–1069 (2012)
16. Zwann, R.: The immersed experiencer: toward an embodied theory of language comprehension. In: Ross, B.H. (ed.) Psychology of Learning and Motivation, vol. 44, pp. 35–62. Academic Press, New York (2004)

Computable Prediction

Kenshi Miyabe[✉]

Department of Mathematics, Meiji University, Kawasaki, Kanagawa, Japan
research@kenshi.miyabe.name
http://kenshi.miyabe.name/wordpress

Abstract. We try to predict the next bit from a given finite binary string when the sequence is sampled from a computable probability measure on the Cantor space. There exists the best betting strategy among a class of effective ones up to a multiplicative constant, the induced prediction from which is called algorithmic probability or universal induction by Solomonoff. The prediction converges to the true induced measure for sufficiently random sequences. However, the prediction is not computable.

We propose a framework to study the properties of computable predictions. We prove that all sufficiently general computable predictions also converge to the true induced measure. The class of sequences along which the prediction converges is related to computable randomness. We also discuss the speed of the convergence. We prove that, even when a computable prediction predicts a computable sequence, the speed of the convergence cannot be bounded by a computable function monotonically decreasing to 0.

Keywords: Algorithmic probability · Universal induction · Computable randomness

1 Introduction

Given data, one finds regularity and predicts the future. This is what all living things are doing and what we want to make machines do. Is there a universal way of doing this? If so, what properties should the prediction have?

Solomonoff's algorithmic probability or universal induction answers. For simplicity, consider the case of infinite binary sequences, that is, the Cantor space 2^ω. We try to predict the next bit from a given finite binary string. It is known that there is an optimal c.e. semi-measure M on the Cantor space. Here, a function is c.e. if it can be computably approximated from below and optimality means that it dominates all c.e. semi-measures up to a multiplicative constant. See the definition in Sect. 2.1. By the usual correspondence between measures and martingales (or semi-measures and supermartingales), this roughly means that the prediction by M behaves at least as well as one by any c.e. semi-measure. The prediction induced from an optimal c.e. semi-measure is called *algorithmic probability* or *universal induction*.

© Springer Nature Switzerland AG 2019
P. Hammer et al. (Eds.): AGI 2019, LNAI 11654, pp. 137–147, 2019.
https://doi.org/10.1007/978-3-030-27005-6_14

Algorithmic probability has some desirable properties. One of them is the convergence to the true induced measure (Theorem 2.3 below). This roughly means that algorithmic probability can find any computable regularity unknown in advance.

In this paper, we propose a framework showing that all sufficiently general prediction should have some properties. That a program has a property does not mean that the program is general enough, however, that a program does not have a property means that the program can be modified to a more general one. By evaluating computational complexity that a function with a property should have, we can also discuss how difficult to add the property although we do not discuss much this in this paper.

We focus on the speed of the convergence. One of our results (Theorem 4.4) says that, for all sufficiently general computable predictions, the speed of the convergence to the true measure cannot be bounded by a computable function. Thus, incomputability of the rate of the convergence is not by the incomputability of algorithmic probability. Rather than that, it is by the existence of computable measures that are "close" to each other.

The structure of the paper as follows. In Sect. 2 we review some notions and results on algorithmic randomness and algorithmic probability. In Sect. 3 we prove the convergence result for computable predictions along computably random sequences. In Sect. 4 we consider the case of Dirac measures and show the incomputability of the rate of the convergence.

2   Preliminaries

2.1   Algorithmic Randomness

We follow the notation in computability theory (see e.g. [10]) or the theory of algorithmic randomness (see e.g. [1,8]).

The Cantor space 2^ω is the class of all infinite binary sequences equipped with the topology generated by the base elements of the cylinders $[\sigma] = \{X \in 2^\omega : \sigma \prec X\}$ where $\prec$ denotes the prefix relation. A function $f : \omega \to \omega$ is *computable* if it is computable by a Turing machine. The computability on $\mathbb{Q}$ or $2^{<\omega}$ is naturally induced by their natural representation by ω. A real $x \in \mathbb{R}$ is called *computable* if there exists a computable sequence $(a_n)_{n \in \omega}$ of rationals such that $|x - a_n| \le 2^{-n}$ for all n. A real $x \in \mathbb{R}$ is called *left-c.e.* if there exists an increasing computable sequence $(a_n)_{n \in \omega}$ of rationals.

A function $f : 2^{<\omega} \to \mathbb{R}$ is called *computable* or *c.e.* if $f(\sigma)$ is computable or left-c.e. uniformly in $\sigma \in 2^{<\omega}$, respectively. A measure μ on 2^ω is *computable* if the function $\sigma \mapsto \mu([\sigma]) =: \mu(\sigma)$ is computable. A *semi-measure* is a function $\mu : 2^{<\omega} \to [0,1]$ such that $\mu(\lambda) \le 1$ and $\mu(\sigma) \ge \mu(\sigma 0) + \mu(\sigma 1)$ for every $\sigma \in 2^{<\omega}$ where λ denotes the empty string. A measure μ with $\mu(\lambda) = \mu(2^\omega) = 1$ is called a *probability* measure. Notice that each semi-measure μ satisfying $\mu(\lambda) = 1$ and $\mu(\sigma) = \mu(\sigma 0) + \mu(\sigma 1)$ for every $\sigma \in 2^{<\omega}$ can be seen as a probability measure.

Let μ, ν be measures or semi-measures on 2^ω. We say μ *multiplicatively dominates* (or m-dominates) ν if, there exists $C \in \omega$ such that $\nu(\sigma) \le C\mu(\sigma)$ for all

$\sigma \in 2^{<\omega}$. A c.e. semi-measure μ is called *optimal* if μ m-dominates every c.e. semi-measure. An optimal c.e. semi-measure exists.

Fix a computable probability measure μ. Martin-Löf randomness (or ML-randomness) is an important concept to talk about randomness of individual sequences. ML-randomness is usually defined by tests, but we give an equivalent characterization to compare it with the definition of computable randomness below. Let $X_{\leq n} = X_1 X_2 \cdots X_n$ be the initial segment of X with length n.

Theorem 2.1 ([6]). *A sequence $X \in 2^\omega$ is ML-random w.r.t. μ (or μ-ML-random) if and only if there exists a constant $C \in \omega$ such that $\xi(X_{\leq n}) \leq C\mu(X_{\leq n})$ for all n, where ξ is an optimal c.e. semi-measure.*

By the optimality, this is equivalent to the following statement: For every c.e. semi-measure ξ, there exists a constant $C \in \omega$ such that $\xi(X_{\leq n}) \leq C\mu(X_{\leq n})$ for all n.

The central notion in this paper is computable randomness. Computable randomness for the uniform measure is defined by martingales. However, Rute [9] has suggested the following definition for a general computable probability measure.

Definition 2.2. *A sequence $X \subset 2^\omega$ is computably random w.r.t. μ (or μ-computably random) if $\mu(X_{\leq n}) > 0$ for all n and $\limsup_n \xi(X_{\leq n})/\mu(X_{\leq n}) < \infty$ for all computable measures ξ.*

It is not difficult to see that this is equivalent to the following statement: For every computable measure ξ, there exists a constant $C \in \omega$ such that $\xi(X_{\leq n}) \leq C\mu(X_{\leq n})$ for all n. ML-randomness implies computable randomness, but the converse does not hold in general.

2.2 Algorithmic Probability

We review some results from algorithmic probability. For details, see e.g. [2].

Let μ be an optimal c.e. semi-measure. Fix a sequence $X \in 2^\omega$. We are interested in the ratio

$$\mu(k|X_{<n}) = \frac{\mu(X_{<n}k)}{\mu(X_{<n})},$$

where $X_{<n} = X_1 \cdots X_{n-1}$ and $k \in \{0,1\}$. Notice that X_0 denotes the empty string. The function $k \mapsto \mu(k|X_{<n})$ is a measure on $\{0,1\}$ but the measure of the whole space $\{0,1\}$ need not be 1. The ratio can be understood as the conditional probability of the n-th bit given the initial $(n-1)$ bits of X, and is called *algorithmic probability*.

One of the desirable properties of algorithmic probability is the following convergence to the true induced measure.

Theorem 2.3. *Let μ be a computable probability measure on 2^ω and ξ be an optimal c.e. semi-measure. Suppose $X \in 2^\omega$ is sampled from μ. Then,*

$$\xi(k|X_{<n}) - \mu(k|X_{<n}) \to 0 \ as \ n \to \infty \tag{1}$$

for both $k \in \{0,1\}$ and

$$\frac{\xi(X_n|X_{<n})}{\mu(X_n|X_{<n})} \to 1 \ as \ n \to \infty \tag{2}$$

with μ-probability 1.

The convergence (1) is called the *convergence in difference* by Solomonoff [11]. The convergence (2) is called the *convergence in ratio* in Li-Vitányi's book [7, Theorem 5.2.2, p. 433]. Remark the difference between on-sequence and off-sequence. The speed of the convergence is one of our interest, which has been discussed briefly in [3] but has not been established.

2.3 Distance Measures Between Probability Measures

The following notions are important in the proof of the convergence. For probability measures μ, ξ on $\{0,1\}$, we define the *squared Hellinger distance* $H^2(\nu, \xi)$ by

$$H^2(\mu, \xi) = \frac{1}{2} \sum_{k \in \{0,1\}} (\sqrt{\mu(k)} - \sqrt{\xi(k)})^2 = 1 - \sum_{k \in \{0,1\}} \sqrt{\mu(k)\xi(k)}.$$

From the equalities above, $0 \le H^2(\mu, \xi) \le 1$. We also use the Kullback-Leibler divergence (or KL-divergence) of μ with respect to ξ defined by

$$D(\mu||\xi) = \sum_{k \in \{0,1\}} \mu(k) \ln \frac{\mu(k)}{\xi(k)}$$

where ln is the natural logarithm and $0 \cdot \ln \frac{0}{z} = 0$ for $z \ge 0$ and $y \ln \frac{y}{0} = \infty$ for $y > 0$. The two notions are related by the following inequality:

$$2H^2(\mu, \xi) \le D(\mu||\xi). \tag{3}$$

One can check this by direct calculation or see Hutter [2, Lemma 3.11h].

3 Convergence Along Computable Random Sequences

3.1 Convergence Results

Algorithmic probability is computably approximable or Δ_2^0 but not computable while all the functions we can implement are computable. The correct or ideal prediction may have some properties that algorithmic probability has, however, implementing a program with one of such properties may be impossible. Thus, this does not say anything about whether our implementable prediction should have the properties. That a program does not have one of such properties does not say that the program is not general enough.

The goal of this paper is to give a framework to study the properties of computable measures or predictions. Algorithmic probability uses an optimal c.e. semi-measure while no computable measure m-dominates all computable measures. We abandon to pursue the unique correct prediction. Instead, we ask the following:

Which properties do all sufficiently general predictions have?

Notice that this statement is about a prediction that can be implemented in reality.

As a definition of the "generality" above, we use m-domination inspired by the definition of optimality. More concretely, we construct a computable measure ν such that a property P holds for all computable measures m-dominating ν. This means that P holds for all sufficiently general predictions. There are many quantifiers, and we will see that their order is important.

Suppose that, a property P is witnessed by a computable measure ν_P, that is, all computable measures ξ m-dominating ν_P have the properties P. Similarly, suppose that a property Q is witnessed by a computable measure ν_Q. Then, the property $P \wedge Q$ is witnessed by the computable measure $(\nu_P + \nu_Q)/2$. The composition of properties can be extended into computable countable sum.

Some property P may be witnessed by a measure μ executable in feasible time. If some good prediction induced from ν does not have the property P, then the prediction by $\epsilon\mu + (1-\epsilon)\nu$ for a positive rational ϵ is more general than ν in the sense above, and the computation cost may be still reasonable.

Now, we give computable versions of Theorem 2.3 as follows.

Theorem 3.1. *Let μ be a computable probability measure on 2^ω. For all computable probability measures ξ m-dominating μ and for all μ-computably random sequence $X \in 2^\omega$, we have*

$$\sum_{n=1}^{\infty} D(\mu(\cdot|X_{<n}) \,\|\, \xi(\cdot|X_{<n})) < \infty.$$

In particular,

$$\xi(k|X_{<n}) - \mu(k|X_{<n}) \to 0 \ as \ n \to \infty$$

for both $k \in \{0,1\}$.

Theorem 3.2. *Let μ be a computable probability measure. For all computable probability measure ξ m-dominating μ and for all μ-computably random sequence $X \in 2^\omega$, we have*

$$\frac{\xi(X_n|X_{<n})}{\mu(X_n|X_{<n})} \to 1 \ as \ n \to \infty.$$

Notice that both Theorems 3.1 and 3.2 claim the existence of a computable measure $\nu(=\mu)$ such that for all computable measures ξ m-dominating ν have some properties, that is, all sufficiently general computable measures have some properties.

Hutter and Muchnik [3] has shown that "μ-probability 1" in Theorem 2.3 cannot be replaced by "for all μ-ML-random sequences X." The above theorem says that, for a computable probability measure, we only need μ-computable randomness.

3.2   Martingale Characterization and Convergence

We use a martingale characterization of computable randomness and a convergence theorem of martingales. The following characterization is due to [9].

Definition 3.3. *Let μ be a computable probability measure. A martingale M with respect to μ is a partial function $M :\subseteq 2^{<\omega} \to \mathbb{R}^+$ such that the following two conditions hold:*

(i) *(Impossibility condition) If $M(\sigma)$ is undefined, then $\mu(\sigma) = 0$.*
(ii) *(Fairness condition) For all $\sigma \in 2^{<\omega}$, we have*

$$M(\sigma 0)\mu(\sigma 0) + M(\sigma 1)\mu(\sigma 1) = M(\sigma)\mu(\sigma)$$

where undefined $\cdot\, 0 = 0$ and $\mathbb{R}^+$ is the set of all non-negative reals.

We say M is an almost-everywhere computable martingale *(or a.e. computable martingale) if M is a partial computable function. We say M succeeds on $X \in 2^\omega$ if $\limsup_{n\to\infty} M(X_{\le n}) = \infty$.*

Proposition 3.4. *Let μ be a computable probability measure on 2^ω. Then, $X \in 2^\omega$ is μ-computably random if and only if $\mu(X_{\le n}) > 0$ for all n and there is no a.e. computable martingale M which succeeds on X.*

Computable randomness with respect to the uniform measure can be characterized as the existence of the limit along the sequence for all computable martingales (see, e.g. [1, Theorem 7.1.3]) by using Doob's upcrossing argument. The same method can be applied for any computable measure.

Proposition 3.5. *Let μ be a computable probability measure on 2^ω. Then, $X \in 2^\omega$ is μ-computably random if and only if $\lim_{n\to\infty} M(X_{\le n})$ exists for all a.e. computable martingales M.*

3.3   Proof of Theorem 3.1

Proof. Since ξ m-dominates μ, there exists a constant $C \in \omega$ such that

$$\mu(\sigma) \le C\xi(\sigma) \tag{4}$$

for all $\sigma \in 2^{<\omega}$. Let $D(\sigma)$ be the KL-divergence of μ w.r.t. ξ at σ, that is,

$$D(\sigma) = D(\mu(\cdot|\sigma) \| \xi(\cdot|\sigma)).$$

We define a function $M :\subseteq 2^{<\omega} \to \mathbb{R}^+$ by

$$M(\sigma) = \ln C - \ln \frac{\mu(\sigma)}{\xi(\sigma)} + \sum_{t=1}^{|\sigma|} D(\sigma_{<t})$$

for every $\sigma \in 2^{<\omega}$.

We claim that M is an a.e. computable martingale w.r.t. μ. The function M is non-negative because of (4) and the non-negativeness of D. For the impossibility condition of Definition 3.3, notice that, if $\mu(\sigma) > 0$, then $\xi(\sigma) > 0$ because ξ m-dominates μ, thus $M(\sigma)$ is defined. Then, the a.e. computability of M follows from the computability of μ, ξ, and D. For the fairness condition,

$$\sum_{k \in \{0,1\}} \mu(\sigma k)M(\sigma k) - \mu(\sigma)M(\sigma) = - \sum_{k \in \{0,1\}} \mu(\sigma k) \ln \frac{\mu(k|\sigma)}{\xi(k|\sigma)} + \mu(\sigma)D(\sigma) = 0.$$

Since X is μ-computably random, we have $\limsup_n M(X_{\leq n}) < \infty$. Since both $\ln C - \ln \frac{\mu(\sigma)}{\xi(\sigma)}$ and $D(\sigma)$ are always non-negative, $\sum_{n=1}^{\infty} D(X_{\leq n})$ also converges. Finally, the last claim of the theorem follows by (3). $\qquad\square$

3.4   Proof of Theorem 3.2

Proof. Suppose that ξ is a computable measure m-dominating the measure μ. We define a function $M : 2^{<\omega} \to \mathbb{R}^+$ by

$$M(\sigma) = \frac{\xi(\sigma)}{\mu(\sigma)}.$$

Then, M is a a.e. computable martingale w.r.t. μ. Hence, $\lim_n M(X_{\leq n}) = \alpha$ exists for all μ-computably random sequences $X \in 2^{\omega}$.

Since ξ m-dominates μ, there exists $C \in \omega$ such that $\mu(\sigma) \leq C\xi(\sigma)$ for every $\sigma \in 2^{<\omega}$. Then,

$$M(X_{\leq n}) = \frac{\xi(X_{\leq n})}{\mu(X_{\leq n})} \geq \frac{1}{C}$$

for every n. Thus, $\alpha \geq \frac{1}{C}$.

Fix $\epsilon > 0$. Then, there exists $N \in \omega$ such that

$$\left| \frac{\xi(X_{\leq n})}{\mu(X_{\leq n})} - \alpha \right| = |M(X_{\leq n}) - \alpha| \leq \frac{\epsilon}{3C}$$

for all $n \geq N$. Thus,

$$\frac{\xi(X_n|X_{\leq n})}{\mu(X_n|X_{\leq n})} = \frac{\xi(X_{\leq n})}{\mu(X_{\leq n})} \cdot \frac{\mu(X_{<n})}{\xi(X_{<n})} \leq \frac{\alpha + \epsilon/(3C)}{\alpha - \epsilon/(3C)} = 1 + \epsilon \cdot \frac{2}{3\alpha C - \epsilon} < 1 + \epsilon$$

for all $n \geq N + 1$ if ϵ is sufficiently small. Similarly, $\frac{\xi(X_n|X_{\leq n})}{\mu(X_n|X_{\leq n})} > 1 - \epsilon$ for all $n \geq N + 1$. Since ϵ is arbitrary, the claim follows. $\qquad\square$

4   Non-computability of the Convergence

From now on, we only consider the case that μ is the Dirac measure on a point $A \in 2^\omega$. If μ is computable, then A should be computable. Theorem 3.1 in this case can be written as follows.

Corollary 4.1. *Let $A \in 2^\omega$ be a computable sequence. There exists a computable measure ν such that*

$$\sum_n (1 - \xi(A_n|A_{<n})) < \infty \tag{5}$$

for all computable measures ξ m-dominating ν. In particular, $\xi(A_n|A_{<n}) \to 1$ as $n \to \infty$.

Proof. Let μ be the Dirac measure on the point $A \in 2^\omega$. Then, A is μ-computably random. By Theorem 3.1, we have $\sum_{n=1}^\infty \ln \frac{1}{\xi(A_n|A_{<n})} < \infty$. Finally, notice that

$$\sum_n \ln(1 - (1 - \xi(A_n|A_{<n}))) > -\infty \iff \sum_n (1 - \xi(A_n|A_{<n})) < \infty.$$

$\square$

All sufficiently general computable measures can detect the pattern of a computable sequence A while no computable measure can detect the pattern of all computable sequences. One needs to pay attention to the order or quantifiers.

Remark 4.2. *For each computable measure ξ, there exists a computable sequence A such that $\xi(A_n|A_{<n})$ does not converge to 1.*

This claim is essentially the same as a famous fact in algorithmic learning theory that the class of all computable sequences is not BC-learnable. See e.g. [12] for a survey on algorithmic learning theory. A stronger result in the context of universal induction is in [4, Lemma 5.2.4]. For the sake of self-containedness, we give a short proof here in our terminology.

Proof. Let $(\epsilon_n)_n$ be a computable sequence of positive rationals such that $\epsilon_n < \frac{1}{2}$ for all n and $\prod_n (1 + \epsilon_n) < \infty$. For each σ, at least one of $i \in \{0,1\}$ satisfies $\xi(\sigma i) < \frac{1+\epsilon_{|\sigma|}}{2}\xi(\sigma)$. This is a c.e. relation and one can compute such i from σ uniformly. By iterating this, one can compute a sequence A such that $\xi(A_{\leq n}) < \frac{1+\epsilon_n}{2}\xi(A_{<n})$ for all n. Since $\epsilon_n \to 0$, we have

$$\limsup_n \xi(A_n|A_{<n}) \leq \limsup_n \frac{1 + \epsilon_n}{2} \leq \frac{1}{2}.$$

$\square$

The following theorem says that all sufficiently general predictions $\xi(A_n|A_{<n})$ are not too close to 1; they have almost the same convergence speed (5) up to a multiplicative constant. The convergence speed $\xi(\overline{A_n}|A_{<n})$ to 0 is the slowest one among the sequences whose sum converge. Let $\overline{k} = 1 - k$ for $k \in \{0,1\}$.

Theorem 4.3. *Let $A \in 2^\omega$ be a computable sequence and $(a_n)_n$ be a computable sequence of positive rationals such that $\sum_n a_n < \infty$. Then, there exists a computable measure ν with the following property: For each computable measure ξ m-dominating ν, there exists a natural number $C \in \omega$ such that*

$$\xi(\overline{A_n}|A_{<n}) \geq \frac{a_n}{C}$$

for all n.

Notice that $(a_n)_n$ need not be monotone.

Proof. Without loss of generality, we can assume that $s = \sum_n a_n < 1$. Define a measure ν by

$$\nu = \sum_n a_n \mathbf{1}_{A_{<n}\overline{A_n}0^\omega} + (1-s)\mathbf{1}_A$$

where $\mathbf{1}_X$ is the point-mass measure on $X \in 2^\omega$.

We claim that this measure ν is computable. It suffices to show that $\nu(\sigma)$ is computable uniformly in $\sigma \in 2^{<\omega}$. If $\sigma \prec A$, then

$$\nu(\sigma) = \sum_{n \geq |\sigma|} a_n + 1 - s = 1 - \sum_{n < |\sigma|} a_n.$$

If $\sigma = A_{<k}\overline{A_k}0^i$ for some $k, i \in \omega$, then

$$\nu(\sigma) = a_k.$$

If $\sigma = A_{<k}\overline{A_k}0^i1\tau$ for some $k, i \in \omega$ and $\tau \in 2^{<\omega}$, then

$$\nu(\sigma) = 0.$$

In any case, $\nu(\sigma)$ is computable from n.

Suppose that a computable measure ξ m-dominates ν. Then, there exists $C \in \omega$ such that $\nu(\sigma) \leq C\xi(\sigma)$ for all $\sigma \in 2^{<\omega}$. Then,

$$\xi(\overline{A_n}|A_{<n}) = 1 - \frac{\xi(A_{\leq n})}{\xi(A_{<n})} = \frac{\xi(A_{<n}\overline{A_n})}{\xi(A_{<n})} \geq \frac{\nu(A_{<n}\overline{A_n})}{C} = \frac{a_n}{C}.$$

$\square$

The rate of convergence of $\xi(\overline{A_n}|A_{<n})$ to 0 is not monotone. In fact, it cannot be bounded by a decreasing computable function converging to 0.

Theorem 4.4. *Let $A \in 2^\omega$ be a computable sequence. Then, there exists a computable measure ν such that no decreasing computable sequence $(b_n)_n$ converging to 0 m-dominates $\xi(\overline{A_n}|A_{<n})$ for all computable measures ξ m-dominating ν.*

Proof. Let $U :\subseteq 2^{<\omega} \to 2^{<\omega}$ be a universal prefix-free machine. By the usual convention, $U(\sigma)[s] \uparrow$ for each $s < |\sigma|$. For all n, let

$$a_n = \sum_{\sigma} \{2^{-|\sigma|} : U(\sigma) \downarrow \text{ at stage } n\}.$$

Note that $(a_n)_n$ is a computable sequence because the possible σ should satisfy $|\sigma| \leq n$ by the convention. Furthermore,

$$\sum_n a_n = \sum_{\sigma \in \text{dom}(U)} 2^{-|\sigma|} < 1.$$

Then, by Theorem 4.3, there exists a computable measure ν such that $\nu(\overline{A_n}|A_{<n})$ m-dominates $(a_n)_n$.

Suppose that there exists a decreasing computable $(b_n)_n$ such that $b_n \to 0$ as $n \to \infty$ and $(b_n)_n$ m-dominates $\nu(\overline{A_n}|A_{<n})$. Then, $(b_n)_n$ also m-dominates $(a_n)_n$, and let $C \in \omega$ such that $a_n \leq 2^C b_n$ for all n.

For each σ, search the least $n \in \omega$ such that $b_n < 2^{-|\sigma|-C}$. If $U(\sigma)[n] \uparrow$ and $U(\sigma)[s] \downarrow$ for some $s > n$, then $a_s \geq 2^{-|\sigma|}$ by the definition of $(a_n)_n$, and

$$a_s \leq 2^C b_s \leq 2^C b_n < 2^{-|\sigma|},$$

which is a contradiction. Thus, $U(\sigma) \downarrow$ if and only if $U(\sigma)[n] \downarrow$. Since n is computable from σ uniformly, this means that the halting problem is computable, which is a contradiction. Hence, such $(b_n)_n$ does not exist. $\square$

It may be interesting to compare the above result to Laplace's answer to the sunrise problem. The answer $\frac{n}{n+1}$ is slightly slower than (5). Theorem 4.4 means that all sufficiently general prediction violates Nicod's criterion as the usual Solomonoff induction does [5].

References

1. Downey, R.G., Hirschfeldt, D.R.: Algorithmic randomness and complexity. Theory and Applications of Computability. Springer, New York (2010). https://doi.org/10.1007/978-0-387-68441-3
2. Hutter, M.: Universal Artificial Intelligence: Sequential Decisions Based on Algorithmic Probability. Springer, Heidelberg (2005). https://doi.org/10.1007/b138233
3. Hutter, M., Muchnik, A.: On semimeasures predicting Martin-Löf random sequences. Theor. Comput. Sci. **382**, 247–261 (2007)
4. Legg, S.: Machine super intelligence. Ph.D. thesis, Università della Svizzera italiana (2008)
5. Leike, J., Hutter, M.: Solomonoff induction violates Nicod's criterion. In: Chaudhuri, K., Gentile, C., Zilles, S. (eds.) ALT 2015. LNCS (LNAI), vol. 9355, pp. 349–363. Springer, Cham (2015). https://doi.org/10.1007/978-3-319-24486-0_23
6. Levin, L.A.: On the notion of a random sequence. Sov. Math. Dokl. **14**, 1413–1416 (1973)

7. Li, M., Vitányi, P.: An introduction to Kolmogorov complexity and its applications. Graduate Texts in Computer Science, 3rd edn. Springer, New York (2009). https://doi.org/10.1007/978-0-387-49820-1

8. Nies, A.: Computability and Randomness. Oxford Logic Guides, vol. 51. Oxford University Press, Oxford (2009). https://doi.org/10.1093/acprof:oso/9780199230761.001.0001

9. Rute, J.: Computable randomness and betting for computable probability spaces. Math. Log. Q. **62**(4–5), 335–366 (2016)

10. Soare, R.I.: Turing Computability. Theory and Applications of Computability. Springer, Heidelberg (2016). https://doi.org/10.1007/978-3-642-31933-4

11. Solomonoff, R.J.: Complexity-based induction systems: comparisons and convergence theorems. IEEE Trans. Inf. Theor. **IT-24**, 422–432 (1978)

12. Zeugmann, T., Zilles, S.: Learning recursive functions: a survey. Theor. Comput. Sci. **397**, 4–56 (2008)

Cognitive Module Networks for Grounded Reasoning

Alexey Potapov[1,2(✉)], Anatoly Belikov[1], Vitaly Bogdanov[1],
and Alexander Scherbatiy[1]

[1] SingularityNET Foundation, Amsterdam, The Netherlands
{alexey, abelikov, vitaly,
alexander.scherbatiy}@singularitynet.io
[2] ITMO University, St. Petersburg, Russia

Abstract. The necessity for neural-symbolic integration becomes evident as more complex problems like visual question answering are beginning to be addressed, which go beyond such limited-domain tasks as classification. Many existing state-of-the-art models are designed for a particular task or even benchmark, while general-purpose approaches are rarely applied to a wide variety of tasks demonstrating high performance. We propose a hybrid neural-symbolic framework, which tightly integrates the knowledge representation and symbolic reasoning mechanisms of the OpenCog cognitive architecture and one of the contemporary deep learning libraries, PyTorch, and show how to implement some existing particular models in our general framework.

Keywords: Grounded reasoning · Cognitive architectures ·
Neural module networks · Visual question answering

1 Introduction

Most contemporary cognitive architectures (CAs) are considered as hybrid [1]. However, it is difficult to find an architecture that tightly integrates a powerful symbolic reasoning with modern deep neural networks (DNNs). At the same time, such neural-symbolic integration of learning and reasoning constitutes a separate important field of research[1]. Unfortunately, there are just a few attempts to create a general framework, within which neural-symbolic models for solving different tasks can be developed. Moreover, conceptually sound approaches usually don't rely on the contemporary frameworks and practical models of deep learning and efficient engines of symbolic reasoning, but implement a particular type of models with specific inference procedures, for which mapping between neural networks and logical expressions is established (e.g. [2]).

Some general-purpose neural-symbolic frameworks, which combine contemporary DNN and symbolic reasoning tools, do exist. DeepProbLog [3] is one such frameworks. Unfortunately, examples of its applications are mostly limited to such toy

---

[1] http://www.neural-symbolic.org/.

© Springer Nature Switzerland AG 2019
P. Hammer et al. (Eds.): AGI 2019, LNAI 11654, pp. 148–158, 2019.
https://doi.org/10.1007/978-3-030-27005-6_15

problems as recognizing a pair of MNIST digits conditioned on their known sum. Other works on a hybrid neural-symbolic approach based on deep probabilistic programming (e.g. [4]) also don't show how state-of-the-art models for various benchmarks can be created within them. At the same time, one cán encounter a variety of modern individual solutions to specific problems based on ad hoc hybrid models, which are quite efficient, but narrowly applicable (e.g. the Transparency by Design, TbD, model [5]).

One of the prominent examples of this situation can be found in the field of visual reasoning, in particular, Visual Question Answering (VQA) that requires explicit reasoning capabilities. In particular, VQA implies variable binding, handling which is considered as a classical problem for connectionist models [6]. Although contemporary attention models incorporated into DNNs (in particular, in VQA [7]) partially address this problem, but without compositionality featured by symbolic approach.

On the one hand, DNNs achieve state-of-the-art results on some VQA datasets containing real-world images, and the use of contemporary DNN models and frameworks in visual processing seems essential. However, it is convincingly argued [8] that pure neural models tend to learn statistical biases in datasets (in particular, strong language priors, e.g. [9]) and to map inputs to outputs directly instead of explicitly modeling the underlying reasoning processes that results in a considerable decrease of performance on specially designed datasets (such as CLEVR [10] or GQA [11]). On the other hand, application of pure symbolic reasoning systems, which supposes that the input images are preliminarily processed by a vision subsystem and converted into symbolic form, is not robust and has low performance.

Apparently, hybrid solutions are desirable in order to account for all aspects of VQA. However, state-of-the-art VQA models frequently use narrow imperative program executors instead of general declarative reasoning systems (see, e.g. [5, 8]).

In this work, we propose a framework of hybridization of the integrative cognitive architecture OpenCog with symbolic inference engine operating on declarative knowledge bases with modern deep learning libraries supporting gradient descent optimization of differentiable functions over real-valued (subsymbolic) parameters.

Attempts to bridge the symbolic/subsymbolic gap via such hybridization of symbolic reasoning and deep neural networks in OpenCog has been done before [12, 13]. However, they were aimed at specific DNN architectures (a version of DeSTIN system and a hierarchical attractor neural network), and didn't support end-to-end training of the DNN model as a component of a pipeline that includes symbolic reasoning.

The proposed framework enables integration of OpenCog with arbitrary DNN models providing means to backpropagate errors from conclusions to DNNs through symbolic inference trees. This allowed us not only to reproduce the example used to illustrate DeepProbLog [3], but also to re-implement the TbD model [5] with the use of the general symbolic reasoning engine operating over declarative knowledge instead of imperative program executor specifically design for CLEVR VQA dataset.

2 Motivation: Grounded Reasoning

As it is shown in [14], the OpenCog's language Atomese suits well to express queries
about image content, for example, in the task of semantic image retrieval. These queries
are executed by OpenCog's reasoning subsystems such as the Unified Rule Engine
(URE), in particular, with the Probabilistic Logic Networks (PLN) rule set, and the
Pattern Matcher over the labels assigned by DNNs to the detected objects.

For example, the following query in Atomese can retrieve a video frame that
contains a bounding box recognized as a helicopter (and easily can be extended to more
complex queries):

```
BindLink
  VariableList
    VariableNode "$Frame"
    VariableNode "$BB"
  AndLink
    InheritanceLink
      VariableNode "$Frame"
      ConceptNode "Frame"
    InheritanceLink
      VariableNode "$BB"
      ConceptNode "Helicopter"
    MemberLink
      VariableNode "$BB"
      VariableNode "$Frame"
  ListLink
    VariableNode "$Frame"
    VariableNode "$BB"
```

Here, BindLink specifies the rule with three parts: a variable declaration, a pattern
to be found in Atomspace, a graph to be formed for each matched subgraph (for
different variable groundings). InheritanceLink is used to indicate that some
bounding box (which is distinguished by its name, e.g. ConceptNode "BB-03-11") is
recognized as an object of some specific class, and MemberLink is used to indicate that
the bounding box belongs to a certain frame. In order to successfully retrieve information, OpenCog will just need inheritance and member links for frames and bounding
boxes (each of which is represented as an atom, e.g. ConceptNode) to be stored in
Atomspace.

However, the simplest way to perform visual reasoning, which consists in preliminary processing images with DNNs and inserting the descriptions of the images
into Atomspace with consequent pure symbolic reasoning, is far from enough even in
the case of image retrieval. One may want to find images with either a happy child or a
jumping boy, which can be the same. This means that assigning one label per object or
bounding box in image is not enough.

The problem is even more obvious if we consider the task of VQA, in which more complex questions are frequent, e.g. "are the people looking in the same direction?" or "are the chairs similar?" Apparently, to answer these questions, one should not simply reason over symbolic labels, but should go down to the level of image features that implies a deeper neural-symbolic integration. Although complete disentanglement of reasoning from vision and language understanding can work for such datasets as CLEVR [15], we consider such disentanglement not as an achievement, but as over-simplification, which is not scalable to real-world reasoning.

Thus, what we want to make our system to reason about is not mere symbols, but symbols with their groundings (e.g. grounded predicates), which are calculated by demand in the course of reasoning.

Let us assume for example that we have a VQA system, which detects a number of bounding boxes (BBs) in the image and describes them with some high-level features (that is quite typical for models developed for some benchmarks [7]). A naïve neural-symbolic system will apply a multinomial classifier to these features to produce most probable labels for bounding boxes (maybe a few such classifiers to recognize objects and their attributes). Each output neuron of such classifier can be considered as a grounded predicate corresponding to a certain concept (e.g. "boy", "happy", etc.).

Instead of precomputing truth values of all these predicates, the system can compute only those predicates, which are necessary. For example, the question "Is the boy happy?" requires to check predicates "boy" and "happy", while the question "What color is the car?" can use a symbolic knowledge base to select predicates corresponding to concepts inherited from the concept "color".

Of course, this requires using a one-class classifier for each concept instead of a multinomial classifier, which can only calculate truth values of all predicates simul-taneously. However, this is not really a drawback, because no two concepts are pre-cisely mutually exclusive. A boy is also a child (and interestingly, we can frequently recognize children without recognizing them as boys or girls, so it is more likely that we use different grounded predicates to recognize classes and subclasses instead of recognizing subclasses only and inferring classes symbolically). Even more, an object can be simultaneously black and white, and even a boat can have a shape of a banana.

One can argue that all these predicates can still be pre-calculated before reasoning without too large overhead. However, it is not really the case, when we are talking about relations between objects in images, especially those, which require descending on the level of image features or even pixels.

Moreover, the reasoning system can influence the sequence of operations per-formed by the vision system or influence the output of different levels of the vision system by imposing priors dependent on the current state of the cognitive system (e.g. in neural-symbolic generative models). For example, in the TbD model, a sequence of applications of DNN modules is constructed in a symbolic (although not declarative) way (see Fig. 1).

Here, grounded predicates or functions are applied to the whole image instead of bounding boxes, and they produce attention maps and features that are fed to the next DNN modules, although one can imagine that modules are selected by the reasoning system dynamically depending on the already obtained results and background knowledge.

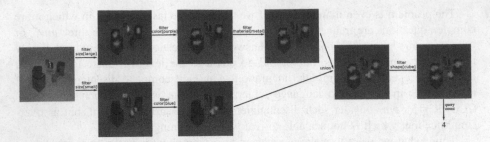

Fig. 1. Module network answering, "How many blocks are tiny blue objects or big purple metallic objects" (Color figure online)

Here, we aim not at discussing, what models better fit to visual (or, more generally, grounded) reasoning, but at designing a framework, which allows combining dynamically arbitrary DNN models with knowledge-based symbolic reasoning. Since one of the main motivations for this is to replace an ad hoc hand-coded imperative "reasoner" (program executor) in Neural Module Networks with an entire cognitive architecture, we call this approach Cognitive Module Networks.

3 Cognitive Module Networks

The best way to achieve the stated above goal would be to keep the possibility of using the DNN modules in the existing Neural Module Networks while replacing only hard-coded program executors with a general reasoning engine. Thus, what we need from OpenCog is to chain forward applications of DNN modules in a similar way as the program executors do. Technically important issue is the necessity to construct this chain of applications as an uninterrupted computation graph that supports error backpropagation by the corresponding DNN library.

On the side of OpenCog, such application can be carried out by executing `GroundedSchemaNodes` and `GroundedPredicateNodes` (which differ in that the former returns Atoms while the latter returns `TruthValues`). Some restrictions of the existing API for `GroundedSchemaNode` were to be overcome to achieve the necessary functionality. In particular, execution of methods of dynamically created objects rather than static objects, and passing tensors (data structures specific to a certain DNN library) between calls to `GroundedSchemaNodes` without conversion are desirable. Different solutions to these problems are possible. However, we will not go into technical detail here and focus more on a conceptual level.

Consider the following code in Atomese that corresponds to the question "Is the zebra fat?" (or more precisely, "Is there a fat zebra in the image?").

```
SatisfactionLink
  VariableNode "$X"
  AndLink
    InheritanceLink
      VariableNode "$X"
      ConceptNode "BoundingBox"
    EvaluationLink
      GroundedPredicateNode "py:runNN"
      ListLink(VariableNode("$X"), ConceptNode("zebra"))
    EvaluationLink
      GroundedPredicateNode "py:runNN"
      ListLink(VariableNode("$X"), ConceptNode("fat"))
```

Its execution by Pattern Matcher will cause the enumeration of all ConceptNodes that inherit from "BoundingBox" and pass them to the wrapper function runNN, which will take visual features for the given bounding box (e.g. attached as Values to ConceptNodes) and pass them to the DNN that corresponds to the provided class to be recognized (e.g. "zebra" or "fat"). Depending on implementation, it can be one DNN that accepts word embeddings as input, or there can be many small classifiers over high-level visual features (e.g. taken from ResNet or such) – each classifier for each concept. Then, runNN should convert the DNN output to OpenCog's Truth-Value, over which AndLink acts. Thus, all bounding boxes will be retrieved that classified simultaneously as "zebra" and "fat".

This simple code already does a sort of variable grounding for neural networks and use of declarative knowledge, which neural networks lack otherwise. However, this solution didn't allow for training DNNs based on conclusions made by the reasoner, and it has an ad hoc interface to run particular networks.

In the companion paper [16], we describe how differentiable rules for URE can be constructed that enables both learning tensor truth values and learning formulas for rules themselves by gradient descent. In this paper, we extend this approach by using predicates and schemas grounded in DNN models. More precisely, we focus more on a DNN-centered framework, which can be adopted by the deep learning community. Current implementation supports PyTorch backend, although Tensorflow and other backends can be added in the future.

As described in [16], if formulas attached to URE rules are implemented as operations on PyTorch tensors, application of a sequence of formulas corresponding to the chain of reasoning steps found by URE will yield a PyTorch computation graph, over which errors from final conclusions to PyTorch variables can be backpropagated. For example, PLN rule set for URE can help us to infer the truth value of the conclusion.

```
EvaluationLink
    PredicateNode "green"
    ConceptNode "apple-001"
```

using modus ponens from the truth values of premises:

```
ImplicationLink
    PredicateNode "apple"
    PredicateNode "green"
EvaluationLink
    PredicateNode "apple"
    ConceptNode "apple-001"
```

With the use of tensor truth values and PyTorch implementation of the formula for modus ponens, the error can be propagated from the truth value of the conclusion to the truth values of the premises.

If we replace `PredicateNode` in the above example with `GroundedPredicateNode`, which can in particular execute a DNN that outputs the probability that some object in an image can be recognized as an apple, then the PyTorch computation graph will include this DNN as a subgraph, and error will be propagated through the truth value (probability) produced by it to its weights. Instead of just adjusting truth values, we will train neural networks to output such values that lead to correct conclusions inferred by the reasoning system. Since the OpenCog reasoning subsystems perform the process of rewriting subgraphs of a (hyper)graph composed of Atoms, they can compose and execute an arbitrary graph (architecture) of neural modules.

In order to make this possible, DNN modules should be attached to atoms, to which variables in queries can be bound. CogNets library (its experimental implementation can be found here[2]) provides class `CogModule` that inherits from `torch.nn.Module`. On the one hand, `CogModule` objects can behave as ordinary `torch.nn.Module` objects implying that if we take some module network and change the inheritance of its modules to `CogModule`, it will continue working correctly. On the other hand, each `CogModule` object also attaches itself (through Values) to the specified Atom in Atomspace. Execution of neural modules attached to Atoms is done through a special `GroundedSchemaNode` that extracts `CogModule` objects from Atoms and passes arguments to them.

The basic application of CogNets will be to just inherit all modules in the TbD model from `CogModule`. Then, we will be able to use OpenCog to execute queries represented in the form of `BindLinks`. One question, which we don't consider in detail here, is how to obtain such queries from question in natural language. OpenCog contains natural language processing components, in particular RelEx, that can be used to parse questions and then convert them to Atomese queries. However, these components have some limitations. Another possibility is to reuse the pre-trained LSTM-based program generator from [8] (used in the TbD model also), which produces

[2] https://github.com/singnet/semantic-vision/tree/master/experiments/opencog/cog_module.

programs from questions, which they can be easily translated into Atomese. This approach works well for CLEVR, although cannot be applied to the COCO VQA benchmark in contrast to RelEx.

"Reasoning" in the TbD model is performed by executing an imperative program, composed of a sequence of applications of DNN modules. For example, the question "What color is the cylinder?" will be transformed to the consequent application of `filter_shape[cylinder]` module and `query_color` module. The `query_color` module will take as input the image features masked by the attention map produced by `filter_shape[cylinder]` module and outputs new feature map, which is then passed to the final classifier. The multinomial classifier will calculate the probabilities of all answers.

Thus, if we directly apply the TbD model just replacing its program executor with OpenCog, we will gain not too much, because these Atomese queries will be nested applications of `GroundedSchemaNodes`. Although these `GroundedSchemaNodes` will be presented in Atomspace knowledge base, OpenCog's reasoning capabilities will not be involved.

However, we can explicitly introduce the query variable $X, replace the query module with the corresponding filter module `filter_color[$X]`, and ask the reasoning engine to find such value of $X which will produce a non-empty final attention map. Therefore, the question "What color is the cylinder?" can be represented declaratively in Atomese:

```
AndLink
  InheritanceLink
    VariableNode "$X"
    ConceptNode "color"
  EvaluationLink
    GroundedPredicateNode "py:filter"
    ConceptNode "cylinder"
  EvaluationLink
    GroundedPredicateNode "py:filter"
    VariableNode "$X"
```

if we use a specially coded static Python function filter, which executes a corresponding DNN module depending on the name of the given argument. Here, we will need to add to Atomspace such facts as

```
InheritanceLink(ConceptNode("red"),ConceptNode("color"))
```

Pattern Matcher will be able to enumerate different colors and call different `filter_color` modules, for which PLN will infer the truth value of the given `AndLink`.

CogNets provide a general wrapper function `CogModule.callMethod` to extract Python objects attached to Atoms and call their method with automatic unwrapping of their arguments from Atoms and wrapping their results back into Atoms in such a way that, in particular, forward methods of `torch.nn.Module` objects can be used as is. Thus, the above code with the use of CogNets will look like

```
AndLink
    InheritanceLink
        VariableNode "$X"
        ConceptNode "color"
    EvaluationLink
        GroundedPredicateNode "py:CogModule.callMethod"
        ListLink
            ConceptNode "cylinder"
            ConceptNode "call_forward_tv"
            ConceptNode "image"
    EvaluationLink
        GroundedPredicateNode "py:CogModule.callMethod"
        ListLink
            VariableNode "$X"
            ConceptNode "call_forward_tv"
            ConceptNode "image"
```

`CogModule.callMethod` will extract the Python object (which will be a DNN module as `CogModule` object here) attached to `ConceptNode` "cylinder" and execute its `call_forward_tv` method (which is the method of `CogModule` inherited from `torch.nn.Module`), which will extract Python object (PyTorch tensor here) from `ConceptNode` "image" and execute forward method of the DNN module reducing its output to the tensor truth value. CogNets library provides a syntactic sugar in Python to form the necessary Atomese expressions concisely.

One can see that this allows for assembling modules in neural module networks using symbolic knowledge and reasoning over (probabilistic) logic expressions with variable grounding. This opens the path to real visual reasoning. For example, Atomspace can contain the fact that left(X, Y) :- right(Y, X). Applying this fact during the chain of reasoning performed by URE will result in transforming the module network and using `relation[right]` module instead of `relation[left]` module of TbD. In particular, given the question "To the left of what object is the green pyramid?" humans will most likely find the green pyramid first and then look to the right of it. Direct conversion of the question into the imperative program cannot represent such visual reasoning, while it can appear naturally within our approach.

In contrast to the TbD model with its hard-coded program executor, our approach can naturally be applied not to CLEVR, but also to COCO VQA and even to the example given in the paper on ProbLog [3], namely to recognize digits on a pair of MNIST digits conditioned on their sum. The premise for the query (requiring the sum to be 7) with two `VariableNodes` of `NumberNode` type will look like

```
AndLink
    EqualLink
    PlusLink
        VariableNode("$X")
        VariableNode("$Y")
    NumberNode "7"
    EvaluationLink
        GroundedPredicateNode "py:CogModule.callMethod"
        ListLink
            VariableNode "$X"
            ConceptNode "call_forward_tv"
            ConceptNode "image1"
    EvaluationLink
        GroundedPredicateNode "py:CogModule.callMethod"
        ListLink
            VariableNode "$Y"
            ConceptNode "call_forward_tv"
            ConceptNode "image2"
```

4 Conclusion

We have considered an approach to neural-symbolic integration, within which knowledge-based reasoning is carried out over symbols grounded in perception through deep neural networks, that, in particular, allows the symbolic reasoner to interoperate with execution of neural modules and to assemble a neural module network on fly depending on the current input and background knowledge.

We have implemented a framework, which embodies this approach with the use of the contemporary cognitive architecture and deep learning library, namely OpenCog and PyTorch. This implementation enables such integration of OpenCog with arbitrary DNN models that allows for error backpropagation from conclusions to DNNs through symbolic inference trees.

On example of neural-symbolic models widely used for the CLEVR benchmark, we have shown how a domain-specific program executor, which assembles neural module networks using given linear sequences of imperative commands, can be replaced with a general-purpose reasoning engine operating over a declarative knowledge base that can equally be used to reproduce models implemented within other frameworks, in particular, ProbLog.

References

1. Duch, W., Oentaryo, R.J., Pasquier, M.: Cognitive architectures: where do we go from here. In: Proceedings of 1st AGI Conference. Frontiers in Artificial Intelligence and Applications, vol. 171, pp. 122–136 (2008)

2. Besold, T.R., et al.: Neural-symbolic learning and reasoning: a survey and interpretation. arXiv preprint, arXiv:1711.03902 (2017)
3. Manhaeve, R.M., et al.: DeepProbLog: neural probabilistic logic programming. arXiv preprint, arXiv:1805.10872 (2018)
4. Overlan, M.C., Jacobs, R.A., Piantadosi, S.T.: Learning abstract visual concepts via probabilistic program induction in a Language of Thought. Cognition **168**, 320–334 (2017)
5. Mascharka, D., Tran, Ph., Soklaski, R., Majumdar, A.: Transparency by design: closing the gap between performance and interpretability in visual reasoning. arXiv preprint, arXiv: 1803.05268 (2018)
6. Fodor, J.A., Pylyshyn, Z.W.: Connectionism and cognitive architecture: a critical analysis. Cognition **28**(1–2), 3–71 (1988)
7. Singh, J., Ying, V., Nutkiewicz, A.: Attention on attention: architectures for Visual Question Answering (VQA). arXiv preprint, arXiv:1803.07724 (2018)
8. Johnson, J.: Inferring and executing programs for visual reasoning. arXiv preprint, arXiv: 1705.03633 (2017)
9. Agrawal, A., et al.: Don't just assume; look and answer: overcoming priors for visual question answering. In: Proceedings of IEEE Conference on Computer Vision and Pattern Recognition, pp. 4971–4980 (2018)
10. Johnson, J., et al.: CLEVR: a diagnostic dataset for compositional language and elementary visual reasoning. arXiv preprint, arXiv:1612.06890 (2016)
11. Hudson, D.A., Manning, Ch.D.: GQA: a new dataset for real-world visual reasoning and compositional question answering. arXiv preprint, arXiv:1902.09506 (2019)
12. Goertzel, B.: Perception processing for general intelligence: bridging the symbolic/subsymbolic gap. In: Bach, J., Goertzel, B., Iklé, M. (eds.) AGI 2012. LNCS (LNAI), vol. 7716, pp. 79–88. Springer, Heidelberg (2012). https://doi.org/10.1007/978-3-642-35506-6_9
13. Goertzel, B.: OpenCog NS: a deeply-interactive hybrid neural-symbolic cognitive architecture designed for global/local memory synergy. In: Proceedings of AAAI Fall Symposium Series FS-09-01, pp. 63–68 (2009)
14. Potapov, A., Zhdanov, I., Scherbakov, O., Skorobogatko, N., Latapie, H., Fenoglio, E.: Semantic image retrieval by uniting deep neural networks and cognitive architectures. In: Iklé, M., Franz, A., Rzepka, R., Goertzel, B. (eds.) AGI 2018. LNCS (LNAI), vol. 10999, pp. 196–206. Springer, Cham (2018). https://doi.org/10.1007/978-3-319-97676-1_19
15. Yi, K., et al.: Neural-symbolic VQA: disentangling reasoning from vision and language understanding. arXiv preprint, arXiv:1810.02338 (2018)
16. Potapov, A., Belikov, A., Bogdanov, V., Scherbatiy, A.: Differentiable probabilistic logic networks. arXiv preprint, arXiv:1907.04592 (2019)

Generalized Diagnostics with the Non-Axiomatic Reasoning System (NARS)

Bill Power[✉], Xiang Li[✉], and Pei Wang[✉]

Department of Computer and Information Sciences, Temple University,
Philadelphia, USA
{tug00038,xiangliAGI,pei.wang}@temple.edu

Abstract. Symbolic reasoning systems have leveraged propositional logic frameworks to build diagnostics tools capable of describing complex artifacts, while also allowing for a controlled and efficacious search over failure modes. These diagnostic systems represent a complex and varied context in which to explore general intelligence. This paper explores the application of a different reasoning system to such frameworks, specifically, the Non-Axiomatic Reasoning System. It shows how statements can be built describing an artifact, and that NARS is capable of diagnosing abnormal states within examples of said artifact.

Keywords: Diagnostics · Model Based Diagnostics ·
Abductive inference

1 Introduction

The task of diagnosis highlights many of the core issues in general intelligence. It is a process that works from insufficient knowledge, building hypotheses and testing them to explain an observed state. These steps, each of which encompasses a wide body of work on their own, are combined into a process that feels uniquely human. As such, the field of Artificial Intelligence (AI) has made many attempts to understand these elements, and to compose their understanding into methods of automated diagnosis [1,3,13].

The general approach is to somehow encode a description of the artifact under diagnosis into a logic or model. Then, compare observations about the true artifacts behaviour, with observations of the predicted output of the model. The differences between the output are then the starting point to understand, or diagnose the physical artifact. This forms the basis of the Model Based Diagnostic Framework [12].

The goal of this paper is to show that the Non-Axiomatic Reasoning Logic, and associated reasoning system, can be used to build descriptions of systems, and similarly encode examples of the artifact for diagnosis. It will also show that the resulting descriptions can be fed into an "off the shelf" implementation of NARS, which yields expected results.

© Springer Nature Switzerland AG 2019
P. Hammer et al. (Eds.): AGI 2019, LNAI 11654, pp. 159–167, 2019.
https://doi.org/10.1007/978-3-030-27005-6_16

2   Prior Work

Prior to the work of Reiter, these attempts were largely separate, context dependant endeavours. Reiters work took these varied symbolic approaches, and create a generalized abstraction he referred to as Model Based Diagnostics. MBD could be considered the first formal 'consistency based' diagnostic method. The general approach is to encode a description of the artifact under diagnosis into a logical model. Then, compare observations about the true artifacts behaviour, with observations of the predicted output of the model. The differences between the output are then the starting point to understand, or diagnose the physical artifact [8]. Model Based Diagnosis describes a way to encode a model of an artifact in a predicate logic. This system description consists of predicate statements that connect components of the system. These components are encoded with their proper behaviour using the language of the predicate logic. Then, these component descriptions are conjuncted with the negation of a reserved predicate; "AB(x)", intuitively meaning "if the situation is abnormal".

This system description can then be combined with observations of the workings of a physical realization of the model. Again, such observations are also written in the language of the predicate logic used to describe the system. If these observations include statements that produce contradictions in the system, then it can be assumed that some subset of the components are behaving abnormally. In other words, there is a set of components, where if the predicate "AB(X)" is no longer negated, then the system description, along with the observations, becomes consistent [10].

Various methods have been developed to search for the resolution of these contradictory statements [2,5,9].

Extensions of the consistency based methods have been proposed. These incorporate more information into the system description. Instead of limiting the state of components to either normal or abnormal, abductive systems allow for a richer set of "failure states" that could be applied to a component [7]. These states relate failure to specific behaviours of the components. For instance, in the canonical example of the adder system, a gate component could be in a failure mode corresponding to "always outputs a value of true". The resolution of a diagnosis is then the minimal set of failure modes that must be applied in order for the system to be brought into a consistent state.

In addition to these new failure modes, abductive based systems also make new distinctions between the types and kinds of observations the system can have made on it. [11] introduces two main classes of observation. First, the set of observations that describe the context of the problem, yet do not require an 'explanation' via the diagnosis. Second, the set of observations that require an explanation. These two sets are referred to as CONTEXT and SYMPTOMS, respectively. This distinction is required to ensure that the resulting diagnosis is truly parsimonious, and does not include unnecessary explanations of contextual observations.

A unique approach to diagnosis comes from [8] extending the work of Reiter to handle multiple-fault diagnosis. In this, de Kleer develops an extension of truth maintenance systems that allows for tracking and tagging of assumptions.

Truth maintenance systems are a two part system. First, a problem solver, working in the language of some logic. The statements it derives and operates on are passed to the second component, a truth-maintenance system. This component views the logical statements on their own, and attempts to identify, correct, and isolate the inconsistencies that may develop in the running of the problem solver [4].

De Kleers system applies these notions to the arena of diagnosis. The problem solver sees the logical description of the artifact, its components, their relations, and then the observations of physical instances of the artifact. If the statements regarding an instance of the artifact bring the problem solver into an inconsistency, then the working of the truth maintenance system will isolate the minimal sets of components that need be labeled abnormal to bring the system back to 'working' order.

This combination of truth maintenance system with a system description most closely matches the approach presented in this work. While a truth maintenance system solely works by inducing consistency amongst observed statements, NARS would also include its additional methods of inference with prior knowledge to find conclusions.

3   NARS Overview

NARS (Non-Axiomatic Reasoning System) is a general purpose AI built in the framework of a reasoning system. It operates under a definition of intelligence that includes a notion of insufficient resources, specifically: "Intelligence" in NARS is defined as the ability for a system to adapt to its environment and to work with insufficient knowledge and resources. Detailed discussions can be found in many publications, including two main books [14,15], describing the full logic. The following will highlight the elements of the logic that are used by this paper to encode the system description of an artifact under diagnosis.

Narsese is the formal language which is used by NARS for its knowledge representation, defined using a formal grammar in [14]. The logic is developed from the traditional "term logic", where a "term" is the smallest element of each statements. Statements in this logic have the form *subject-copula-predicate*.

Inheritance statements are the most basic statement in Narsese, with the form "S → P", where S is the subject, and P is the predicate term. The "→" is the *inheritance* copula, defined in ideal situations as a reflexive and transitive relation from one term to another term. The intuitive meaning of $S \rightarrow P$ is "S is a special case of P" and "P is a general case of S". For example, the statement "$CRV \rightarrow Honda$" intuitively means "CRV is a type of Honda vehicle".

A compound term (con, $C_1, C_2...C_n$) is formed by a term connector, "con" and one or more components terms $(C_1, C_2, ...C_n)$. The term connector is a logical constant with predefined meaning in the system. Major types of compound terms in Narsese include the following:

- **Sets:** Term $\{Honda, Toyota\}$ is an *extensional set* specified by enumerating its instances; term $[coupe, SUV]$ is an *intensional set* specified by enumerating its properties.
- **Products and images:** The relation "Mike is the patient of Dylan" is represented as "$(\{Mike\} \times \{Dylan\}) \rightarrow patient\text{-}of$", "$\{Mike\} \rightarrow (uncle\text{-}of\ /\ \diamond \{Dylan\})$", and "$\{Dylan\} \rightarrow (patient\text{-}of\ /\ \{Mike\}\diamond)$", equivalently.
- **Statement:** "Bill notices check engine light is on" can be represented as a *higher-order statement* "$\{Bill\} \rightarrow (notice\ /\ \diamond\ \{\texttt{check\_engine\_light} \rightarrow [on, off]\})$", where the statement "$\texttt{check\_engine\_light} \rightarrow [on]$" is used as a term.
- **Compound statements:** Statements can be combined using term connectors for disjunction('$\vee$'), conjunction('$\wedge$'), and negation('$\neg$'), which are intuitively similar to those in propositional logic, but not defined using truthtables [14].

4   System Descriptions in NAL

Artifacts can typically be described as a hierarchical set of components, along with some type of indication, or feedback about the state of an artifact. That is, we can break apart an artifact into components, which themselves can be composed of other components. The relations between these entities must account for relationships that would cause the 'parent' to behave abnormally, if any of their children were to behave abnormally.

In addition, it is assumed that there are classes of components that provide feedback to an observer. These are essentially the set of "senseable" components. They are the manner in which an example artifact can be described, because it is assumed that an example is simply a list of values, corresponding to a set of 'sensor readings'.

Encoding a system description then requires a representation for the components, a representation of the possible states of the senseable nodes, and a representation of the possible relations between the sensable values, and relevant components.

The relationship between parent components and their constituent parts can be expressed with the following inheritance statement.

$$Component_P \rightarrow (*, C_1, C_2, \ldots, C_N)$$

This roughly translates to "$Component_P$ inherits from the set of components: $C_1, C_2, \ldots, C_N$."

The relationship between components and their sensors is slightly more complicated. We need to encode the possible states sensors can be in, then describe the relationship between these states and the working state of components. The sensor states are encoded as possible properties for each sensor.

$$SensorX \rightarrow (\|, [on, off])$$
$$SensorY \rightarrow (\|, [state_1, state_2, \ldots, state_n])$$

An implication is used to describe the relation between these sensor properties and the possible 'not working' property of components.

$$(\text{SensorX} \rightarrow [\text{on}]) \Longrightarrow (\text{ComponentY} \rightarrow [\text{Not Working}])$$
$$(\text{Check\_Engine\_Light} \rightarrow [\text{on}]) \Longrightarrow (\text{Engine} \rightarrow [\text{Not Working}])$$

This simplifies the method in which an instance of an object is presented to the system. We want to find the components that have a high frequency of having the property "Not Working", after listing the set of sensor properties for a particular object. For the example of a car, we would provide a conjunction of statements, where each statement is describing the properties of the car's components.

$$(\&, \text{SX} \rightarrow [\text{PA}], \text{SY} \rightarrow [\text{PB}], \ldots, \text{SN} \rightarrow [\text{PQ}]) \Longrightarrow (? \rightarrow [\text{Not Working}])$$

The above roughly translates to "Given a conjunction of properties, what Components have the property 'Not Working'".

Two types of inference are typically involved in a complete diagnostic process; forward and backward inference. The goal of forward inference is to apply the current knowledge to the problem directly. An example of this is the simple chain of logic that starts with a cars 'check engine light'. The fact that the engine light is on, can be carried forward with the fact that 'engine light implies the engine is not working' to arrive at the fact that the engine is indeed not functioning.

In contrast, backward inference is used when the system does not have complete information, or a complete set of rules to use to arrive at a 'straight forward' inference. This typically occurs when different components of the system have an overlap in symptoms, or when the rules describing the system do not explicitly contain a mention of a particular combination of symptoms. In these situations, the system must 'work backwards' from what it knows to determine where it lacks appropriate information. In these situations, the system may need to prompt for additional rules.

Consider the car example. In our formulation, the engine itself is comprised of multiple sub components. The indicator for these components have some overlap; the check engine light could indicate a 'general' engine problem, or a 'specific' problem with the alternator. If the system assumes there are some cases, say the presence of smoke, that could be applied to only one of these sub components, then asking the clarifying question "is smoke observed?" is an example of backward inference.

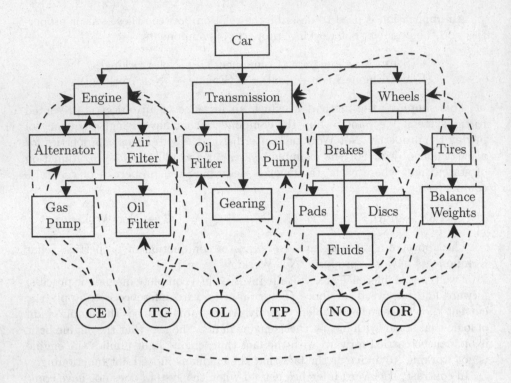

Symbol	Interpretation	Values
CE	Check Engine Light	On, Off
TG	Temperature Gauge	Low, High
OL	Oil Level	Low, Middle, High
TP	Tire Pressure Indicator	On, Off
NO	Noise	None, High, Low
OR	Odometer Reading	Low, Middle, High

Fig. 1. Senseables

5 Automotive Example

The detailed car use case breaks down the object to be diagnosed, the car, according to the following diagram. In this diagram, two types of nodes exist, one denoting a component, and one denoting a facet of the system that can be sensed. These nodes represent items that would be 'sensed' by a user of the vehicle. This list was created from the point of view of a lay user describing issues to a mechanic, and try to reflect the high level indicators that exist on common dashboards.

The goal with this graph is to capture enough complexity for the system to have fodder for interesting and useful derived inferences. A key part of this complexity is ensuring that there are many-to-one relationships between components and the indicators. In addition, there is a deeper hierarchy of components, where the relationships with indicator nodes can span multiple levels.

The links between components (solid lines) indicate the relevant "required by" or "composed of" relations. These are implemented with the inheritance operator. A higher level component inherits its lower level constituent components.

There is a second type of edge/relationship in the graph; the relation between a component and a sensible thing (dashed lines). These represent the possible relations between an indicator and the components it might 'indicate' a problem for. Figure 1 shows the set of senseables exposed to the system, and the possible values they can take.

The actual NAL statements that encode the relations above are as follows.

```
//Engine, Transmission and Wheels are main components of the car
<{Engine, Transmission, Wheels} --> Main_Component>.

//Alternator, Air_Filter and so on are sub-components of the car
<{Alternator, Air_Filter} --> Sub_Component>.
<{Gas_Pump, Oil_Filter, Oil_Pump} --> Sub_Component>.
<{Gearing, Brakes, Tires} --> Sub_Component>.
<{Pads, Discs, Fluids, Balances_Weights} --> Sub_component>.

//Alternator, Air_Filter, Gas_Pump, Oil_Filter are parts of Engine
<{Alternator, Air_Filter, Gas_Pump, Oil_Filter} --> Engine>.
//Oil_Filter, Oil_Pump, Gearing are parts of Transmission
<{Oil_Filter, Oil_Pump, Gearing} --> Transmission>.
//Brakes and tires are components of wheel
<{Brakes, Tires} --> Wheels>.
//Pads, Discs and fluids are components of brakes
<{Pads, Discs, Fluids} --> Brakes>.
//Balance weights is component of tire
<{Balances_Weights} --> Tires>.

//Check engine light has no stage, ON or Off
<{CE} --> (||, [ON, OFF])>.
<{TG} --> (||, [LOW, HIGH])>.
<{OL} --> (||, [LOW, MIDDLE, HIGH])>.
<{TP} --> (||, [ON,OFF])>.
<{NO} --> (||, [NONE, HIGH, LOW])>.
<{OR} --> (||, [LOW, MIDDLE, HIGH])>.

// If check engine light is on, then alternator might not working
<<{CE} --> [ON]> ==> <Alternator --> [Not_Working]>>.
<<{CE} --> [ON]> ==> <Engine --> [Not_Working]>>.
<<{TG} --> [High]> ==> <Air_Filter --> [Not_Working]>>.
<<{TG} --> [High]> ==> <Engine --> [Not_Working]>>.
```

```
<<{OL} --> [High]> ==> <Oil_Filter --> [Not_Working]>>.
<<{OL} --> [low]> ==> <Oil_Pump --> [Not_Working]>>.
<<{TP} --> [ON]> ==> <Tires --> [Not_Working]>>.
<<{TP} --> [ON]> ==> <Wheels --> [Not_Working]>>.
<<{NO} --> [High]> ==> <Engine --> [Not_Working]>>.
<<{NO} --> [High]> ==> <Wheels --> [Not_Working]>>.
<<{NO} --> [High]> ==> <Brakes --> [Not_Working]>>.
<<{NO} --> [High]> ==> <Balances_Weights --> [Not_Working]>>.
<<{OR} --> [High]> ==> <Transmission --> [Not_Working]>>.
<<{OR} --> [High]> ==> <Engine --> [Not_Working]>>.
```

6   Results

The encoded system description was provided to an off-the-shelf version of the
OpenNARS implementation of the NARS [6]. The system was run with its stock
control mechanisms and parameters, and allowed to settle on answers to simple
diagnostic queries. The resulting output is as follows.

```
// Car1's check engine light is on
<{Car1} ==> <CE --> [ON]>>.g
<{Car1} ==> <TG --> [High]>>.
<{Car1} ==> <NO --> [High]>>.
<{Car1} ==> <OR --> [High]>>.

// Car1 has a diagnosis on main components
<{Car1} --> [Diagnosis_On_Main_Component]>.
<{Car1} --> [Diagnosis_On_Sub_Component]>.
<{Diagnosis_On_Main_Component} --> Main_Component>.
<{Diagnosis_On_Sub_Component} --> Sub_component>.
//Which main component is not working?
<Diagnosis_On_Main_Component <-> ?x>?
<Diagnosis_On_Sub_Component <-> ?y>?

// Transmission is not working
Answer: <Diagnosis_On_Main_Component <-> Transmission>. %1.00;0.42%
// Alternator is not working
Answer: <Alternator <-> Diagnosis_On_Sub_Component>. %1.00;0.42%
// Engine is not working
Answer: <Engine <-> Diagnosis_On_Main_Component>. %1.00;0.59%
Answer: <Alternator <-> Diagnosis_On_Sub_Component>. %1.00;0.56%
```

7   Conclusion

This work shows that a separate logical framework can indeed solve the same
problems covered by Model Based Diagnosis. However, this simplified representation does not leverage the full set of language levels, and mental operations

available in the NARS. Future work will include a closer inspection of the different types of operations that could be beneficial to automated diagnosis, while also developing a more robust control mechanism for generalized diagnostics. In addition, it would be useful to test the framework on more complex artifacts, such as models of human biological systems, or complex circuit designs.

References

1. Brusoni, V., Console, L., Terenziani, P., Dupré, D.T.: A spectrum of definitions for temporal model-based diagnosis. Artif. Intell. **102**(1), 39–79 (1998)
2. Ceriani, L., Zanella, M.: Model-based diagnosis and generation of hypothesis space via AI planning. In: 25th International Workshop on the Principles of Diagnosis (DX-14) (2014)
3. Console, L., Torasso, P.: A spectrum of logical definitions of model-based diagnosis1. Comput. Intell. **7**(3), 133–141 (1991)
4. De Kleer, J.: An assumption-based TMS. Artif. Intell. **28**(2), 127–162 (1986)
5. Felfernig, A., Friedrich, G., Jannach, D., Stumptner, M.: Consistency-based diagnosis of configuration knowledge bases. Artif. Intell. **152**(2), 213–234 (2004)
6. Hammer, P., Lofthouse, T., Wang, P.: The OpenNARS implementation of the non-axiomatic reasoning system. In: Steunebrink, B., Wang, P., Goertzel, B. (eds.) AGI -2016. LNCS (LNAI), vol. 9782, pp. 160–170. Springer, Cham (2016). https://doi.org/10.1007/978-3-319-41649-6_16
7. ohan de Kleer, J., Williams, B.C.: Diagnosis with behavioral modes. Proc. IJ CAI **1**(989), 1324–1330 (1989)
8. de Kleer, J., Williams, B.C.: Diagnosing multiple faults. Artif. Intell. **32**(1), 97–130 (1987)
9. Koitz, R., Wotawa, F.: SAT-based abductive diagnosis. In: International Workshop on Principles of Diagnosis, vol. 26, p. 10 (2015)
10. McCarthy, J.: Applications of circumscription to formalizing common-sense knowledge. Artif. Intell. **28**(1), 89–116 (1986)
11. Peng, Y., Reggia, J.A.: Abductive Inference Models for Diagnostic Problem-Solving. Springer, New York (2012). https://doi.org/10.1007/978-1-4419-8682-5
12. Reiter, R.: A theory of diagnosis from first principles. Artif. Intell. **32**(1), 57–95 (1987)
13. ten Teije, A., van Harmelen, F.: An extended spectrum of logical definitions for diagnostic systems. In: Proceedings of DX-94 Fifth International Workshop on Principles of Diagnosis, pp. 334–342 (1994)
14. Wang, P.: Rigid Flexibility: The Logic of Intelligence. Springer, Dordrecht (2006). https://doi.org/10.1007/1-4020-5045-3
15. Wang, P.: Non-Axiomatic Logic: A Model of Intelligent Reasoning. World Scientific, Singapore (2013)

Cognitive Model of Brain-Machine Integration

Zhongzhi Shi[1(✉)] and Zeqin Huang[1,2]

[1] Key Laboratory of Intelligent Information Processing,
Institute of Computing Technology, Chinese Academy of Sciences,
Beijing 100190, China
{shizz,huangzeqin17g}@ict.ac.cn
[2] University of Chinese Academy of Sciences, Beijing 100049, China

Abstract. Brain-machine integration is a new intelligent technology and system, which is a combination of natural intelligence and artificial intelligence. In order to make this integration effective and co-adaptive biological brain and machine should work collaboratively. A cognitive model of brain-machine integration will be proposed. Environment awareness and collaboration approaches will be explored in the paper.

Keywords: Brain-machine integration · Environment awareness · Collaboration · Motivation · Joint intention

1 Introduction

Machines have advantages that humans can't match in terms of search, computing, memory, etc. However, machines are far less intelligent and efficient than human intelligence in terms of perception, reasoning and learning. In order to realize artificial intelligence with common attributes, it is necessary to combine the advantages of machine intelligence and human intelligence to achieve deep integration of brain with machine. Brain-machine integration is a new intelligent technology and system generated by the interaction of human and machine. It combines the advantages of human and machines, and is the next generation of intelligent systems [1].

At present, brain-machine integration is an active research area in intelligence science. In 2009, DiGiovanna et al. developed the mutually adaptive brain computer interface system based on reinforcement learning [2], which regulates brain activity by the rewards and punishment mechanism. The machine adopts the reinforcement learning algorithm to adapt motion control of mechanical arm, and has the optimized performance of the manipulator motion control. In 2010, Fukayarna et al. control a mechanical car by extraction and analysis of mouse motor nerve signals [3]. In 2011, Nicolelis team developed a new brain-machine-brain information channel bidirectional closed-loop system reported in Nature [4], turn monkey's touch information into the electric stimulus signal to feedback the brain while decoding to the nerve information of monkey's brain, to realize the brain computer cooperation. In 2013, Zhaohui Wu team of Zhejiang University developed a visual enhanced rat robot [5]. Compared with the general robot, the rat robot has the advantage in the aspects of flexibility, stability and environmental adaptability.

Brain-machine integration system has three remarkable characteristics: (a) More comprehensive perception of organisms, including behavior understanding and decoding of neural signals; (b) Organisms also as a system of sensing, computation body and executive body, and information bidirectional exchange channel with the rest of the system; (c) Comprehensive utilization of organism and machine in the multi-level and multi-granularity will achieve system intelligence greatly enhanced.

Supported by the project of National Program on Key Basic Research we are engaging in the research on Computational Theory and Method of Perception and Cognition of Brain-machine Integration. The main goal of the project is the exploration of cyborg intelligence through brain-machine integration, enhancing strengths and compensating for weaknesses by combining the biological cognition capability with the computer computational capability. In order to make this integration effective and co-adaptive, brain and computer should work collaboratively. We mainly focus on four aspects, environment awareness, cognitive modeling, joint intention and action planning, to carry out the research of cognitive computational model.

In this paper, a model of brain-machine integration is proposed. Environment awareness is an important for brain-machine integration and will be explored. The collaboration methods between brain and machine will be explored by motivation and joint intention. The conclusions and future works are given at the end.

2   A Model of Brain-Machine Integration

An effective approach to implementing engineering systems and exploring research problems in cyborg intelligence is based on brain-machine integration methods [6]. Using these methods, computers can record neural activity at multiple levels or scales, and thus decode brain representation of various functionalities, and precisely control artificial or biological actuators. In recent decades, there have been continuous scientific breakthroughs regarding the directed information pathway from the brain to computers. Meanwhile, besides ordinary sensory feedback such as visual, auditory, tactile, and olfactory input, computers can now encode neural feedback as optical or electrical stimulus to modulate neural circuits directly. This forms the directed information pathway from the computer to the brain. These bidirectional information pathways make it possible to investigate the key problems in cyborg intelligence.

How to interact between brain and computer is a critical problem in brain-machine integration. On the basis of the similarity between brain function partition and corresponding computing counterparts, a hierarchical and conceptual framework for brain-machine integration is proposed. The biological part and computing counterparts are interconnected through information exchange, and then cooperate to generate perception, awareness, memory, planning, and other cognitive functions.

For the brain part, abstracted the biological component of cyborg intelligence into three layers: perception and behavior, decision making, memory and consciousness shown in Fig. 1. We also divided the computer functional units into three corresponding layers: awareness and actuator, planning, motivation and belief layers. We also defined two basic interaction and cooperation operations: homogeneous interaction (homoraction) and heterogeneous interaction (heteraction). The former represents information exchange and function recalls occurring in a single biological or computing component, whereas the latter indicates the operations between the function units of both biological and computing parts. Homoraction is also modeled as the relationship between units within the same part. In the case of a single part in a brain-machine integration system, it will reduce to a biological body or computing device just with homoraction inside. Consequently, verifying the existence of heteraction is necessary for cyborg intelligent systems.

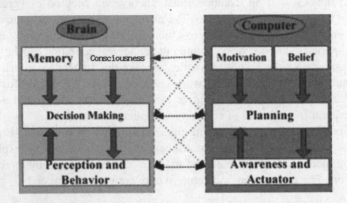

Fig. 1. Cognitive model of BMI

As typical Brain-machine integration system of "animal as the actuators", rat cyborgs [7, 8], were developed to validate how the animals can be enhanced by the artificial intelligence. Ratbots are based on the biological platform of the rat with electrodes implanted in specific brain areas, such as the somatosensory cortex and reward area [9]. These electrodes are connected to a backpack fixed on the rat, which works as a stimulator to deliver electric stimuli to the rat brain.

3   Environment Awareness

For brain-machine bidirectional information perception characteristics, the integration of visual features of the Marr visual theory and Gestalt whole perception theory in the wide range, research on the environment group awareness model and method by combination of brain and machine. The discriminative, generative and other methods are applied to analyze the features of environment perception information, mine perception information patterns and knowledge, generate high-level semantics, and understand well the environment awareness.

In 1995, Endsley proposed a classic theory of situational awareness, which is a three-level model. It is defined as the ability of people to perceive, comprehend and predict the various elements in the environment in a certain space and time [10]. In the three-level model of situational awareness, perception acquires information, and under high-load cognitive conditions, information acquisition mainly depends on the sensor of the machine, and then is presented to the operator through computer processing. The machine plays an important role in the perception phase in the three-level model. In the decision-making stage after the forecast, the collaborative judgment and analysis between machines and people is also needed. The integration of brain and machines in dynamic situational awareness is the key to achieving good performance in understanding the environment.

Awareness is the state or ability to perceive, to feel events, objects or sensory patterns, and cognitive reaction to a condition or event. Awareness has four basic characteristics:

– Awareness is knowledge about the state of a particular environment.
– Environments change over time, so awareness must be kept up to date.
– Agents maintain their awareness by interacting with the environment.
– Awareness establishes usually an event.

Based on the integration of Marr visual theory and Gestalt whole perception theory, applying statistic and deep learning and other methods to analyze environment information and generate high-level semantics, we can build the brain-machine awareness model.

The brain-machine awareness model is defined as 2-tuples: {Element, Relation}, where Element of awareness is described as follows:

(a) Who: describes the existence of agent and identity the role, answer question who is participating?
(b) What: shows agent's actions and abilities, answer question what are they doing? And what can they do? Also can show intentions to answer question what are they going to do?
(c) Where: indicates the location of agents, answer question where are they?
(d) When: shows the time point of agent behavior, answer question when can action execute?

Basic relationships contain task relationship, role relationship, operation relationship, activity relationship and cooperation relationships.

(a) Task relationships define task decomposition and composition relationships. Task involves activities with a clear and unique role attribute.
(b) Role relationships describe the role relationship of agents in the multi-agent activities.
(c) Operation relationships describe the operation set of agent.
(d) Activity relationships describe activity of the role at a time.
(e) Cooperation relationships describe the interactions between agents. A partnership can be investigated through cooperation activities relevance between agents to ensure the transmission of information between different perception of the role and tasks for maintenance of the entire multi-agent perception.

Agent can be viewed as perceiving its environment information through sensors and acting environment through effectors. As an internal mental model of agent, BDI model has been well recognized in philosophical and artificial intelligence area. As a practical agent existing in real world should consider external perception and internal mental state of agents. In terms of these considerations we propose a cognitive model through 4-tuple <Awareness, Belief, Goal, Plan>, and the cognitive model can be called ABGP model [11].

There are several methods developed for visual awareness. Here we describe how CNN is used for visual awareness. Convolutional neural networks (CNN) is a multiple-stage of globally trainable artificial neural networks. CNN has a better performance in 2 dimensional pattern recognition problems than the multilayer perceptron, because the topology of the two-dimensional model is added into the CNN structure, and CNN employs three important structure features: local accepted field, shared weights, sub-sampling ensuring the invariance of the target translation, shrinkage and distortion for the input signal. CNN mainly consists of the feature extraction and the classifier. The feature extraction contains the multiple convolutional layers and sub-sampling layers. The classifier is consisted of one layer or two layers of fully connected neural networks. For the convolutional layer with the local accepted field and the sub-sampling layer with sub-sampling structure, they all have the character of sharing the weights.

The architecture of ABGP-CNN agent is shown in Fig. 2. In the ABGP-CNN, the awareness module has been implemented by CNN, which is completely different from the original single pre-defined rule implementation. The parameters of CNN will become the knowledge in the belief library, and other modules have not changed. In Fig. 2, the ABGP-CNN based agent implements behavior planning through motivation-driven intentions, and the motivation drive adopts a series of internal events. Interesting to achieve planning choices. Each internal mental action of ABGP-CNN must be transformed into an event that drives introspective search to select the most interesting event planning method using novelty and interest. Events consist primarily of internal events (which occur inside the agent) and external events (from external scene perception or other agents). Often, the formation of motivation is motivated by demand and curiosity, but is primarily motivated by curiosity in the ABGP-CNN agent. A goal consisting of a motivational position drives an agent. Unlike most traditional BDI systems, ABGP-CNN does not simply target the target as a special set of events, nor does it assume that all targets must be consistent.

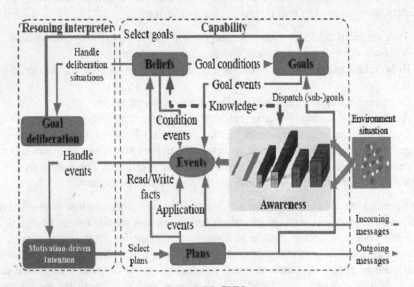

Fig. 2. ABGP-CNN agent

4 Collaboration

Collaborations occur over time as organizations interact formally and informally through repetitive sequences of negotiation, development of commitments, and execution of those commitments. Both cooperation and coordination may occur as part of the early process of collaboration, collaboration represents a longer-term integrated process. Gray describes collaboration as a process through which parties who see different aspects of a problem can constructively explore their differences and search for solutions that go beyond their own limited vision of what is possible [12].

In this project we propose multi-level collaboration for brain-machine integration [13]. Here we only introduce motivation-based collaboration and joint-intention based collaboration.

4.1 Motivation Based Collaboration

Motivation is defined by psychologists as an internal process that activates, guides, and maintains behavior over time. Maslow proposed hierarchy of needs which was one of first unified motivation theories [14]. Since it introduced to the public, the Maslow's theory has a significant impact to the every life aspect in people's life. Various attempts have been made to either classify or synthesize the large body of research related to motivation.

Curiosity is a form of motivation that promotes exploratory behavior to learn more about a source of uncertainty, such as a novel stimulus, with the goal of acquiring sufficient knowledge to reduce the uncertainty. In fact, most of curiosities are caused by novelty. Novelty detection is useful technology to find curiosity. Novelty detection is the identification of new or unknown data or signal.

Detecting novel events is an important ability of any signal classification scheme. Given the fact that we can never train a machine learning system on all possible object classes whose data is likely to be encounter by the system, it becomes important to differentiate between known and unknown object information during testing.

Interestingness is defined as novelty and surprise. It depends on the observer's current knowledge and computational abilities. The interestingness of a situation is a measure of the importance of the situation with respect to an agent's existing knowledge. Interestingness will make attention to an event, leading to collaborative work of brain and machine.

4.2 Joint Intention Based Collaboration

The abstraction concept of the joint intention is convenient to support describe and analyze the social behavior among the agents. A joint intention to perform a particular action is a joint commitment to enter a future state wherein the agents mutually believe the collaborative action is imminent just before they perform it.

In 1990, Bratman's philosophical theory was formalized by Cohen and Levesque [15]. In their formalism, intentions are defined in terms of temporal sequences of agent's beliefs and goals. In 1992, Jennings claimed the need to describe collectives as well as individuals [16]:

- Agents must agree on a common goal.
- Agents must agree they wish to collaborate to achieve their shared objective.
- Agents must agree a common means of reaching their objective.
- Action inter-dependencies exist and must be catered for in general terms.

In multi-agent systems, agents achieve a formula together. Joint intention embody all agents' joint activity selection, so the selective and joint are the basic factors. Intuitively, joint intention has the list properties:

- **Selective**: Intention is the choice of the agent about the future, it will have effect on its activities.
- **Joint**: Joint intention is that which all the team member want to achieve. As a team member, each one knows it specifically and needs collaboration to achieve.
- **Satisfaction**: The satisfaction makes the notion of a formula being true under an interpretation. Then intention is satisfiable means the intention is achievable.
- **Consistency**: Joint intention is the same as the single agent's intention. Different intentions among the team will make the joint intention conflict. What's more, one agent's belief and intention should be consistent.
- **Continuity**: Continuity is one of the properties of joint intention. All the agents will keep their intention until it is impossible to achieve or achieved.

Agent joint intention means agent wants to achieve a formula, which corresponds to agent's goal. For the joint intention, each agent has three basic knowledge: first each one should select ϕ as its intention; second, each one knows its neighbors who also select the intention ϕ; third, each one knows they are on the same team. Distributed dynamic description logic (D3L) is adopted to describe joint intention [17].

Since the brain-machine integration is a multi-agent system as a distributed system, the dynamic description logic is only suitable for processing isomorphic information, and can't provide a reasonable logical basis for multi-agent system. For this reason, D3L is proposed to extend the dynamic description logic for distributed, heterogeneous information integration. Distributed dynamic description logic is a unified representation and reasoning mechanism for studying multi-agent systems.

Distributed dynamic description logic propagates knowledge through bridge rules, but it only deals with the case where two local DDL ontology are connected by bridge rules, and the propagation of knowledge between ontology is not used for distributed reasoning. Knowledge dissemination is the main feature of D3L that is different from traditional dynamic description logic. In the case that multiple DDL agents form a chain between bridge rules, they do not always propagate in the expected way, so the combination consistency is introduced and distributed dynamic description logic supporting chain bridge rules is proposed (CD3L). The CD3L component is divided into three parts: a distributed TBox, a distributed ABox, and a distributed ActBox. Therefore, it can better provide a logic basis for multi-agent systems.

5 Simulation Experiment

ABGP-CNN as the detailed implementation for the conceptual framework of brain-machine integration, here we give a simulation application to significantly demonstrate feasibility of conceptual framework of brain-machine integration based ABGP-CNN Agent model. The following will mainly represent the actual design of the rat agent based on ABGP-CNN supported by the conceptual framework of brain-machine integration.

Under belief knowledge conditions, the goals (here mainly visual information) constantly trigger the awareness module to capture environment visual information, and the event module converts the visual information into the unified internal motivation signal events which are transferred to action plan module. Then the action plan module will select proper actions to response the environment.

In simulation application, we construct a maze and design a rat agent based on ABGP-CNN to move in the maze depending on the guidepost of maze path in Fig. 3. The task of the rat agent is to start moving at the maze entrance (top-left of maze), and finally reach the maze exit (bottom right of maze) depending on all guideposts.

Fig. 3. Rat agent activities in maze

In order to fulfill the maze activity shown in Fig. 3, the rat agent is implemented all the three basic modules, <Awareness>, <Motivation>, <Action Plan>. In the rat maze activity experiment, the rat agent is designed to have 3 basic behaviors moving on, turning left and turning right in the maze. In order to guide rat's behaviors we construct a true traffic guidepost dataset means 3 different signals, moving on, turning left and turning right. The different signal corresponds to different guidepost images like in Fig. 4.

(a) Moving on   (b) Turning left   (c) Turning right

Fig. 4. Traffic guideposts in maze

When rat agent moves on the path, its goals constantly drive awareness module to capture environment visual information (here guideposts in the maze) and generate the motivation signal events to drive its behaviors plan selection. In the experiment, there are 3 motivation signals, moving on, turning left and turning right according to the guideposts in the maze path, which means the agent can response 3 types of action plans to finish the maze activities.

6 Conclusions

At present, brain-machine integration is an active research area in intelligence science. A cognitive model of brain-machine integration has been presented in this paper. The paper explained environment awareness. Motivation is the cause of action and plays important roles in collaboration. The motivation based collaboration has been explored in terms of event curiosity, which is useful for sharing common interest situations. Joint intention based collaboration is also discussed in terms of a sharing goal.

The future of brain-machine integration may lead towards many promising applications, such as neural intervention, medical treatment, and early diagnosis of some neurological and psychiatric disorders. The goal of artificial general intelligence (AGI) is the development and demonstration of systems that exhibit the broad range of general intelligence. The brain-machine integration is one approach to reach AGI. A lot of basic issues of brain-inspired intelligence are explored in details in the book [1].

Acknowledgements. This work is supported by the National Program on Key Basic Research Project (973) (No. 2013CB329502), National Natural Science Foundation of China (No. 61035003).

References

1. Shi, Z.: Mind Computation. World Scientific Publishing, Singapore (2017)
2. DiGiovanna, J., Mahmoudi, B., Fortes, J., et al.: Coadaptive brain-machine interface via reinforcement learning. IEEE Trans. Biomed. Eng. **56**(1), 54–64 (2009)
3. Fukuyama, O., Suzuki, T., Mabuchi, K.: RatCar: a vehicular neuro-robotic platform for a rat with a sustaining structure of the rat body under the vehicle. In: Annual International Conference of the IEEE Engineering in Medicine and Biology Society (2010)
4. O'Doherty, J.E., Lebedev, M.A., Ifft, P.J., et al.: Active tactile exploration using a brain-machine-brain interface. Nature **479**(7372), 228–231 (2011)

5. Wang, Y.M., Lu, M.L., Wu, Z., et al.: Ratbot: a rat "understanding" what humans see. In: International Workshop on Intelligence Science, in conjunction with IJCAI-2013, pp. 63–68 (2013)
6. Wu, Z., et al.: Cyborg intelligence: research progress and future directions. IEEE Intell. Syst. **31**(6), 44–50 (2016)
7. Berger, T.W., et al.: A cortical neural prosthesis for restoring and enhancing memory. J. Neural Eng. **8**(4) (2011). https://doi.org/10.1088/1741-2560/8/4/046017
8. Wu, Z., Pan, G., Zheng, N.: Cyborg intelligence. IEEE Intell. Syst. **28**(5), 31–33 (2013)
9. Wu, Z., Zheng, N., Zhang, S., et al.: Maze Learning by hybrid brain-computer systems, Scientific Report, 9 (2016). https://doi.org/10.1038/srep31746
10. Endsley, M.R.: Toward a theory of situation awareness in dynamic systems. Hum. Factors **37**(1), 32–64 (1995)
11. Shi, Z., Zhang, J., Yue, J., Yang, X.: A cognitive model for multi-agent collaboration. Int. J. Intell. Sci. **4**(1), 1–6 (2014)
12. Gray, B.: Collaborating: Finding Common Ground for Multiparty Problems. Jossey-Bass, San Francisco (1989)
13. Shi, Z., Zhang, J., Yang, X., Ma, G., Qi, B., Yue, J.: Computational cognitive models for brain–machine collaborations. IEEE Intel. Syst. **29**, 24–31 (2014)
14. Maslow, A.H.: Motivation and Personality. Addison-Wesley, Boston (1954, 1970, 1987)
15. Cohen, P.R., Levesque, H.J.: Intention is choice with commitment. Artif. Intell. **42**(2–3), 213–361 (1990)
16. Jennings, N.R., Mamdani, E.H.: Using Joint Responsibility to Coordinate Collaborative Problem Solving in Dynamic Environments. AAAI1992, pp. 269–275 (1992)
17. Zhao, X., Tian, D., Chen, L., Shi, Z.: Reasoning theory for D3L with compositional bridge rules. In: Shi, Z., Leake, D., Vadera, S. (eds.) IIP 2012. IAICT, vol. 385, pp. 106–115. Springer, Heidelberg (2012). https://doi.org/10.1007/978-3-642-32891-6_15

Exploration Strategies for Homeostatic Agents

Patrick Andersson[✉], Anton Strandman, and Claes Strannegård

Department of Computer Science and Engineering,
Chalmers University of Technology, Gothenburg, Sweden
andersson.patrick95@gmail.com

Abstract. This paper evaluates two new strategies for investigating artificial animals called *animats*. Animats are homeostatic agents with the objective of keeping their internal variables as close to optimal as possible. Steps towards the optimal are rewarded and steps away punished. Using reinforcement learning for exploration and decision making, the animats can consider predetermined optimal/acceptable levels in light of current levels, giving them greater flexibility for exploration and better survival chances. This paper considers the resulting strategies as evaluated in a range of environments, showing them to outperform common reinforcement learning, where internal variables are not taken into consideration.

Keywords: Artificial general intelligence ·
Multi-objective reinforcement learning · Exploration strategies ·
Homeostatic regulation · Animat

1 Introduction

One way to approach *artificial general intelligence* (AGI) is to construct artificial animals, or *animats*, endowed with sensors and motors: i.e., sensorimotor capabilities. These agents act to satisfy predefined needs [11]. By simulation of more and more complex agents and environments, one can hope to obtain progressively better insight into the general nature of intelligence [12].

The notion of a homeostatic agent comes from physiology [2]. Through homeostasis, the agent attempts to minimize deviation of some number of key internal variables from their optimal levels [1], thus satisfying basic "needs"; for many animals, these are things like food and water. All living organisms are homeostatic agents. That said, the concept of homeostasis can be extended in careful, limited fashion to non-living systems that require balancing of multiple parameters: e.g., a hydroelectric power plant that "needs" to balance energy generation with water levels.

Research supported by the Torsten Söderberg Foundation Ö110/17.

While the notion of a homeostatic animat addresses the "what" and "why" of intelligent behaviour, it provides no clear answers concerning the "how". Reinforcement learning (RL) fills this gap by providing a framework for sequential decision making. RL maps states (sensory perceptions) to actions (motor actions) via the feedback of a reward signal.

A crucial task for agents operating in any environment is to balance exploration with exploitation. This paper evaluates exploration strategies that use internal variables to help agents survive longer by responding more robustly to parametric changes: i.e., adapting dynamically to the environment.

Section 2 describes how the homeostatic agent is modeled and how its exploration strategies take advantage of changes in its internal variables. Section 3 explains how those strategies are best evaluated. Finally, Sect. 5 discusses the results to conclude that RL as traditionally carried out can, indeed, be improved upon.

2 Homeostatic Agents

While the techniques used for RL share many similarities with those used for designing animats – notably those for observation and control – there is one key difference. The homeostatic animat must satisfy its needs and balance its internal variables by considering multiple objectives simultaneously. RL as traditionally conceived is only concerned with one objective: optimizing a single scalar return [10]. The problem of balancing internal variables must be imported into RL.

A homeostatic agent can be modeled in many ways [3,5–7,9]. For present purposes, two things are key: determining a scalar reward from the internal variables and, consequently, giving the agent access to those variables. This can be accomplished with a simple computational model known as *homeostatic drive reduction* [3].

First, one must convert the homeostatic problem into a single objective maximization problem appropriate for RL. Then, one must consider how the information gained from the internal variables can be applied to an exploration strategy.

2.1 Homeostatic RL

In our homeostatic agent, internal variables $\mathbf{h}$ are scaled $-1 \leq h_i \leq 1$ with optimal value $h_i^* = 0$. They are applied in three ways. First, they are fed into the drive-reduction framework [3] to calculate drive using Eq. 1. The "reward" is based on the change in drive at each time step, as seen in Eq. 2. This reward is what the reinforcement learning algorithm tries to maximize.

$$d(\mathbf{h}_t) = \sqrt[m]{\sum_{i=1}^{N} |h_i^* - h_{i,t}|^n} \tag{1}$$

$$r_t = d(\mathbf{h}_t) - d(\mathbf{h}_{t+1}) = d(\mathbf{h}_t) - d(\mathbf{h}_t + \mathbf{k}_t) \tag{2}$$

Vector **k** represents the outcome at a given time step: i.e., the change that has occurred in the internal variables. Hyper-parameters $n > m > 1$ push drive away from the optimum. By analogy, eating when hungry is more rewarding than eating when full. This creates an incentive to fulfill needs that lie further from the optimum, as a change in these needs will have a larger effect on reward.

Second, the internal variables are used as input to the RL algorithm along with observations from the environment. This increases the state space by enabling the algorithm to be "aware" of the agent's internal state. We chose to use a deep Q network (DQN) architecture [8]. Within the drive reduction framework, the Q-values for each action depend on internal state and external observations. An action indicating "eat" should have higher Q-value if the agent is hungry.

Third, the internal variables are fed into the agent's exploration strategy, becoming a part of the action decision process: the focus of this paper.

The resulting transformation of the traditional RL agent can be seen in Fig. 1. Note that the animat receives no explicit reward from its environment; instead, reward is calculated using drive reduction on the internal variables, which are perturbed but not determined by the environment.

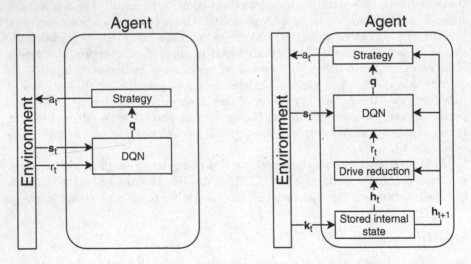

Fig. 1. Diagram visualizing the difference between a traditional RL agent, left, and a multi-objective homeostatic RL agent, right.

2.2   Homeostatic Exploration

The typical exploration strategy used in RL is ϵ-greedy [10]. It takes a random action with probability ϵ or, otherwise, the action with highest Q-value. It is typically implemented as annealed ϵ-greedy, where ϵ decays over time toward some lower bound. While this strategy has proven successful in numerous settings, it has drawbacks – the most obvious being that it is often a function of t.

That requires the hyper-parameters to be manually tuned for every environment to find the right amount of exploration. If the environment changes, the agent requires retraining with human intervention. Ideally, the agent should be capable of adapting – retraining itself – without such intervention.

By contrast, we apply a simple heuristic to the agent's internal variables to create two exploration strategies: *explore when good* (EWG) and *explore when bad* (EWB). These are dynamic strategies capable of balancing exploration with exploitation continuously, based on how the agent performs over the course of its lifetime. They operate similarly to ϵ-greedy but calculate ϵ's value at each time step based on Eqs. 3 and 4, where θ is the hyper-parameter *threshold*. The values of ϵ are represented for the agent by two internal variables, as shown in Fig. 2. It should be clear that, for EWG, the value of ϵ is highest when both variables are near optimal, whilst for EWB it is highest when they are furthest away.

$$\text{EWG:} \quad \epsilon = \max\left(0, 1 + \frac{\max_i |h_i|}{\theta - 1}\right) \tag{3}$$

$$\text{EWB:} \quad \epsilon = \max\left(0, \frac{\theta - \max_i |h_i|}{\theta - 1}\right) \tag{4}$$

Threshold parameter $0 \leq \theta < 1$ defines an interval for which the agent should be maximally greedy, selecting only the best possible actions for itself. For EWG, this threshold is set near the limit of the internal variables' acceptable levels, while for EWB it is set near the optimum. In consequence, EWG will stop exploring when any internal variable approaches the acceptable limits, while EWB will only start exploring when one or more variables are no longer close to optimum. These strategies are not dependent on time but instead change the rate of exploration dynamically, moment by moment, based on how the agent is performing in relation to optimal levels of its internal variables.

3 Method

The EWG and EWB strategies are compared to annealed ϵ and constant ϵ in a number of environments designed to evaluate various properties of the strategies. The agent balances two internal variables both of which decay when an action is performed, simulating energy usage. The variables increase or decrease according to actions in certain states. In all, thirteen environments are used, at three levels of complexity.

3.1 Environments

First are the simple worlds having no observable external state, though the agent still observes its internal state: "Greed", "Random" and "Dual". "Greed" is a static world where action outcomes are predetermined: i.e., all actions modify

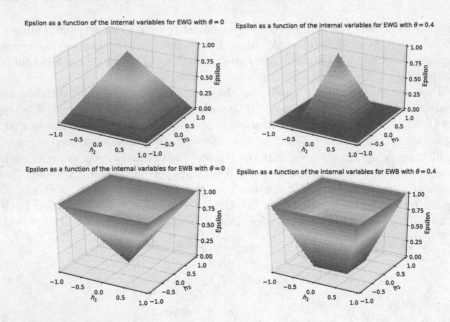

Fig. 2. A visual representation of ϵ as a function of internal variables under the EWG and EWB strategies. Threshold θ creates a buffer zone in which the agent only exploits and does not explore.

internal variables in a strictly predictable manner. "Greed" tests the strategies' ability to adopt a greedy policy quickly. "Random" randomly determines the outcome of an action once the action has been selected. This tests the strategies' ability to adapt to a highly stochastic world. "Dual" is a combination of "Greed" and "Random". Every fifty time steps, the world switches its behaviour. This tests the strategies' ability to adapt to temporal instability.

Next are grid-world variants that give the agent access to its coordinate position. The action set allows movement in the cardinal directions as well as the option of not moving, with the benefit of reduced resource decay. Four variants of a 3×3 grid world and two corridor worlds – "Corridor A" (10×1) and "Corridor B" (20×1) – are implemented.

The 3×3 grid worlds are designed to test the same properties as the simple environments, using both static and dynamic environments. Food sources change position when consumed. The agent's ability to balance its internal variables is evaluated by means of a "hostile" tile (coordinate position) that reduces one of the variables, whereas the safe environment lacks this tile. The corridor environments are designed to favour the annealed ϵ strategies. A successful agent initially explores to find both ends of the corridor, then uses this knowledge to be "greedy". The hyper-parameters are chosen so that too many exploratory actions will cause the agent's premature death.

The final set of worlds are grid-world variants adding observations of the RGB color triplets for the 3×3 set of tiles (coordinate positions) centered on the agent. The same properties as in the smaller grid worlds are evaluated in four environmental variants. As these worlds are more complex, their size is limited to a 5×5 grid initially, gradually expanded every 10,000 time steps with one tile in each cardinal direction.

The environments are non-trivial and survival is not guaranteed. The dynamic variants require exploration throughout the simulations, while the static variants promote greedy policies. The hostile environments increase environmental complexity and reduce internal variable symmetry. For subsequent discussion, the environment names are shortened to **G** for "grid world" and **ECG** for "expanding color grid world" followed by a suffix: **SS** for "static safe", **SH** for "static hostile", **DS** for "dynamic safe" and **DH** for "dynamic hostile".

3.2   Agent

The agent uses the DQN architecture [8] with one of two configurations, the difference being the size of the underlying network. A larger network with three dense layers of 64 units is used for the color grid worlds and corridor worlds, a smaller dense network with two layers of four units for the remaining environments. The agents have the hyper-parameters drive $m = 3$ and $n = 4$; discount factor $\gamma = 0.9$; and optimizer Adam [4], with learning rate 0.001, batch size 32, and experience-replay size 10^6. Online and target network switch after 200 steps; training starts after 500 steps. To speed up learning, a random, uniform initializer in the range $(-10^{-6}, 10^{-6})$ is used for the output layer.

3.3   Exploration Strategies

Multiple hyper-parameter settings of both annealed ϵ and constant ϵ are used as baselines to ensure that the best possible baseline is found for each environment. $\epsilon \in \{0, 0.01, 0.1, 0.2, 0.3, 0.4, 1\}$ is tested for constant ϵ. For annealed ϵ, all combinations of $\epsilon_{min} \in \{0.1, 0.01\}$ and $\epsilon_\Delta \in \{0.001, 0.0001, 0.00001\}$ are tested. In similar fashion, the EWG and EWB strategies are evaluated with levels of $\theta \in \{0, 0.2, 0.4, 0.6, 0.8\}$.

The agent structure is held constant for all evaluations in each environment, the only differences being the exploration strategy and random seed. Consequently, all agents have the same potential to learn about their environment. How well and how quickly they do so depends on how they explore that environment.

3.4   Evaluation

Each simulation lasts 1,000,000 steps. The primary metric for the strategies' success is the number of deaths they accumulate in each environment. Ten trials are made for each possible combination of strategy and environment. A death (i.e., terminal state) occurs when an internal variable exceeds 1 or falls below -1. Upon death, environment and agent-internal variables are reset, and the simulation continues.

The number of non-optimal actions serves as a secondary metric for gauging the number of exploratory actions [10]. This highlights any differences in strategic behaviour.

4   Results

The results indicate that EWG and EWB outperform the baseline strategies, the agents dying less often over the course of 1,000,000 steps. The agents find equivalent or better policies, faster, which they maintain throughout the simulation despite often having a higher rate of exploratory actions.

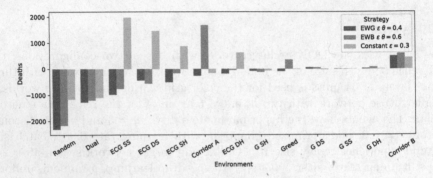

Fig. 3. The average number of deaths under the best-performing strategies of each type, relative to the best annealed baseline strategy ($\epsilon_{min} = 0.1, \epsilon_\Delta = 0.0001$). Lower values are better; a value below zero indicates better than annealed baseline performance.

Figure 3 shows the best hyper-parameter settings of the EWG, EWB, and constant ϵ strategies compared to the best annealed ϵ baseline, with $\epsilon_{min} = 0.1, \epsilon_\Delta = 0.0001$. One can see that, without human interaction, the EWG strategy adapts to environments better than any of the other strategies. This holds even when each strategy is tuned to the environment, as shown in Fig. 4.

Taking a closer look at the effects of the hyper-parameter θ on the EWG strategy, Fig. 5 shows that adding a small threshold makes the strategy more stable across environments. Making the threshold value too high may cause the agent not to explore enough: the internal variables quickly drop below the threshold and the agent becomes greedy, as the corridor environments reveal. However, the strategy appears fairly robust to changes in the threshold, with $\theta \in \{0.2, 0.4, 0.6\}$ performing well in almost all environments.

The EWG and EWB strategies prove capable of quite different levels of exploration depending on environment, without any need for human intervention – as can be seen in Fig. 6. The different environments afford a varying range of possible actions, which changes the number of non-optimal actions slightly. EWG and EWB change rate even within environments of the same type even as the constant ϵ and annealed ϵ do not. This reduces the need for human intervention when the agent is introduced to new or dynamic environments.

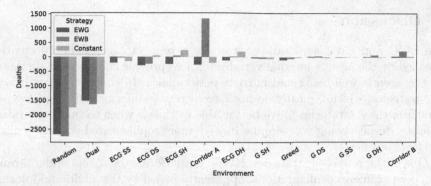

Fig. 4. Even when all strategies are tuned to find the optimal settings, EWG still performs best overall. EWB performs slightly better than EWG in "Random" and "Dual"; however it performs worse than EWG in all others.

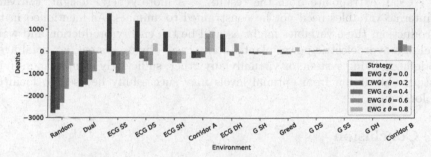

Fig. 5. Comparison of all EWG strategies to the best annealed baseline strategy ($\epsilon_{min} = 0.1, \epsilon_\Delta = 0.0001$). A small value of θ makes the EWG strategy more robust across environments, while a too-high value increases the risk of the agent not exploring enough.

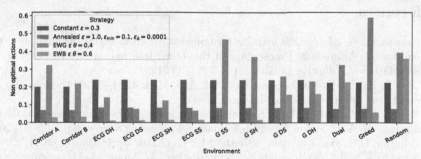

Fig. 6. The percentage of exploratory actions taken in each environment for the best performing hyper-parameter setting of each strategy type. The number changes slightly based on the number of available actions. Both EWG and EWB change their rates of exploration dynamically within the same environment type, based on how well they perform.

5   Discussion

The EWG and EWB exploration strategies take advantage of the information provided by the agent's internal variables. These provide an approximate metric for the agent's well-being and current performance. In contrast to traditional RL strategies, which typically do not have access to information regarding performance, these strategies prove better able to choose when to take exploratory actions – despite being very simple. Indeed, more sophisticated strategies might perform even better.

One of the proposed strategies, EWG, outperforms the others under a range of hyper-parameter configurations, apparently fueled by the additional information it is able to exploit. Simply adding a small threshold to EWG improves performance across most environments. The EWB strategy also performs well, but falls short in some of the environments.

We can extrapolate from the results to a more general insight: the value of internal variables need not be constrained to animats. As mentioned in the introduction, these variables might as well be the energy production and water level of a hydroelectric power plant. In any case – living system, artificial agent modeling a living system, or virtually any other, sufficiently complex non-living system – deviation from optimal levels may successfully be used to facilitate exploration.

6   Conclusion

We introduce two simple strategies for exploration of the homeostatic reinforcement learning problem. These dynamic strategies outperform traditional RL exploration strategies.

References

1. Bersini, H.: Reinforcement learning for homeostatic endogenous variables. In: From Animals to Animats 3: Proceedings of the Third International Conference on the Simulation of Adaptive Behavior, pp. 325–333 (1994)
2. Davies, K.J.: Adaptive homeostasis. Mol. Asp. Med. **49**, 1–7 (2016). Hormetic and regulatory effects of lipid oxidation products
3. Keramati, M., Gutkin, B.S.: A reinforcement learning theory for homeostatic regulation. In: Advances in Neural Information Processing Systems, pp. 82–90 (2011)
4. Kingma, D.P., Ba, J.: Adam: a method for stochastic optimization (2014)
5. Kompella, V.R., Kazerounian, S., Schmidhuber, J.: An anti-hebbian learning rule to represent drive motivations for reinforcement learning. In: del Pobil, A.P., Chinellato, E., Martinez-Martin, E., Hallam, J., Cervera, E., Morales, A. (eds.) SAB 2014. LNCS (LNAI), vol. 8575, pp. 176–187. Springer, Cham (2014). https://doi.org/10.1007/978-3-319-08864-8_17
6. Konidaris, G., Barto, A.: An adaptive robot motivational system. In: Nolfi, S., Baldassarre, G., Calabretta, R., Hallam, J.C.T., Marocco, D., Meyer, J.-A., Miglino, O., Parisi, D. (eds.) SAB 2006. LNCS (LNAI), vol. 4095, pp. 346–356. Springer, Heidelberg (2006). https://doi.org/10.1007/11840541_29

7. Konidaris, G.D., Hayes, G.M.: An architecture for behavior-based reinforcement learning. Adapt. Behav. **13**(1), 5–32 (2005)
8. Mnih, V., et al.: Human-level control through deep reinforcement learning. Nature **518**(7540), 529–533 (2015)
9. Oubbati, M., Fischer, C., Palm, G.: Intrinsically motivated decision making for situated, goal-driven agents. In: del Pobil, A.P., Chinellato, E., Martinez-Martin, E., Hallam, J., Cervera, E., Morales, A. (eds.) SAB 2014. LNCS (LNAI), vol. 8575, pp. 166–175. Springer, Cham (2014). https://doi.org/10.1007/978-3-319-08864-8_16
10. Sutton, R.S., Barto, A.G.: Reinforcement Learning: An Introduction. MIT Press, Cambridge (2018)
11. Wilson, S.W.: Knowledge growth in an artificial animal. In: Narendra, K.S. (ed.) Adaptive and Learning Systems, pp. 255–264. Springer, Boston (1986). https://doi.org/10.1007/978-1-4757-1895-9_18
12. Wilson, S.W.: The animat path to AI. In: Meyer, J.A., Wilson, S.W. (eds.) From Animals to Animats: Proceedings of the First International Conference on Simulation of Adaptive Behavior, pp. 15–21. MIT Press (1991)

Lifelong Learning Starting from Zero

Claes Strannegård[1,2]([✉]), Herman Carlström[1], Niklas Engsner[2],
Fredrik Mäkeläinen[2], Filip Slottner Seholm[1],
and Morteza Haghir Chehreghani[1]

[1] Department of Computer Science and Engineering,
Chalmers University of Technology, Gothenburg, Sweden
`claes.strannegard@chalmers.se`
[2] Dynamic Topologies Sweden AB, Gothenburg, Sweden

Abstract. We present a deep neural-network model for lifelong learning inspired by several forms of neuroplasticity. The neural network develops continuously in response to signals from the environment. In the beginning the network is a blank slate with no nodes at all. It develops according to four rules: (i) *expansion*, which adds new nodes to memorize new input combinations; (ii) *generalization*, which adds new nodes that generalize from existing ones; (iii) *forgetting*, which removes nodes that are of relatively little use; and (iv) *backpropagation*, which fine-tunes the network parameters. We analyze the model from the perspective of accuracy, energy efficiency, and versatility and compare it to other network models, finding better performance in several cases.

Keywords: Lifelong learning · Deep learning · Dynamic architectures

Animals need to respond rapidly and appropriately to all kinds of changes in their environment. To stay alive, they must make sufficiently good decisions at every moment. With few exceptions, they learn from experience; their decision-making improves over time. That requires effective mechanisms for adding, modifying, removing, and using memories.

Memories are arguably only useful to the extent they contribute to better decision-making in future: e.g., memories of vital resources that can be exploited again; memories of dangers that need to be avoided; memories formed recently; and memories used relatively often.

The ability to learn continuously by incorporating new knowledge is called *lifelong learning* [24]: sensory data is available via a continuous data stream; that data comes without any division into e.g. training set and test set; it comes without division into tasks; and sensory input at two consecutive time steps tends to be similar. Within computer science, lifelong learning is often contrasted with learning in *batch mode* where the entire data set is available from the start.

Today, deep-learning models can outperform humans on a number of tasks; see e.g. [13]. When it comes to lifelong learning and general intelligence, however, the success of deep learning has been modest at best. In contrast, insects

Supported by the Torsten Söderberg Foundation Ö110/17.

like the honeybee and fruit fly excel at lifelong learning and adaptation to new environments [10]. These animals have several mechanisms of *neuroplasticity* for altering their nervous systems in response to changes in the environment [25].

The present research was guided by the idea that neural networks with static architectures lack the flexibility needed for effective lifelong learning. Section 1 summarizes research in lifelong learning based on neural networks. Section 2 presents our dynamic model LL0. Section 3 analyzes LL0 from the perspective of accuracy, energy consumption, and versatility. Section 4 draws some conclusions.

1   Related Work

Lifelong learning constitutes a long-standing, central problem in machine learning [12,24]. Many current neural-network-based learning methods assume that all training data is available from the beginning and do not consider lifelong learning. That said, several models for lifelong learning are based on neural networks. *Catastrophic forgetting* is a crucial aspect of lifelong learning [8,19,27] that can lead to abrupt deterioration in performance. To get around it, biologically inspired computational methods integrate new knowledge while preventing it from dominating old knowledge [4,20]. The consequent trade-off is referred to as the *stability-plasticity dilemma* [11].

Various solutions have been proposed. As the network sequentially learns multiple tasks, weight protection [15] counteracts catastrophic forgetting by safeguarding weights that have been important previously. Regularization techniques [9] constrain the update of neural networks to prevent catastrophic forgetting [18]. Pruning can be used toward the same end [28,29]. Both regularization techniques and pruning reduce network size while improving generalization. The neural-network models developed for these purposes can have fixed or dynamic architectures. With fixed architectures, adaptation to new knowledge is achieved via parameter updates that penalize parameter updates to avoid catastrophic forgetting. [30] presents an example of such a model with "synaptic" intelligence.

Among the earliest dynamic models is the *cascade-correlation* architecture [7], which adds one hidden neuron at a time while freezing the network to avoid catastrophic forgetting. *Progressive* neural networks [26] add new layers of neurons progressively while blocking changes to those parts of the network trained on earlier data. Other incremental methods exist, based e.g. on incremental training of an auto-encoder; new neurons are added in response to a high rate of failure with the new data [31] or based on reconstruction error [5]. AdaNet [3] gradually extends its network by evaluation and selection among candidate sub-networks. A *dynamically expandable* network [17] expands via network split/duplication operations, retraining the old network only when necessary. Lifelong learning has been applied to such domains as autonomous learning and robotics. Learning agents are continuously exposed to new data from the environment [1,16] in a strategy markedly different from classical learning performed on finite, prepared data. Lifelong learning is in no way limited to deep neural-network models: consider the methods used for language [21] and topic modeling [2].

2   The LL0 Model

The supervised-learning model LL0 adds and removes nodes and connections dynamically through four network-modification mechanisms, each inspired by a different form of neuroplasticity: (i) *backpropagation* which adjusts parameters, inspired by synaptic plasticity [6]; (ii) *extension*, which adds new nodes, inspired by neurogenesis [14]; (iii) *forgetting*, which removes nodes, inspired by programmed cell death [22]; and (iv) *generalization*, which abstracts from existing nodes, inspired by synaptic pruning [23]. LL0 thus models four forms of neuroplasticity rather than one (i), as in standard deep learning, or two (i+ii), as in the dynamic approaches mentioned above.

LL0 receives a continuous stream of data points (x, y), where x and y are vectors of real numbers with fixed dimensions. The model maintains a neural network that starts without any nodes or connections and develops continuously. Algorithm 1 shows the main loop; the following subsections add details.

Algorithm 1. Main loop of LL0.

---
receive the first data point (x, y)
form $|x|$ input nodes and $|y|$ output nodes
while *true* **do**
  compute network output $\hat{y}$ produced by input x
  if $prediction(\hat{y}) \neq y$ **then**
    generalization
    extension
  else
    backpropagation
  end
  forgetting
  receive a new data point (x, y)
end

LL0's neural network consists of four node types:

input nodes with the identity function as their activation function;
output nodes with softmax as their activation function;
value nodes with a Gaussian activation function and two parameters, (μ, σ), used for storing values; and
concept nodes with a sigmoid activation function and one bias parameter, used for forming the neural counterparts of conjunctions (though training can turn them into something quite different!).

All concept nodes are directly connected to all output nodes. Concept nodes may also have any number of outgoing connections to value nodes. All incoming connections to concept nodes are from value nodes. Each value node has one incoming connection, which originates from either a concept or input node. They have one outgoing connection, always to a concept node.

2.1 Extension

When LL0 makes an incorrect classification, the *extension rule* is triggered. Then an *extension set* is formed. This set consists of all concept nodes and input nodes, whose activation is above a certain threshold and whose position in the network is as deep as possible. Thus no node in the extension set has a downstream node that is also in the extension set. The extension rule essentially connects each node of the extension set to a value node and then connects those value nodes to a concept node, as illustrated in Fig. 1.

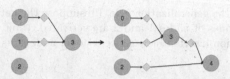

Fig. 1. Illustration of the extension rule. Yellow diamonds represent value nodes, blue circles other nodes. Assuming that nodes 2 and 3 are in the extension set, a new concept node 4 is added along with two new value nodes. (Color figure online)

The parameters are set so that each value node stores the present activation of its parent node and the concept node resembles an AND-gate. The concept node is then connected to all output nodes and the weights of those connections are set so that one-shot learning is ensured.

Imagine an agent learning to distinguish blueberries from blackberries based on taste. Suppose the data points it receives have the form (*sweetness, sourness, bitterness; blueberry, blackberry*). Suppose the first data point is $(0.6, 0.4, 0.2; 1, 0)$. Then LL0 constructs the network shown in Fig. 2.

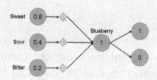

Fig. 2. The network shown is created following receipt of the first data point. The node in the center can be viewed as a conjunction node that "remembers" the taste of the first berry. Here the numbers represent approximate node activation.

2.2 Generalization

The generalization rule is used for feature extraction. Whenever the extension rule is triggered, LL0 checks whether it can generalize before adding the new node. A concept node c gets generalized if it has enough parent value nodes that are activated above a certain threshold. This is done by detaching the activated parents from c and attaching them to a new intermediate concept node c' that is inserted into the network and connected back to c, as illustrated in Fig. 3. The parameters of c' are set so that the original functionality of c is preserved.

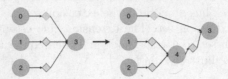

Fig. 3. Illustration of the generalization rule. Presuppose the network to the left. Suppose that the value nodes of nodes 1 and 2 are activated, while that of node 0 is not activated. Generalization inserts a new concept node, node 4, as shown to the right.

2.3 Forgetting

The forgetting rule is used for removing relatively unimportant nodes. Forgetting can be done in either of two ways: (i) setting a fixed limit to the network size and removing the worst performing nodes when the network reaches this limit, or (ii) observing how a node performs and removing it if its performance drops below a certain threshold. In the case of (i), it can clearly be catastrophic *not* to forget and leave room for new memories. The performance $p_c(t)$ of concept node c at time t can be characterized as

$$p_c(t) = \frac{\sum_{i=t_0}^{t} a_i}{t - t_0},$$

where t_0 is the time at which c was added and a_i is the activation of c at time i.

2.4 Backpropagation

The backpropagation step uses the cross-entropy cost function. The partial derivatives are calculated as usual by using the chain rule. Each concept node can be connected to hidden layers further down in the network and to output nodes. The derivative for the concept nodes needs to take all these incoming derivatives into consideration. Three parameters are updated:

- bias for the concept node: $\frac{\partial E}{\partial \theta_c}$;
- weights that are not frozen: $\frac{\partial E}{\partial w_i}$; and
- (σ, μ) for the value nodes' Gaussian activation function: $\frac{\partial E}{\partial \sigma}, \frac{\partial E}{\partial \mu}$.

These parameters are multiplied by the learning rate δ and updated using the gradient-descent algorithm.

3   Results

LL0 was compared to four fully connected, layered networks:

FC0: No hidden layer.
FC10: One hidden layer with 10 nodes.
FC10*2: Two hidden layers with 10 + 10 nodes.
FC10*3: Three hidden layers with 10 + 10 + 10 nodes.

The hyperparameters of all models were optimized for good overall performance and then fixed. The baseline models were trained using stochastic gradient descent with mini-batch size 10, learning rate 0.01, ReLU nodes in the hidden layers, softmax at the output nodes, and the cross-entropy loss function.

Despite their simplicity, these static baselines are highly useful. Dynamic models that construct fully connected layered architectures generally learn more slowly and consume more energy, since they must search for architectures in addition to undergoing the standard training procedure.

Performance of LL0 and the four baseline models was analyzed with respect to four data sets adapted from playground.tensorflow.org and scikit-learn.org: *spirals*, *digits*, *radiology*, and *wine*, in relation to accuracy and energy consumption on previously unseen test sets. An average over ten runs was calculated for each of the baseline models. Energy consumption for the baseline models was calculated as the number of parameters times the number of forward and backward passes. For LL0 it was calculated similarly and then multiplied by three. For the other LL0 rules, energy consumption was estimated conservatively as the number of network parameters times ten.

3.1   Spirals

The *spirals* data set consists of 2,000 two-dimensional data points in the form of two intertwined spirals as shown in Fig. 4 (right). Figure 5 shows the results obtained.

3.2   Digits

The *digits* data set consists of 1,797 labeled 8×8 pixel grayscale images of hand-written digits. Figure 6 shows the results obtained.

3.3   Radiology

The *radiology* data set consists of 569 data points, each a 30-dimensional vector describing features of a radiology image labeled benign or malignant. Figure 7 shows the result obtained.

3.4   Wine

The *wine* data set consists of 178 data points, each a 13-dimensional vector describing taste features of a wine identified by one of three regions of origin. Figure 8 shows the results obtained.

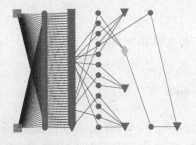
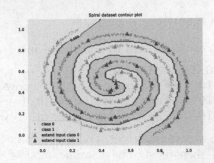

Fig. 4. Left: The network produced by LL0 on the spirals data set, with the two output nodes and their connections omitted for sake of readability. The architecture converged after less than one epoch with about 160 nodes, depth six, and max fan-in five. The yellow node was created by the generalization rule. **Right:** The spirals data set with the generated decision boundary. Input points that triggered the extension rule are marked by triangles. (Color figure online)

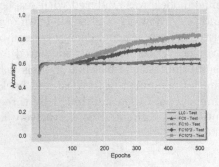
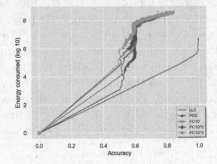

Fig. 5. Results on the spirals data set. **Left:** LL0 reaches 100% accuracy on the test set after less than one epoch. By contrast, the best baseline model FC10*3 reaches 80% accuracy after about 350 epochs. **Right:** FC10*3 consumes over 1000 times more energy than LL0 to reach 80% accuracy.

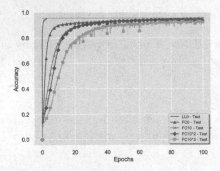
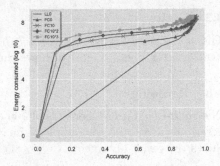

Fig. 6. Results on the digits data set. **Left:** All models eventually reach approximately the same accuracy. LL0 learns relatively fast. **Right:** The energy curves converge.

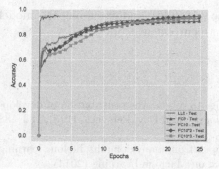

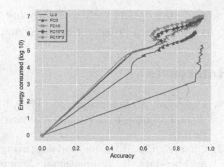

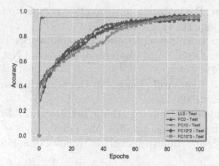

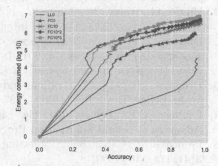

Fig. 7. Results on the radiology data set. **Left:** LL0 learns about ten times faster than the baselines. **Right:** LL0 consumes about 10% as much energy.

Fig. 8. Results on the wine data set. **Left:** LL0 learns much more quickly, but peaks at an accuracy level slightly below the best baseline. **Right:** Energy consumption.

4   Conclusion

This paper has presented a model for lifelong learning inspired by four types of neuroplasticity. The LL0 model can be used for constructing networks automatically instead of manually. It starts from a blank slate and develops its deep neural network continuously. It uses no randomization, builds no fully connected layers, and engages in no search among candidate architectures: properties that set it apart from the dynamic models surveyed in Sect. 1.

The results obtained indicate that LL0 is versatile. The four data sets considered stem from completely different sources: i.e., mathematical functions, handwriting, clinical judgment, and chemical measurements. Still, for each data set, LL0 performs at the level of the best baseline model or better. The reason might be that LL0 uses a form of one-shot learning that counteracts catastrophic forgetting and leads to relatively fast learning and low energy consumption. The fact that LL0 builds sparse networks that are continuously being generalized and trimmed might also play an important role.

The present implementation is a prototype that scales poorly to large data sets although the runtime of the underlying algorithm is linear in the number of nodes. Future plans include improving the scalability and extending the model to dynamic deep Q-networks and dynamic recurrent networks.

References

1. Cangelosi, A., Schlesinger, M.: From babies to robots: the contribution of developmental robotics to developmental psychology. Child Dev. Perspect. **12**(3), 183–188 (2018)
2. Chen, Z., Liu, B.: Topic modeling using topics from many domains, lifelong learning and big data. In: International Conference on Machine Learning (2014)
3. Cortes, C., et al.: AdaNet: adaptive structural learning of artificial neural networks. In: Proceedings of the 34th International Conference on Machine Learning, vol. 70, pp. 874–883. JMLR.org (2017)
4. Ditzler, G., Roveri, M., Alippi, C., Polikar, R.: Learning in nonstationary environments: a survey. IEEE Comput. Intell. Mag. **10**(4), 12–25 (2015)
5. Draelos, T.J., et al.: Neurogenesis deep learning: extending deep networks to accommodate new classes. In: 2017 International Joint Conference on Neural Networks (IJCNN), pp. 526–533. IEEE (2017)
6. Draganski, B., May, A.: Training-induced structural changes in the adult human brain. Behav. Brain Res. **192**(1), 137–142 (2008)
7. Fahlman, S.E., Lebiere, C.: The cascade-correlation learning architecture. In: Advances in Neural Information Processing Systems, pp. 524–532 (1990)
8. French, R.M.: Catastrophic forgetting in connectionist networks. Trends Cogn. Sci. **3**(4), 128–135 (1999)
9. Goodfellow, I., Bengio, Y., Courville, A.: Deep Learning. MIT Press, Cambridge (2016)
10. Greenspan, R.J., Van Swinderen, B.: Cognitive consonance: complex brain functions in the fruit fly and its relatives. Trends Neurosci. **27**(12), 707–711 (2004)
11. Grossberg, S.: How does a brain build a cognitive code? In: Grossberg, S. (ed.) Studies of Mind and Brain, pp. 1–52. Springer, Dordrecht (1982). https://doi.org/10.1007/978-94-009-7758-7_1
12. Hassabis, D., Kumaran, D., Summerfield, C., Botvinick, M.: Neuroscience-inspired artificial intelligence. Neuron **95**, 245–258 (2017)
13. Hatcher, W.G., Yu, W.: A survey of deep learning: platforms, applications and emerging research trends. IEEE Access **6**, 24411–24432 (2018)
14. Kandel, E.R., Schwartz, J.H., Jessell, T.M., et al.: Principles of Neural Science, vol. 4. McGraw-Hill, New York (2000)
15. Kirkpatrick, J., et al.: Overcoming catastrophic forgetting in neural networks. Proc. Natl. Acad. Sci. **114**(13), 3521–3526 (2017)
16. Krueger, K.A., Dayan, P.: Flexible shaping: how learning in small steps helps. Cognition **110**(3), 380–394 (2009)
17. Lee, J., Yoon, J., Yang, E., Hwang, S.J.: Lifelong learning with dynamically expandable networks. CoRR abs/1708.01547 (2018)
18. Li, Z., Hoiem, D.: Learning without forgetting. IEEE Trans. Pattern Anal. Mach. Intell. **40**, 2935–2947 (2018)
19. McCloskey, M., Cohen, N.J.: Catastrophic interference in connectionist networks: the sequential learning problem. In: Bower, G.H. (ed.) Psychology of Learning and Motivation, vol. 24, pp. 109–165. Elsevier, Amsterdam (1989)

20. Mermillod, M., Bugaiska, A., Bonin, P.: The stability-plasticity dilemma: investigating the continuum from catastrophic forgetting to age-limited learning effects. Front. Psychol. **4**, 504 (2013)
21. Mitchell, T., et al.: Never-ending learning. Commun. ACM **61**(5), 103–115 (2018)
22. Oppenheim, R.W.: Cell death during development of the nervous system. Annu. Rev. Neurosci. **14**(1), 453–501 (1991)
23. Paolicelli, R.C., et al.: Synaptic pruning by microglia is necessary for normal brain development. Science **333**(6048), 1456–1458 (2011)
24. Parisi, G., Kemker, R., Part, J., Kanan, C., Wermter, S.: Continual lifelong learning with neural networks: a review. Neural Netw. Off. J. Int. Neural Netw. Soc. **113**, 54–71 (2019)
25. Power, J.D., Schlaggar, B.L.: Neural plasticity across the lifespan. Wiley Interdiscip. Rev. Dev. Biol. **6**(1), e216 (2017)
26. Rusu, A.A., et al.: Progressive neural networks. arXiv preprint arXiv:1606.04671 (2016)
27. Soltoggio, A., Stanley, K.O., Risi, S.: Born to learn: the inspiration, progress, and future of evolved plastic artificial neural networks. Neural Netw. Off. J. Int. Neural Netw. Soc. **108**, 48–67 (2018)
28. Sze, V., Chen, Y.H., Yang, T.J., Emer, J.S.: Efficient processing of deep neural networks: a tutorial and survey. Proc. IEEE **105**(12), 2295–2329 (2017)
29. Wolfe, N., Sharma, A., Drude, L., Raj, B.: The incredible shrinking neural network: new perspectives on learning representations through the lens of pruning. arXiv preprint arXiv:1701.04465 (2017)
30. Zenke, F., Poole, B., Ganguli, S.: Continual learning through synaptic intelligence. In: Proceedings of the 34th International Conference on Machine Learning, vol. 70, pp. 3987–3995. JMLR.org (2017)
31. Zhou, G., Sohn, K., Lee, H.: Online incremental feature learning with denoising autoencoders. Artif. Intell. Stat. **22**, 1453–1461 (2012)

Cumulative Learning

Kristinn R. Thórisson[1,2(✉)], Jordi Bieger[1,3], Xiang Li[4], and Pei Wang[4]

[1] Center for Analysis and Design of Intelligent Agents, Reykjavik University,
Reykjavik, Iceland
thorisson@ru.is
[2] Icelandic Institute for Intelligent Machines, Reykjavik, Iceland
[3] Faculty of Technology, Policy and Management, Delft University of Technology,
Delft, The Netherlands
j.e.bieger@tudelft.nl
[4] Temple University, Philadelphia, USA
{xiangliAGI,pei.wang}@temple.edu

Abstract. An important feature of human learning is the ability to continuously accept new information and unify it with existing knowledge, a process that proceeds largely automatically and without catastrophic side-effects. A generally intelligent machine (AGI) should be able to learn a wide range of tasks in a variety of environments. Knowledge acquisition in partially-known and dynamic task-environments cannot happen all-at-once, and AGI-aspiring systems must thus be capable of *cumulative learning:* efficiently making use of existing knowledge while learning new things, increasing the scope of ability and knowledge incrementally—without catastrophic forgetting or damaging existing skills. Many aspects of such learning have been addressed in artificial intelligence (AI) research, but relatively few examples of cumulative learning have been demonstrated to date and no generally accepted explicit definition exists of this category of learning. Here we provide a general definition of cumulative learning and describe how it relates to other concepts frequently used in the AI literature.

Keywords: Cumulative learning ·
Autonomous knowledge acquisition · Knowledge representation ·
Artificial general intelligence

1 Introduction

To be autonomous, any learner in the physical world must be able to learn incrementally over time, as it is impossible to be in multiple places at once; equally importantly, one cannot know up front everything that may be relevant in the future (in which case learning would be mostly unnecessary). A learning mechanism that avoids putting acquired experience in silos, through generalization and

Partial funding for this work was provided by Isavia Iceland, IIIM, Reykjavik University, and Delft University of Technology.

© Springer Nature Switzerland AG 2019
P. Hammer et al. (Eds.): AGI 2019, LNAI 11654, pp. 198–208, 2019.
https://doi.org/10.1007/978-3-030-27005-6_20

old-new unification, will always be more parsimonious, and thus more effective, than the alternatives. We consider such *cumulative learning* a hallmark of human cognition, and of central importance to artificial general intelligence (AGI).

The concept of cumulative learning offers an integrated view of numerous cognitive processes that largely have been treated in isolation in the AI literature to date, including, in one form or another, pattern matching, reasoning, continuous information acquisition, and old-new integration or unification (which has mostly been ignored outside of [16]). While a fragmented approach to learning may be sufficient for narrow AI research, we consider the current state of fragmentation to be detrimental to AGI research, and call for a more integrated perspective to help the field avoid obscuring important phenomena and slowing down progress towards artificial *general* intelligence. This paper attempts to bring all relevant concerns into one place and set the stage for a long-term vision for cumulative learning in AGI systems.

At the heart of cumulative learning is a process of *unification:* New information enters by default into a process of being integrated with already-acquired knowledge—whether it is in agreement with it or not. This is compression under requirements of *incrementality, realtime,*[1] and *generalization*: Replacing incorrect knowledge and extending current knowledge frequently, while generalizing when possible, prepares knowledge to be efficiently applicable to the largest possible class of situations, tasks, topics, and domains—as soon as possible during the learner's lifetime.

Several aspects of cumulative learning as formulated here[2] have been covered in the machine learning literature, *but its many necessary-but-not-sufficient features* have invariably been addressed *in isolation.* As any student of systems engineering knows, it is infeasible to join disparate mechanisms, based on incompatible theoretical foundations, into a single coherent system. Due to the lack of a coherent, comprehensive theory of learning, research on this topic in various fields has yielded a number of ontologically inconsistent terms for the various aspects of the phenomenon, and the almost complete ignorance of the importance of incremental knowledge unification. *Always-on* learning has for instance variously appeared under the headings 'lifelong', 'perpetual', 'never-ending', 'incremental', 'online', and 'continual' learning [8,15,20,29,30], most of which only have partial overlap. Other examples of concepts prevalent in the literature of varying relevance to cumulative learning include 'learning to learn,' 'multi-task learning,' 'metalearning,' 'transfer learning,' 'domain adaptation,' 'inductive/knowledge transfer,' 'knowledge consolidation,' 'knowledge-based inductive bias,' 'context-sensitive learning,' 'catastrophic forgetting/interference,' and 'semi-supervised learning' [5,11,18,24]. Few systems have proposed to address the full scope of cumulative learning as formulated here. Two systems that explicitly have, and presented empirical evidence of progress towards it, are the Non-Axiomatic

---

[1] Unification must happen frequently, relative to the learner's lifetime, lest we'd be hard-pressed to call it 'cumulative.'.

[2] The term itself has appeared in the AI literature with some overlap of its sense here (cf. [2,6,7]), as well as in AGI research (cf. [23]).

Reasoning System (NARS) [26,27] and Auto-Cataytic Endogenous Reflective Architecture (AERA) [16,17].

In addition to insufficient focus on old-new unification, few of the above concepts have been conceived in the context of (artificial) general intelligence and are thus in one or more aspects at odds with the larger, more complete picture of learning that we find needed for AGI. Here we attempt to present a coherent picture by 'defragmenting' the conceptual space surrounding learning, painting instead a coherent picture more suited as a step towards a theory of cumulative learning.

2   Dimensions of (Cumulative) Learning

Learning is necessary for goal achievement in a changing, novel environment. All learning machines, whether natural or artificial, are limited by the time and energy they have available; the outermost constraint on any learning mechanism is the assumption of insufficient knowledge and resources (AIKR) [9]. However, there is a large number of ways to interpret these constraints when implementing learning mechanisms, and thus there are numerous dimensions along which any learning ability may vary. We have identified 14 dimensions whose settings determine the performance characteristics of any particular cumulative learning implementation. These naturally form three sets: (1) *Memory management*, (2) *temporal capacity and granularity*, and (3) *generality*. In each group there are between four and six different dimensions that we will now outline. While these are not perfectly orthogonal to each other (which would require a proper theory of learning), the breakdown allows us to better place prior work in the context of the present focus. Note that our focus in this paper is not so much on learning *methods* but primarily on externally measurable factors and characteristics of the cumulative learning process as a whole, and related learner performance characteristics.

[A] **Memory Management.** Operational characteristics of processes related to memory and knowledge management. These can of course also be learned, i.e. improved with experience. Having to do with quality, these range from *catastrophic* at one end to *highly effective* at the other.
  (a) **Storage:** Storing relevant aspects of experience in memory.
  (b) **Remembrance:** Bringing relevant knowledge to bear on a task or problem.
  (c) **Forgettance:** Removing the least relevant and necessary knowledge, if needed.
  (d) **Compression:** "Cleaning up" knowledge in ways that can improve the learner in some way, w.r.t. storage, forgettance, remembrance, generality, etc.
  (e) **Old-New Unification:** Integrating new information with existing knowledge so that it becomes more coherent and parsimonious.
  (f) **Defeasibility:** Replacing less correct, less useful and/or less detailed knowledge with new more correct, more useful and/or more detailed knowledge.

[B] **Temporal Capacity & Granularity.** When and how the learner can accept new information. This group contains four important characteristics that define temporal measures of cumulative learning:
  (g) **Concurrent capacity:** How many things[3] can be learned concurrently.
  (h) **Consecutive capacity:** How many things can be learned consecutively.
  (i) **Temporal granularity** of information **acceptance/storage**.
  (j) **Temporal granularity** of old-new information **unification**.[4]

The range of dimensions **Bg** and **Bh** starts with *one thing once* at the lower end, meaning that a single learner can only learn one thing at one (particular) time, and extends towards *many things at any time, concurrently/simultaneously and/or consecutively/sequentially* at the other end, meaning the learner can at any time learn new things, no matter how large or small (ignoring learning time and materials). **Bi** and **Bj** at the lower end range from *a single two-step learn-then-apply pair* (e.g. artificial neural nets), to *concurrently* and/or *consecutively and continuously* (non-discretized) at the other end.

[C] **Generality** of the learning, with respect to task, goal, domain, etc. These parameters range from *one* at the lower end, to *any* at the other.
  (k) **Data Flexibility:** Flexibility in the kind of data that learner can accept (as dictated by cognitive – not sensing – capabilities).
  (l) **Knowledge Flexibility:** Flexibility in what knowledge is leveraged.
  (m) **Knowledge Transfer:** Using knowledge acquired for one purpose in one context to other purposes and contexts.
  (n) **Learning to Learn:** Using acquired knowledge to improve learning ability.
  (o) **Inverse Defeasibility:** New information improves existing knowledge. The more generally a learner can do this (i.e. the less directly the new information is related to current knowledge) the better a learner it is.

3 Functions of Cumulative Learning

A cumulative learner in our conceptualization is a learning controller [23] that, guided by one or more top-level internalized goals (or drives), implements a cumulative modeling process whereby regularities are recursively extracted from the learner's experience (of self and environment) to construct integrated models useful for achieving goals [3,23]. The collection of models form a unified body of knowledge that can be used, by a set of additional and appropriate management processes (see **Aa-f** above), as the basis for making predictions about, and achieving goals with respect to, an environment, and that can be used to

---

[3] A "thing" can be a task, environment, goal, domain, phenomenon, process, etc.— it does not matter so much here which, as long as there is some way to compare systems on these features.

[4] 'Learning' here means the acquisition of knowledge applicable to achieving goals the learner might face, now or in the future; this view does not address "non-actionable knowledge".

improve future learning—in speed, quality, efficiency, or all of these [28]. At the risk of oversimplification, a compact definition of cumulative learning might read something like "using a unified body of knowledge to continually and recursively integrate new information from many contexts into that body." A learner whose models capture in this way an actionable description of measurable, verifiable entities in the environment and their relations, and tends over time towards the pragmatically simplest (interrelated) set of such descriptions, is in some sense an ideal cumulative learner.

We will now turn to the central features of this conceptualization of cumulative learning in light of notable related work. We emphasize that our interest in cumulative learning is limited to a learner that _embodies and unifies all_ of the following learning-related functions _in a single coordinated system_, _throughout its lifetime_, as is necessary for making progress towards AGI.

3.1   Temporal Capacity and Granularity

An important dimension of learning concerns how and when the learner is open to accepting, storing and integrating new information into its knowledge base.

Learning Multiple Things. A cumulative learner must, by definition, be able to learn multiple things – tasks, goals, environmental factors, techniques, rules of thumb, generalizations, modes of reasoning, etc. – cumulatively over time: It must not be restricted to a single function, task, domain or phenomenon. Aspects of this capability have been studied under the term 'multitask learning' (MTL) [4] where the learner learns multiple tasks concurrently (cf. **Bg**). MTL assumes the input representation for each task is the same, and concurrent learning requires predefined and pre-programmed knowledge of the number of tasks, and (ideally) access to a data set where each input is associated with a target output label (in the supervised learning setting for which it was conceived). Fei et al. [7] use the term 'cumulative learning' to describe a variation of this type of MTL, where tasks are added one after the other (cf. **Bh**).

MTL can be extended to control tasks in a reinforcement learning setting [22] by assuming the tasks are encountered consecutively (rather than assuming a single agent simultaneously acting in multiple task-environments; cf. **Bh**). In this setting MTL research often makes use of hierarchical reinforcement learning (HRL), which also involves learning multiple (sub)tasks that together constitute a top-level task. When the top-level task is removed, leaving just the subtasks, this is closely related to both multitask learning and multi-objective reinforcement learning (MORL) where an agent has multiple active goals. This kind of process can happen organically in NARS [26].

An ideal cumulative learner should be capable of learning multiple things both concurrently and consecutively, as appropriate, without constraints on the order of encountered phenomena and task revisitation. NARS [25] can accept input data of any content at any time (cf. **Bi, Bj**), as long as they can be expressed in a format that the system can recognize (cf. **Ck, Cl**). This means

NARS has the ability to solve any problems expressible in its language instead of being limited to a specific type of problems. When solving a problem, all accumulated evidence matters, though different pieces may contribute differently (cf. **Ab, Ae, Af**). In AERA [16] any digital data can become a source of learning (cf. **Ck, Cl**), and the simplest basis on which it can learn is correlation between data types, variables or values (cf. **Aa**). To learn, AERA must from the outset have a drive in its seed that references one or more observable environment variables.

Always-On Learning. An ideal cumulative learner can learn at any time—there are no pre-designated periods where its learning is turned off, no required dedicated special training phase (although it is of course not prevented), and the learning process does not converge to an attractor (cf. **Bi, Bj**). Thus, learning occurs perpetually throughout the operational lifetime of a cumulative learner.

Lifelong machine learning (LML) [6,20], continual learning [19], perpetual learning [30] and never-ending learning [15] all focus on sequentially learning an unknown number of tasks.[5] As a result, learning in these settings never truly ends. However, this does not necessarily mean that learning is always on. For instance, Zhang's perpetual learner [30] only enters a new learning phase when a "learning stimulus" is encountered (i.e. an inconsistency, anomaly or surprise) during each (learning-free) application phase. Furthermore, many lifelong learners consider learning on the current task "done" before starting the new one and it is typically not clear when the learned knowledge is supposed to be applied (and what can be learned from that application), suggesting that even here there is a separation between training/learning and application phases.

The temporal granularity at which incoming information can be accepted, stored and added to the knowledge base are important dimensions of learning (cf. **Bi, Bj**). While many ML systems can only learn in a single designated phase at the beginning of their lifetime followed by a phase in which this knowledge is applied, other systems can alternate between these modes (e.g. Zhang's perpetual learner [30]), while yet others learn constantly with or without explicit learning/application phases (e.g. NARS [25] and AERA [16]). The rate at which new information can be accepted and stored, and the rate at which it can be usefully unified into the knowledge base, are separate dimensions.

Assessing temporal granularity of a learner involves examining how much information it needs before learning can occur. *Offline* or *batch learning* assumes constant on-demand access to all data, no restrictions on time and space for training, and a fixed (often *i.i.d.*) distribution from which the data is pulled, while *online* or *incremental learning* removes these assumptions [8]. In online/incremental learning information is encountered sequentially and there are often restrictions placed on the ability to revisit old data. In the most extreme case, upon encountering some new datum d the learner's model m must

---

[5] While the terms 'lifelong learning' and 'lifelong machine learning' are not always used entirely consistently, they can be considered approximately interchangeable with 'perpetual learning' and 'never-ending learning,' respectively.

be updated based only on m and d, without considering any previously encountered data. A continuum of incrementality could be considered based on how much previous data can be used to update m, where offline/batch learning is at the other extreme because it uses all data.

Incrementality in LML can be evaluated at multiple levels: While e.g. tasks are often encountered sequentially, and data from previous tasks may or may not be available, it is often the case that each individual task is trained offline when it is encountered. Online learning is common in forecasting, sequence prediction, and sequential decision making. Many reinforcement learning algorithms learn online (e.g. Q-learning), although other algorithms (e.g. policy gradient) and function approximations (e.g. using deep learning) may require batches of data.

3.2 Memory Management

For an implemented system, neither memory nor computation speed is infinite [9]. This means all learners must make choices on what knowledge can and should be retained (cf. **Aa**). Systems that cannot forget will inevitably run into memory limits at some point and break down, or demand human intervention, either of which are sub-optimal because processing an ever increasing amount of knowledge will become prohibitive due to the limitation on computation speed (cf. **Ab**, **Ac**).

When learning a new task causes forgetting of critical or all parts of previously learned tasks, this is called *catastrophic forgetting* [12]. Workarounds include e.g. "freezing" of knowledge obtained for previously encountered tasks, and retaining training data to engage in task rehearsal (i.e. continuously retraining on old tasks as well as new ones), but this runs into aforementioned limits of space and time. An important challenge to address in cumulative learning is thus the stability-plasticity balance [14], wherein sufficient plasticity is needed to incorporate new knowledge while retaining old knowledge requires sufficient stability.

Forgetting sensibly is bound to involve several processes, such as replacing wrong or worse knowledge with correct or better knowledge, respectively, whenever possible (cf. **Af**). There should be multiple ways of compressing the knowledge (with or without loss; cf. **Ad**)—induction (generalization) is one way to do so, forgetting permanently is another one (based on empirically-evaluated usefulness). Numerous combinations of various mechanisms are possible, achieving various trade-offs between memory requirements, applicability, manageability, and so on. In addition to selective forgetting, AERA's rewriting rules reduces redundancies and storage requirements through increased generality whereby values are replaced with variables coupled with ranges [16]. In NARS, forgetting has two related senses: (1) relative forgetting: decrease priority to save time, (2) absolute forgetting: remove from memory to save space and time [9].

3.3 Generality

The last set of learning dimensions considered here concerns the generality and generalization ability of the learning system. Ideal cumulative learners can accumulate knowledge of any type and in any situation, and generalize it for use in both unseen future contexts and previously encountered situations. As with the other dimensions, the focus here is not on learning methods, i.e. how generality is achieved, but rather on externally measurable characteristics of cumulative learners and performance.

Domain-, Task- & Goal-Generality. A domain-general (domain-independent) cumulative learner will model any relevant experience, including its own sensors, the quality of data they produce (in relation to other sensors), as well as the quality of data acquired from outside sources (cf. **Ck**, **Cl**]), and even its own cognitive processes. An ideal artificial cumulative learner, in our conceptualization, can therefore acquire knowledge and skills through both experience [21] and explicit teaching [3]. Goal-generality means that knowledge and goal(s) are not fused together (in particular situations and constraints) but can be re-purposed when task- and domain-related parameters change [10].

It is worth pointing out that paradigms like transfer learning, MTL and LML tend to focus on the task as a distinct unit (cf. **Bi**, **Bj**): It is assumed that tasks are explicitly separated from the point of view of the learner, who is typically notified when learning on a new task starts, or of the task that should currently be performed. In the general case of the real physical world, task boundaries are not this clear. (Is playing tennis against well-known tennis player Roger Federer a different task than playing against Rafael Nadal? What about playing doubles? Or against a child? What about playing squash or badminton?) Correctly recognizing contexts and knowing what prior knowledge to bear (and how) is a key part of the challenge that cumulative learning solves: Boundaries between tasks and domains for autonomous learners in the real world are inexplicit. Animals learn continuously, cumulatively adding new knowledge to their current knowledge, as needed. NARS [25] accepts input data and task of any contents, as far as they can be expressed in a recognizable format (cf. **Ck**, **Cl**). AERA [16] is data-general as its learning methods are data-agnostic (while its learning is not) (cf. **Ck**, **Cl**).

Unlike transfer learning, with its explicit focus on the learning period itself, cumulative learning assumes a continually running process of unification—irrespective of how or whether the new knowledge can be, or was, useful in learning the new information (cf. **Bi**, **Bj**). An extreme case of this is using analogies to deepen or broaden knowledge of a set of phenomena. In NARS, for instance, learning involves not only tasks but also effective (re-)organization of knowledge, without respect to specific problems, so that it may later be used on *any* relevant task [28] (cf. **Ae**, **Af**). The idea of such meta-learning ('super-task learning' or 'task-free learning') is naturally only a challenge in a context where multiple things are actually learned, and has only recently received some attention [1,9]. In AERA [16] models are by themselves general in that they are not attached to any particular task (this is always computed on a case-by-case basis on the fly), and each model is thus in principle applicable to any part of any task, as long as its preconditions are met (cf. **Ck, Cl**).[6]

Knowledge Transfer. Cumulative modeling, to achieve effective compression and old-new unification for any new context or situation, needs to find ways of dealing with similar input at different points in time, and note its similarity and differences, so that old knowledge acquired at time t_1 for situation S_1 can be successfully used for a new situation S_2 at time t_2. This can be done by e.g. making analogies [25] (cf. **Cm**). New information should be integrated with old information, at a low level of detail (as low as possible, in each case), producing a growing set of interrelated (fine-grained) models of the task-environment [16] (cf. **Ae**).

Similarly, the goal of transfer learning and domain adaptation is to use knowledge obtained in a set (typically of size one) of previously learned source tasks in order to facilitate learning and/or performance on a target task [18] (cf. **Cm, Cn**). Perhaps more generally, it deals with the situation where (some or all of) the training is obtained in a situation different from the one in which it is to be applied. Making use of existing knowledge ('inductive bias') can enable faster learning from one or a few observations that would otherwise not contain enough information ('one-shot' or 'few-shot' learning), possibly even without ever direct observation ('zero-shot learning') [13].

To make knowledge transfer between tasks and situations positive (helping instead of hurting learning and performance), it is important to consider what, when, and how relevant knowledge is transferred. Most work to date has focused on "how," while relevance of prior knowledge is already assumed, and assumed that most transfer happens right before the learner starts learning a target task. Work on task similarity and transferability is rarer, as is the question of when to transfer. An ideal cumulative learner will always treat new information in a way that makes it generally applicable to future tasks, so there is no explicit knowledge transfer step or stage—just the future application of the most relevant available knowledge in each instance. This is how knowledge transfer and learning works in NARS [25] and AERA [16]. Furthermore, at the present time what we might call "forward transfer" – the effect of current learning on future learning – is considered more important than "backward transfer" (the effects that learning the new task has on the ability to perform the previously learned tasks). In practice, backward transfer in much of current machine learning is typically extremely negative, as catastrophic interference/forgetting [12] occurs where the previous tasks are forgotten almost entirely or performance drops dramatically (cf. **Bc**).

---

[6] Still, if some models are often used together they may be compiled for faster future use, which may be comparable to detecting "tasks" that are meaningful to the learning system).

4   Conclusions

Artificial generally intelligent (AGI) systems will need to handle unknown dynamic environments, where required information cannot be known fully up front and many skills must be acquired. Cumulative learning, as we conceive of it, is important for AGI for numerous reasons, including: (1) Knowledge is created incrementally, matching the needs of partially-known, changing environments, (2) knowledge is built up and improved in small increments, avoiding pitfalls of catastrophic forgetting and errors, (3) new knowledge is immediately available to the learner, and (4) knowledge consisting of fine-grained (low-level) explicit models provides explicitness necessary for comparing, managing, reasoning, etc. To be useful for AGI systems these skills must *all exist in a unified manner in one and the same learner*. In this paper we have tried to clarify why and how the various aspects of cumulative learning relate to key AGI requirements, and place it in the context of prior work. More work is clearly needed to realize true artificial cumulative learning in a single system on par with that found in nature. The systems developed by the authors, NARS [26] and AERA [16], demonstrate some important steps in this direction by bringing several of its features together in single unified systems.

References

1. Aljundi, R., Kelchtermans, K., Tuytelaars, T.: Task-free continual learning. CoRR (2018)
2. Baldassare, G., et al.: The IM-CLeVeR project: intrinsically motivated cumulative learning versatile robots. In: 9th International Conference on Epigenetic Robotics: Modeling Cognitive Development in Robotic Systems, pp. 189–190 (2009)
3. Bieger, J.E., Thórisson, K.R.: Task analysis for teaching cumulative learners. In: Iklé, M., Franz, A., Rzepka, R., Goertzel, B. (eds.) AGI 2018. LNCS (LNAI), vol. 10999, pp. 21–31. Springer, Cham (2018). https://doi.org/10.1007/978-3-319-97676-1_3
4. Caruana, R.A.: Multitask connectionist learning. In: Proceedings of the 1993 Connectionist Models Summer School, pp. 372–379 (1993)
5. Chapelle, O., Schölkopf, B., Zien, A.: Semi-supervised Learning. Adaptive Computation and Machine Learning. MIT Press, Cambridge (2006)
6. Chen, Z., Liu, B.: Lifelong Machine Learning. Morgan & Claypool Publishers, San Rafael (2016)
7. Fei, G., Wang, S., Liu, B.: Learning cumulatively to become more knowledgeable. In: Proceedings of the 22nd ACM SIGKDD International Conference on Knowledge Discovery and Data Mining, KDD 2016, pp. 1565–1574 (2016)
8. Fontenla-Romero, Ó., Guijarro-Berdiñas, B., Martinez-Rego, D., Pérez-Sánchez, B., Peteiro-Barral, D.: Online machine learning. In: Igelnik, B., Zurada, J.M. (eds.) Efficiency and Scalability Methods for Computational Intellect, pp. 27–54. IGI Global, Hershey (2013)
9. Hammer, P., Lofthouse, T., Wang, P.: The OpenNARS implementation of the Non-Axiomatic Reasoning System. In: Proceedings of Artificical General Intelligence Conference (2016)

10. Hammer, P., Lofthouse, T.: Goal-directed procedure learning. In: Iklé, M., Franz, A., Rzepka, R., Goertzel, B. (eds.) AGI 2018. LNCS (LNAI), vol. 10999, pp. 77–86. Springer, Cham (2018). https://doi.org/10.1007/978-3-319-97676-1_8

11. Jiang, J.G., Su, Z.P., Qi, M.B., Zhang, G.F.: Multi-task coalition parallel formation strategy based on reinforcement learning. Acta Automatica Sinica **34**(3), 349–352 (2008)

12. Kirkpatrick, J., et al.: Overcoming catastrophic forgetting in neural networks. Proc. Natl. Acad. Sci. **114**(13), 3521–3526 (2017)

13. Lake, B., Salakhutdinov, R., Gross, J., Tenenbaum, J.: One shot learning of simple visual concepts. In: Proceedings of the Annual Meeting of the Cognitive Science Society, vol. 33 (2011)

14. Mermillod, M., Bugaiska, A., Bonin, P.: The stability-plasticity dilemma: investigating the continuum from catastrophic forgetting to age-limited learning effects. Front. Psychol. **4**, 504 (2013)

15. Mitchell, T., et al.: Never-ending learning. Commun. ACM **61**(5), 103–115 (2018)

16. Nivel, E., et al.: Bounded recursive self-improvement. Technical RUTR-SCS13006, Reykjavik University Department of Computer Science, Reykjavik, Iceland (2013)

17. Nivel, E., et al.: Autocatalytic endogenous reflective architecture. Technical RUTR-SCS13002, Reykjavik University School of Computer Science, Reykjavik, Iceland (2013)

18. Pan, S.J., Yang, Q.: A survey on transfer learning. IEEE Trans. Knowl. Data Eng. **22**(10), 1345–1359 (2010). https://doi.org/10.1109/TKDE.2009.191

19. Ring, M.B.: CHILD: a first step towards continual learning. Mach. Learn. **28**(1), 77–104 (1997)

20. Silver, D.L., Yang, Q., Li, L.: Lifelong machine learning systems: beyond learning algorithms. In: AAAI Spring Symposium: Lifelong Machine Learning (2013)

21. Steunebrink, B.R., Thórisson, K.R., Schmidhuber, J.: Growing recursive self-improvers. In: Proceedings of Artificial General Intelligence, pp. 129–139 (2016)

22. Taylor, M.E., Stone, P.: Transfer learning for reinforcement learning domains: a survey. J. Mach. Learn. Res. **10**, 1633–1685 (2009)

23. Thórisson, K.R., Talbot, A.: Cumulative learning with causal-relational models. In: Iklé, M., Franz, A., Rzepka, R., Goertzel, B. (eds.) AGI 2018. LNCS (LNAI), vol. 10999, pp. 227–237. Springer, Cham (2018). https://doi.org/10.1007/978-3-319-97676-1_22

24. Vilalta, R., Drissi, Y.: A perspective view and survey of meta-learning. Artif. Intell. Rev. **18**(2), 77–95 (2002)

25. Wang, P.: Rigid Flexibility: The Logic of Intelligence. Springer, Dordrecht (2006). https://doi.org/10.1007/1-4020-5045-3

26. Wang, P.: From NARS to a thinking machine. Adv. Artif. Gen. Intell. Concepts, Arch. Algorithms **157**, 75–93 (2007)

27. Wang, P.: Non-Axiomatic Logic: A Model of Intelligent Reasoning. World Scientific Publishing, Singapore (2013)

28. Wang, P., Li, X.: Different conceptions of learning: function approximation vs. self-organization. In: Steunebrink, B., Wang, P., Goertzel, B. (eds.) AGI -2016. LNCS (LNAI), vol. 9782, pp. 140–149. Springer, Cham (2016). https://doi.org/10.1007/978-3-319-41649-6_14

29. Zhan, Y., Taylor, M.E.: Online transfer learning in reinforcement learning domains. arXiv preprint arXiv:1507.00436 (2015)

30. Zhang, D.: From one-off machine learning to perpetual learning: a step perspective. In: IEEE International Conference on Systems, Man, and Cybernetics (SMC) (2018)

Learning with Per-Sample Side Information

Roman Visotsky[1], Yuval Atzmon[1], and Gal Chechik[1,2](✉)

[1] Bar-Ilan University, Ramat Gan, Israel
gal.chechik@biu.ac.il
[2] NVIDIA Research, Tel Aviv, Israel
https://chechiklab.biu.ac.il/

Abstract. Learning from few samples is a major challenge for parameter-rich models such as deep networks. In contrast, people can learn complex new concepts even from very few examples, suggesting that the sample complexity of learning can often be reduced. We describe an approach to reduce the number of samples needed for learning using per-sample side information. Specifically, we show how to speed up learning by providing textual information about feature relevance, like the presence of objects in a scene or attributes in an image. We also give an improved generalization error bound for this case. We formulate the learning problem using an ellipsoid-margin loss, and develop an algorithm that minimizes this loss effectively. Empirical evaluation on two machine vision benchmarks for scene classification and fine-grain bird classification demonstrate the benefits of this approach for few-shot learning.

Keywords: Few-shot learning · Side information · Machine teaching

1 Introduction

People can learn to recognize new classes from a handful of examples. In contrast, deep networks need large labeled datasets to match human performance in object recognition. This gap in performance suggests that there are fundamental factors that could reduce the sample complexity of our current learning algorithms. From the practical point of view, few-shot learning becomes a real challenge in domains where collecting labeled samples is hard or costly. For example, when the number of classes is large, tail-concepts often have too few samples for effective training. Also, in numerous applications where the data is non-stationary, classifiers have to learning in an online manner, continuously suffering a cost for every wrong decision. In these cases, it is important to learn quickly from a few samples.

Many approaches to few-shot learning and zero-shot learning (ZSL) are based on learning a representation using well-sampled classes and then using that representation to learn new classes with few samples [1,2,10,18,19]. In a second line of approaches, *meta-learning*, a learner is trained to find an inductive bias over the set of model architectures that benefits FSL [9,15]. Unfortunately, these approaches may not be feasible in the online learning setup where a cost is incurred for every prediction made.

© Springer Nature Switzerland AG 2019
P. Hammer et al. (Eds.): AGI 2019, LNAI 11654, pp. 209–219, 2019.
https://doi.org/10.1007/978-3-030-27005-6_21

This paper proposes a complementary approach, inspired by how people learn faster by integrating side information about samples, classes and features. Specifically, when people learn new concepts from few labeled samples x_i, y_i, they can also effectively use additional per-sample information z_i which provides an inductive bias about the model to be learned. We name this source of side information: **Rich supervision** (RS).

Learning with rich human supervision has to address two major challenges. First, one has to collect rich supervision from human raters, which may be hard to scale. Second, one needs to find ways to integrate the rich supervision into the model effectively. Most previous approaches focused on providing localization information as side information. Here we focus on a specific type of RS and address these two challenges. We study a learning architecture that has an intermediate representation with named entities, like attributes or detected objects. In this setup, we show that it is possible to use open-world tags provided by raters by mapping them to the intermediate entities. This approach also addresses the second challenge, collecting sparse information about features at scale [3]. We demonstrate two different datasets where such information is available, and show how the text tags can be mapped onto an internal network representation.

We formulate the problem in the context of online learning. We design a new ellipsoid-margin loss that takes into account the side-information available, and describe an online algorithm for minimizing that loss efficiently. We test the algorithm with two datasets and find that it improves over two baselines. First, with visual scene classification using object occurrence as RS. Second, with bird species recognition using visual attributes as RS.

The novel contributions of this paper are as follows: (1) First, we describe the general setup of learning with per-sample side-information and discuss the special case of learning with per-sample information about feature uncertainty and relevance as a special case; (2) We prove a theorem showing how per-sample information can reduce the sample complexity; (3) We then describe Ellipsotron, an online learning algorithm for learning with rich supervision about feature uncertainty, which efficiently uses per-class and per-sample information; (4) We demonstrate empirically how rich supervision can help even in a case of strong-transfer, where expert feedback is provided in an unrestricted language, and that feedback is transferred *without learning* to a pretrained internal representation of the network; (5) Finally, we demonstrate the benefit of empirical supervision at the sample level and class level on two standard benchmarks for scene classification and fine-grained classification.

2   Related Work

Learning with Feature Feedback. A special case of rich supervised learning occurs when feedback is available about the accuracy or confidence of given features. This setup was studied for batch learning. [7] incorporated user-provided information about feature-label relations into the objective. [17] augmented SVM using a set of order constraints over weights, e.g., the weight of one feature should be larger than another. [4] described a large-margin approach to handle structurally missing features, which in the current context can be viewed as features with infinite uncertainty. [3] describes a visual recognition method with a human-in-the-loop at inference time. [14] studied an active learning setup where raters are asked about relevance of features. Other approaches provided localization information as a source of side information, see references in [20].

Most relevant to this paper is the recent work by [13]. They studied user-provided feedback about features for binary classification and proposed an algorithm based SVM applied to rescaled features (Algorithm 4, SVM-FF). It differs from the Ellipsotron algorithm described here in several important ways. First, the fundamental difference is that SVM-FF rescales all data using a single shared matrix, while *our approach is class-specific or sample-specific*. Second, we present an online algorithm. Third, our loss is different, in that samples are only scaled to determine if the margin constraint is obeyed, but the loss is taken over non-scaled samples. This is important since rescaling samples with different matrices may change the geometry of the problem. Indeed, our evaluation of an online-variant of SVM-FF performed poorly (see Sect. 7.1 below) compared to the approach proposed here. Also relevant is the work of [6], which address learning a multi-class classifier using simple explanations viewed as "discriminative features", and analyze learning a particular subclass of DNF formulas with such explanations.

3   Rich Supervised Learning

The current paper considers using information about features per-sample. It is worth viewing it in the more general context of rich supervision (RS). As in standard supervised learning, in RS we are given a set of n labeled samples ($x \in \mathcal{X}, y \in \mathcal{Y}$) drawn from a distribution D, and the goal is to find a mapping $f_W : X \to Y$ to minimize the expected loss $E_D[loss(f_W(\mathbf{x}_i), y_i)]$. In RS, at training time, each labeled sample is also provided with an additional side information $z \in \mathcal{Z}$. Importantly, z is not available at test time, and only used as an inductive bias when training f. Rich supervision can have many forms. It can be about a class (hence $z_i = z_j$ iff $y_i = y_j \ \forall$ samples i, j), as with a class description in natural language ("zebras have stripes"). It can be about a sample, e.g., providing information about the uncertainty of a label y_i, about the importance of a sample $\mathbf{x}_i$ ("this sample is important"), or the importance of features per sample ("look here"). Here we study z_i about the per-sample detection of high-level concepts characterized using natural language terms.

4   Learning with Per-Sample Feature Information

We focus here on the online learning setting for multiclass classification. An online learner repeatedly receives a labeled sample $\mathbf{x}_i$ (with $i = 1, \ldots, n$), makes a prediction $\hat{y}_i = f_W(\mathbf{x}_i)$ and suffers a cost $loss(\mathbf{w}; \mathbf{x}_i, y_i)$. We explore a specific type of rich supervision z_i, providing feedback about features per samples.

Specifically, in many cases it is easy to collect information from raters about high-level features being present and important in an image. For instance, raters could easily point out that an image of a bathroom contains a sink, and that side information can be added to pre-trained detectors of a sink in images.

The key technical idea behind our approach is to define a sample-dependent margin for each sample whose multidimensional shape is based on the known information about the uncertainty about features for that particular sample. Importantly, this is fundamentally different from scaling the samples. This point is often overlooked because when all samples share the same uncertainty structure, the two approaches become equivalent. Unfortunately, when each sample has its own multidimensional uncertainty scale, scaling samples might completely change the geometry of the problem. We show how to avoid this issue by rescaling the margins, rather than the data samples.

To take this information into account, we treat each sample i as if it is surrounded by an ellipsoid centered at a location $\mathbf{x}_i$. The ellipsoid is parametrized by a matrix $z_i = S_i \in \mathbb{R}_+^{d \times d}$, and represents the set of points where a sample might have been if there was no measurement noise. It can also be thought of as reflecting a known noise covariance around a measurement. When that covariance has independent features, S_i is a positive diagonal matrix $S_i = diag(s_1, ..., s_d)$ $(s > 0, j = 1, ..., d)$ that represents the uncertainty in each dimension of the sample $\mathbf{x}_i$. In this case, linearly transforming the space using S_i^{-1} makes the uncertainty ellipsoid S_i a symmetric sphere.

We first define an ellipsoid loss for the binary classification case and later extend it to the multiclass case:

$$loss(\mathbf{w}; \mathbf{x}, y) = \begin{cases} 0 & \min_{\hat{\mathbf{x}} \in \mathcal{X}_S} y\mathbf{w}^T\hat{\mathbf{x}} > 0 \\ 1 - y\mathbf{w}^T\mathbf{x} & \text{otherwise} \end{cases} \tag{1}$$

where $\mathcal{X}_S = \{\hat{\mathbf{x}} : ||\hat{\mathbf{x}} - \mathbf{x}||_{S^{-\infty}} \leq \infty/||\mathbf{w}||_S\}$ and $||\mathbf{x}||_S^2 = \mathbf{x}^T S^T S \mathbf{x}$ is the Mahalanobis norm corresponding to the matrix $S^T S$, hence minimization is over the set of points $\hat{\mathbf{x}}$ that are "inside", or S-close to, the centroid $\mathbf{x}$. Intuitively, the conditions in the loss mean that if all points inside the ellipsoid are correctly classified, no loss is incurred.

This definition extends the standard margin hinge loss. When S is the identity matrix, we have $\min_{||\hat{\mathbf{x}} - \mathbf{x}|| \leq 1/||\mathbf{w}||} y w^T \hat{\mathbf{x}} = \min_{||\mathbf{u}|| \leq 1/||\mathbf{w}||} y\mathbf{w}^T(\mathbf{x} + \mathbf{u}) = y\mathbf{w}^T\mathbf{x} + \min_{||\mathbf{u}|| \leq 1/||\mathbf{w}||} y\mathbf{w}^T\mathbf{u}$. The 2nd term is minimized when $\mathbf{u} = -\mathbf{w}/||w||$, yielding $y\mathbf{w}^T\mathbf{x} - 1$, hence the loss of Eq. (1) becomes equivalent to the standard margin loss: $loss(\mathbf{w}; \mathbf{x}, y) = 0$ when $y\mathbf{w}^T\mathbf{x} > 1$ and $1 - y\mathbf{w}^T\mathbf{x}$ otherwise.

For the multiclass case, we have k weight vectors, corresponding to k classes, together forming a matrix $W \in \mathbb{R}^{d \times k}$. We follow [5] and consider a weight vector that is the difference between the positive class and the hardest negative class $\Delta\mathbf{w} = \mathbf{w}_{pos} - \mathbf{w}_{neg}$, and define a loss

$$loss_{El}(W; \mathbf{x}, y) = \begin{cases} 0 & \min_{\hat{\mathbf{x}} \in \mathcal{X}_S} \Delta\mathbf{w}^T\hat{\mathbf{x}} > 0 \\ 1 - \Delta\mathbf{w}^T\mathbf{x} & \text{otherwise.} \end{cases} \tag{2}$$

Algorithm 1.

1: **inputs:** A dataset $\{\mathbf{x}_i, y_i, S_i\}_{i=1}^N$ of samples, labels and rich-supervision about feature uncertainty; A constant C. $x_i \in \mathbb{R}^d$, y_i from k classes.
2: **initialize:** Set $W \leftarrow 0$, a matrix of size $d \times k$.
3: **for each** sample $i \in [1 \ldots N]$ **do**
4:    Set $pos \leftarrow y_i$; index of the true label.
5:    Set $neg \leftarrow \underset{n \neq pos}{\mathrm{argmax}}\, \mathbf{w}_n^T \mathbf{x}_i$; index of hardest negative label.
6:    Update $\mathbf{w}_{pos}, \mathbf{w}_{neg}$ using Eq. (4)
7: **end for**

In the spherical case, where the per-sample uncertainty matrix is the identity matrix $S_i = I$, this loss also becomes equivalent to the standard hinge loss.

5   Ellipsotron

We now describe an online algorithm for learning with the loss of Eq. (2).

Since it is hard to tune hyper parameters when only few samples are available, we chose here to build on the passive-aggressive algorithm [PA, 5], which is generally less sensitive to tuning the aggressiveness hyper parameter. Our approach is also related to the *Ballseptron* [16]. The idea is to transform each sample to a space where it is spherical, then apply standard PA steps in the scaled space. The algorithm solves the following optimization problem for each sample:

$$\min_W \left\| W - W^{t-1} \right\|_{S_i^{-1}}^2 + C \, \mathrm{loss}_{El}(W; \mathbf{x}, y). \tag{3}$$

Similar to PA, it searches for a set of weights W that minimize the loss, while keeping the weights close to the previous W^{t-1}. As opposed to PA, the metric it uses over W is through the S matrix of the current example. This reflects the fact that similarity over W should take into account which features are more relevant for the sample $\mathbf{x}$.

Proposition: *The solution to Eq. (3) is obtained by the following updates:*

$$(\mathbf{w}_{pos}^{new})^T \leftarrow \mathbf{w}_{pos}{}^T + \eta S_i^{-1}{}^T S_i^{-1} \mathbf{x}_i, \quad (\mathbf{w}_{neg}^{new})^T \leftarrow \mathbf{w}_{neg}{}^T - \eta S_i^{-1}{}^T S_i^{-1} \mathbf{x}_i. \tag{4}$$

where $\eta = \frac{\mathrm{loss}_{El}}{2\|S_i^{-1}\mathbf{x}_i\|^2 + \frac{1}{2C}}$. The proof is based on transforming each $\mathbf{x}_i$ using the matrix S_i^{-1}, then applying a PA update step [5] for each sample in its own transformed space. Specifically, we use $\mathbf{w}^T \mathbf{x}_i = \mathbf{w}^T S_i S_i^{-1} \mathbf{x}_i$ to rewrite the loss for new variables $\mathbf{v}^T = \mathbf{w}^T S_i$, $\mathbf{u}_i = S_i^{-1} \mathbf{x}_i$, so $\mathbf{w}^T \mathbf{x}_i = \mathbf{v}^T \mathbf{u}_i$. With this transformation, the loss of Eq. (2) becomes equivalent to a standard PA loss over $\mathbf{v}$ and $\mathbf{u}_i$. Taking a PA update step and transforming the variables back completes the proof. The proof is provided in details in [20].

6   Generalization Error Bound

We prove a generalization bound for learning linear classifiers from a hypothesis family $\mathcal{F}$ for a set of n i.i.d. labeled samples $(\mathbf{x}_i, y_i)$. Each sample has its own uncertainty matrix S_i^{-1}. Let $\mathcal{L}$ be the empirical loss $\hat{\mathcal{L}} = \sum_{i=1} loss(\mathbf{w}^T \mathbf{x}_i, y_i)$, and the true loss $\mathcal{L} = E_{p(x,y)} loss(\mathbf{w}^T \mathbf{x}_i, y_i)$. The following relation holds:

Theorem: For a loss function that is upper bounded by a constant M_l and is Lipschitz in its first argument, for the family of linear separators $\mathcal{F} = \{\mathbf{w} : \sum_i \|\mathbf{w}\|_{S_i^{-1}} \leq \sum_i \|\mathbf{w}^*\|_{S_i^{-1}}\}$, and for any positive δ we have with probability $\geq 1 - \delta$ and $\forall f \in \mathcal{F}$:

$$\mathcal{L}(f) \leq \hat{\mathcal{L}}(f) + 2\|\mathbf{w}^*\|_2 \max_{\mathbf{x}_i \in \mathcal{X}} \sqrt{\|\mathbf{x}_i\|_{S_i^{-1}}} \sqrt{\frac{2}{n}} + M_l \sqrt{\frac{1}{2n} \log(\frac{1}{\delta})}, \quad (5)$$

where $\mathbf{w}^*$ is the target classifier and the maximization is taken over the space of samples, with each sample having its predefined corresponding uncertainty matrix S_i^{-1}.

The meaning of this theorem is as follows: Consider a case where some dimensions of $\mathbf{x}_i$ are more variable, for example if contaminated with noise that has different variance across different features. Also assume that the uncertainty matrix S_i^{-1} matches the dimensions of $\mathbf{x}_i$ such that higher-variance dimensions correspond to smaller magnitude S_i^{-1} entries. In this case, $|\mathbf{x}_i|_{S^{-1}} < |\mathbf{x}_i|_2$, hence the theorem leads to a tighter generalization bound, reducing the sample complexity. As a specific example, for a diagonal S_i^{-1} with k non-zero values on the diagonal, **the effective dimension of the data is reduced from d to k, even if these k values vary from one sample to another**. This can dramatically reduce sample complexity in practice, because very often, even if a dataset occupies a high dimensional manifold, a handful of features are sufficient for classifying each sample, and these **features vary from one sample to another**.

Proof: The proof is based on the case of a single uncertainty matrix [13], and is provided in [20].

7   Experiments

We evaluate the Ellipsotron using two benchmark datasets and compare its performance with two baseline approaches. First, in a task of scene classification using SUN [22], a dataset of visual scenes accompanied by list of present objects. Second, in a task of recognizing fine-grained bird classes using CUB [21], a dataset of bird images annotated with semantic attributes.

7.1 Compared Methods

(1) Ellipsotron. Algorithm 1 above. We used a diagonal matrix S_i^{-1}, obtaining a value of 1 for relevant features and $\epsilon = 10^{-10}$ for irrelevant features.

(2) Lean supervision (LS). No rich supervision signal, linear online classifier with hinge loss trained using the standard passive-aggressive algorithm [5] with all input features.

(3) Feature scaling (FS). Rescale each sample $\mathbf{x}_i$ using its S_i^{-1}, then train with the passive-aggressive algorithm [5] with the standard hinge loss. Formally, the loss in this approach is $loss_{FS} = 0$ when $(\mathbf{w}_{pos} - \mathbf{w}_{neg})^T S_i^{-1} \mathbf{x}_i > 1$ and $loss_{FS} = 1 - (\mathbf{w}_{pos} - \mathbf{w}_{neg})^T S_i^{-1} \mathbf{x}_i$ otherwise. The update steps are: $\mathbf{w}_{pos} \leftarrow \mathbf{w}_{pos} + \eta S_i^{-1} \mathbf{x}_i$ and, $\mathbf{w}_{neg} \leftarrow \mathbf{w}_{neg} - S_i^{-1} \mathbf{x}_i$, with $\eta = \frac{loss_{FS}}{2||S_i^{-1} \mathbf{x}_i||^2 + \frac{1}{2C}}$.

Comparing this loss with the Ellipsotron, Eq. (2), reveals two main differences. First, the margin criteria in the FS loss is w.r.t. to the scaled samples $S_i^{-1} \mathbf{x}_i$, while in the Ellipsotron loss the criteria is that the ellipsoid surrounding $\mathbf{x}_i$ would be correctly classified. Second, when a loss is suffered, the Ellipsotron loss is w.r.t. the original sample $\mathbf{x}_i$ while the FS loss is w.r.t. the scaled samples $S_i^{-1} \mathbf{x}_i$. In the case of "hard" focus, namely setting S_i^{-1} to 1 for relevant features and 0 for irrelevant features, this is equivalent to setting to zero the irrelevant features during learning. In this case, weights corresponding to irrelevant features are not updated when a sample is presented.

7.2 Visual Scene Classification

SUN [22] is a large-scale dataset for visual scene recognition. Each SUN image is accompanied by human-annotated objects visible in the scene and marked with free-text tags like "table" or "person" (for a total of 4,917 unique tags). We removed suffixes and duplicates and fixed tag typos, yielding 271,737 annotations over a vocabulary of 3,772 unique object tags. Typically, object tags appear more than once in an image (the median object count over images is 2).

Representing Images with Textual Terms. Object tags in SUN used free-form tags and were not restricted to a predefined vocabulary. To match them with images we used an intermediate representation. Specifically, we used *visual concepts* (VC), a vocabulary of 1000 terms inferred from images by [8]. The VC network was originally trained on MS-COCO images and captions [12], yielding a vocabulary that differs from SUN vocabulary of object tags, and we did a simple mapping of stemmed SUN tags to VC concepts.

Importantly, the feature representation was never trained to predict the identity of a scene. In this sense, we perform a *strong-transfer* from one task (predicting MS-COCO terms) to a different task (scene classification) on a different dataset (SUN). This differs from the more common transfer learning setup where classifiers trained over a subset of classes are transferred to other classes in the same task. Such a strong transfer is a hallmark of high-level abstraction that people exhibit, and is typically hard to achieve.

Rich Supervision. We used the objects detected for each image as rich super-vision. The intuition is that any object marked as present in a scene can be treated more confidently as being detected in any specific image. Importantly, this rich supervision is weak, because the raters were not instructed to mark objects that are discriminative or particularly relevant. Indeed, some objects ("people") commonly appear across many scenes.

The set of SUN objects was mapped to VC terms using string matching after stemming. Objects without a matching VC term were removed. Overall 1631 SUN objects were matched to 531 VC terms. The rich-supervision is viewed as a sample-based binary signal, indicating if an object is present in an image sample.

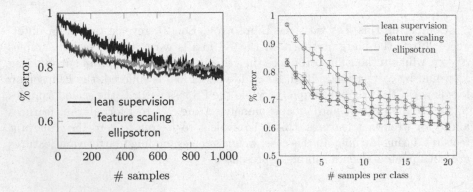

Fig. 1. SUN dataset. Mean over 5 random-seed data splits. **Left:** Percent test error as a function of training samples observed. 100 classes. **Right:** Percent test error vs number of samples per class. Analyzed classes with 40 to 100 samples (41 classes). Error bars denote the standard error deviation.

Evaluation. For each scene we used 50% of samples for testing and the rest for training. Accuracy was stable for a wide range of the complexity parameter C in early experiments, so we used $C = 1$. Weights were initialized to zero.

Results. We first tested Ellipsotron and baselines in a standard online setup where samples are drawn uniformly at random from the training set. Here we used classes that had at least 20 samples and at most 100 samples, yielding 100 classes. Figure 1 (left) shows the accuracy as a function of the number of samples (and updates) for SUN data, showing that Ellipsotron outperforms the two baselines when the number of samples is small.

SUN classes differ by their number of samples, so averaging across classes unfairly mixes heavy-sampled and poorly-sampled classes. For a more controlled analysis, Fig. 1 (right) shows the accuracy as a function of the number of samples per class. Ellipsotron is consistently more accurate than baselines for all training-set sizes tested, with a larger gap for smaller training sets. Results were not sensitive to the number of scenes, details in [20].

7.3   Bird Species Classification

We further tested Ellipsotron using CUB [21] - a dataset with 11K images of 200 bird species, accompanied by 312 predefined attributes like "head is red" and "bill is short". Attribute annotations were made by non-experts and are often missing or incorrect. We used the attributes as a source of rich supervision for training a bird classifier, on top of a set of attribute predictors. At test time, the classifier maps images to bird classes without the need to specify attributes.

Mapping Pixels to Attributes. We used 150 species to learn a map from pixels to attributes, yielding a representation that interacts with the rich supervision. The remaining 50 classes (2933 images) were used for evaluation.

Each image is represented using a predefined set of 312 attributes, predicted using a trained attribute detector, based on a resNet50 [11] trained on ImageNet. We replaced its last, fully-connected, layer with a new fully-connected layer having sigmoid activation. The new layer was trained with a multilabel binary cross-entropy loss, keeping the weights of lower layers fixed. We used 100 bird species drawn randomly to train the attribute predictors, and 50 classes for validation to tune early stopping and hyper parameters. Final models were retrained on all 150 (training and validation) classes with best hyper parameters

Rich Supervision. We use attribute annotations as a signal about confidence, because when a rater notes an attribute, it can be treated with more confidence if detected in the image. In practice, attribute annotations vary across same-class images. This happens due to variance in appearance across images in view point and color, or due to different interpretations by different raters.

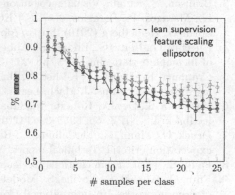

Experimental Setup. We randomly selected 25 samples of each class for training, and the rest was used as a fixed test set making evaluation more stable. Hyper-parameters were set based on the experiments above with SUN data, setting the aggressiveness at $c = 1$.

Fig. 2. Percent error on CUB data. Test error for 50 classes as a function of the number of training samples. Error bars denote the standard error of the mean over 5 repetitions.

Results. Figure 2 depicts percent error as a function of the number of training samples on CUB. Ellipsotron consistently improves over lean supervision and feature scaling. With 10 samples, the accuracy over both baselines improves by 44% (from 18% to 26%).

8   Summary

We presented an online learning approach where labeled samples are also accompanied with rich-supervision. Rich-supervision entails knowledge a teacher has about class features or image features, which in our setup is given in the form of feature uncertainty. The crux of our online approach is to define a sample-dependent margin for each sample, whose multidimensional shape is based on the given information about the uncertainty of features for that particular sample. Experiments on two fine-grained classification benchmarks of real-world complex images demonstrate the benefits of the approach.

Acknowledgement. Supported by the Israeli Science Foundation grant 737/18.

References

1. Atzmon, Y., Chechik, G.: Probabilistic and-or attribute grouping for zero-shot learning. In: UAI (2018)
2. Atzmon, Y., Chechik, G.: Adaptive confidence smoothing for generalized zero-shot learning. In: CVPR (2019)
3. Branson, S., et al.: Visual recognition with humans in the loop. In: Daniilidis, K., Maragos, P., Paragios, N. (eds.) ECCV 2010. LNCS, vol. 6314, pp. 438–451. Springer, Heidelberg (2010). https://doi.org/10.1007/978-3-642-15561-1_32
4. Chechik, G., Heitz, G., Elidan, G., Abbeel, P., Koller, D.: Max-margin classification of incomplete data. In: NIPS, pp. 233–240 (2007)
5. Crammer, K., Dekel, O., Keshet, J., Shalev-Shwartz, S., Singer, Y.: Online passive-aggressive algorithms. J. Mach. Learn. Res. **7**(Mar), 551–585 (2006)
6. Dasgupta, S., Dey, A., Roberts, N., Sabato, S.: Learning from discriminative feature feedback. In: NIPS, pp. 3955–3963 (2018)
7. Druck, G., Mann, G., McCallum, A.: Reducing annotation effort using generalized expectation criteria. Technical report, Mass. Univ Amherst (2007)
8. Fang, H., et al.: From captions to visual concepts and back. In: CVPR (2015)
9. Finn, C., Abbeel, P., Levine, S.: Model-agnostic meta-learning for fast adaptation of deep networks. In: International Conference on Machine Learning, vol. 70, pp 1126–1135 (2017)
10. Hariharan, B., Girshick, R.: Low-shot visual recognition by shrinking and hallucinating features. In: Proceedings of the IEEE International Conference on Computer Vision, pp. 3018–3027 (2017)
11. He, K., Zhang, X., Ren, S., Sun, J.: Deep residual learning for image recognition. In: CVPR, pp. 770–778 (2016)
12. Lin, T.-Y., et al.: Microsoft COCO: common objects in context. In: Fleet, D., Pajdla, T., Schiele, B., Tuytelaars, T. (eds.) ECCV 2014. LNCS, vol. 8693, pp. 740–755. Springer, Cham (2014). https://doi.org/10.1007/978-3-319-10602-1_48
13. Poulis, S., Dasgupta, S.: Learning with feature feedback: from theory to practice. In: Artificial Intelligence and Statistics, pp. 1104–1113 (2017)
14. Raghavan, H., Madani, O., Jones, R.: Active learning with feedback on features and instances. J. Mach. Learn. Res. **7**, 1655–1686 (2006)
15. Ravi, S., Larochelle, H.: Optimization as a model for few-shot learning. In: ICLR (2017)

16. Shalev-Shwartz, S., Singer, Y.: A new perspective on an old perceptron algorithm. In: Auer, P., Meir, R. (eds.) COLT 2005. LNCS (LNAI), vol. 3559, pp. 264–278. Springer, Heidelberg (2005). https://doi.org/10.1007/11503415_18
17. Small, K., Wallace, B., Trikalinos, T., Brodley, C.E.: The constrained weight space SVM: learning with ranked features. In: ICML, pp. 865–872 (2011)
18. Snell, J., Swersky, K., Zemel, R.: Prototypical networks for few-shot learning. In: NIPS, pp. 4077–4087 (2017)
19. Vinyals, O., Blundell, C., Lillicrap, T., Wierstra, D., et al.: Matching networks for one shot learning. In: NIPS, pp. 3630–3638 (2016)
20. Visotsky, R., Atzmon, Y., Chechik, G.: Few-shot learning with per-sample rich supervision. arXiv preprint arXiv:1906.03859 (2019)
21. Welinder, P., et al.: Caltech-UCSD Birds 200. Technical report CNS-TR-2010-001, CalTech (2010)
22. Xiao, J., Hays, J., Ehinger, K.A., Oliva, A., Torralba, A.: Sun database: large-scale scene recognition from abbey to zoo. In: CVPR, pp. 3485–3492 (2010)

Author Index

Printed in the United States
By Bookmasters